Space Is Never Empty
2010 - 2013

Veronica Caven Aldous

First published by Ingram Spark 2022

ISBN:
Print: 978-0-6451693-8-6
Ebook: 978-0-6451693-9-3

Cover Image: Veronica Caven Aldous

Cover design: Busybird Publishing

Layout and typesetting: Busybird Publishing

Busybird Publishing

2/118 Para Road
Montmorency, Victoria
Australia 3094
www.busybird.com.au

Contents

Introduction

At the end of 2009, I planned to continue with my art practice and exhibitions when possible. I also applied to stay at the VCA to do a practice-based PhD. This project would be based on the use of light and light boxes. Although not accepted there, lacking clear research questions and supervisors, I did receive a scholarship offer from Melbourne University. This encouraged me to keep trying to pull it all together.

I spent a lot of time in 2010 meeting potential supervisors at both Melbourne and Monash Universities. I was accepted at Monash in April of 2011. From 2011 until 2013 I worked only with light as a medium in my art practice and researched art, artists and philosophical references to light that would build my exegesis in the following and final years of the PhD.

In terms of my artwork, I noticed that when people viewed my lightboxes, many of them came up with metaphors about light. This kind of commentary had not happened with my painting practice. So even as I considered the project as being within the expanded field of painting, my thoughts and research expanded to include light in space and light as metaphor.

Because I was using light as a medium, I needed to understand more about the history of light metaphors. So, I attended lectures at Melbourne University about the History and Philosophy of Science. I learnt about the changing understandings of metaphors over the centuries to do with the sun, moon, planets, and stars.

The motivation for the use of light by artists is diverse. And viewers interpret the works in diverse ways. To some viewers, light and the spreading of light in the space around the artwork, suggested meaning. For some, the work evoked emotions, visceral responses, or reverie. While others responded to the materiality of the works or had ambiguous reactions.

As I continued to make light boxes, and exhibited some, I considered the space around the work as part of the work. I considered how I hung the light boxes. I considered the extended space. I made free-standing boxes. I learnt light-mixing on boards that programmed the light boxes. Using stage lighting equipment, I made the light in space much stronger.

I sometimes switched off the lights. I worked in the dark. At times I enjoyed the wilder psychedelic effects of coloured light, rather than the controlled and defined effect of white light. I learnt how to slow everything down visually, so the work encouraged a reduced breath rate.

I also read a lot, wrote lot, and made some public presentations and exhibitions at MADA. I was contrasting my artificial light works with natural light, sunrises, and sunsets. Rather than relating my work to European metaphors of light, I saw parallels with Vastu, a branch of historical Indian architecture that related design of buildings and towns to the sun, the cardinal points, and extended space. I had learnt about Vastu through a long-term interest in Vedic literature. In 2011, I went to India to live in a town built according to Vastu. My research questions considered Vastu principles of space in the studio and gallery.

In 2013, I also went to an ACME art residency based in London and Paris. https://acme.org.uk/artist-support/alumni/veronica-aldous/ This was based around the Hayward *Light Show* and *Dynamo - A Century of Light and Motion in Art, 1913-2013* at the Grand Palais, Paris.

After these experiences and studying the history of light art, I felt more consciously aware of space. Light set up boundaries for the space I was in, and the senses interacted within that space. Being in space was an experience. Attention could be in a room or in the body. It could appear to be bound but could also appear to not be. It is whatever context I wanted to set in place. Space involved relationship and the paradigms can keep changing.

Studying the history of light art, I understood that many established light artists had come to use the medium of light as a departure from, or as part of the conversation with, non-representational painting. This resonated with my own practice, moving from traditional to non-traditional materials.

For many years, I had carbon offset my art practice and making light work allowed me to reuse some components and materials for many years. I continue to try for a lighter touch on the environment.

This book presents examples from my art practice between 2010 and 2013, when I took many thousands of photos and videos in my studio as part of my initial years of PhD work. It presents a pivotal collection of these images as a visual archive. Some of the images, and videos, also moved beyond documentation and became works themselves. This is the fourth of a series of books that covers my art practice up to the present. The aim of these books is to expand and ground my archive in the images of work.

This collection of books weaves together threads of interest displayed in my work since the 1970s. My multivalent practice has always conjoined minimalist expression with the materiality of space, textural colour fields, and hybrid modes of participatory encounter to create objects, installations, and possibilities. My practice deploys diverse material investigations to create works and spatial environments of equilibrium.

My career spans five decades. It builds on my lifelong interest in meditation, philosophy, and feminism as conduits of freedom and peace. I aim to manifest works that are supportive of nuance, of mindful attentiveness, and that create a moment of counterpoint to the ubiquitous, anxious complexity of information overload today.

2010

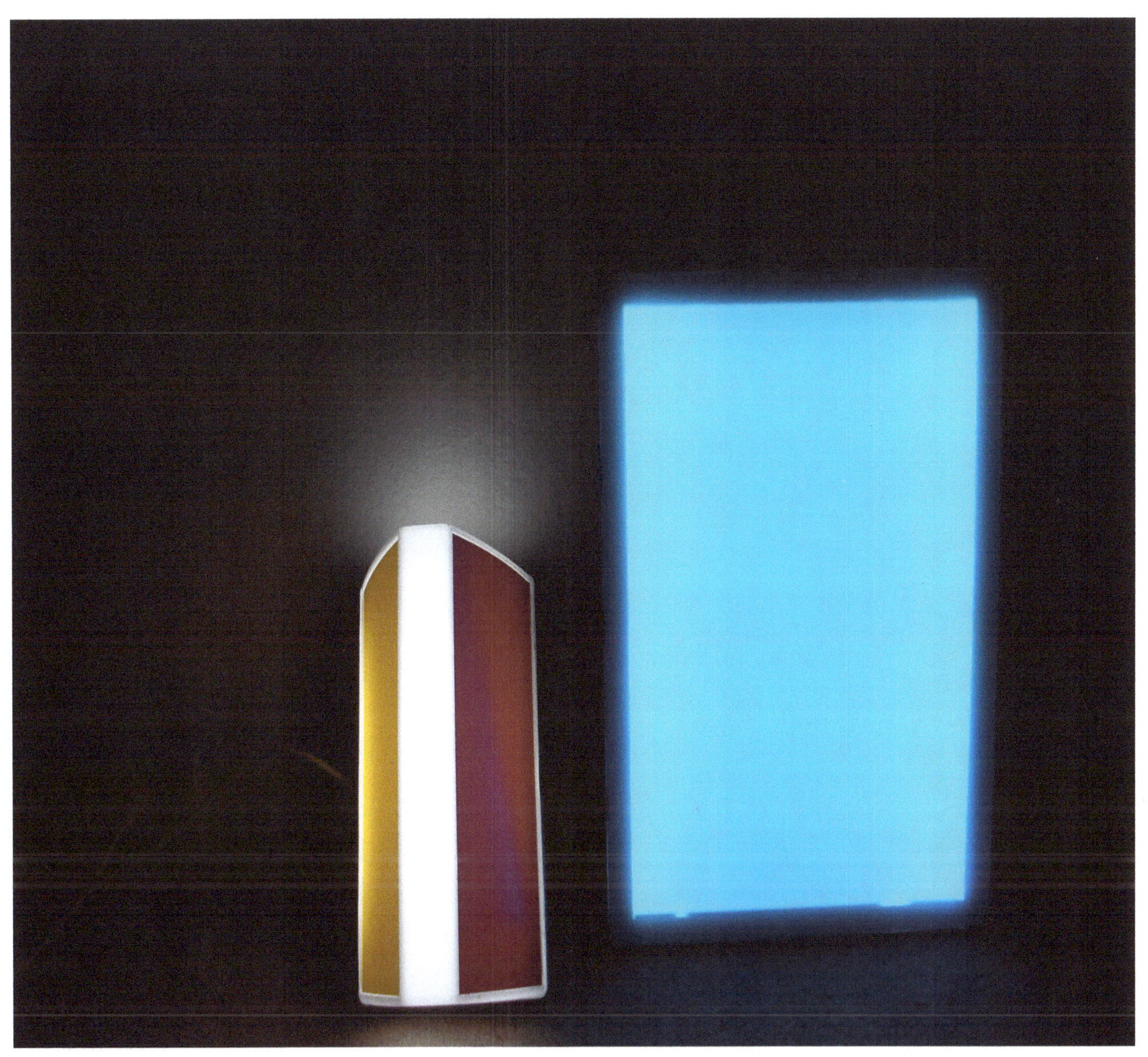

Exit sign and A4 light box, 2010, recycled exit sign, vinyl and LED light box, 80 x 70 cm

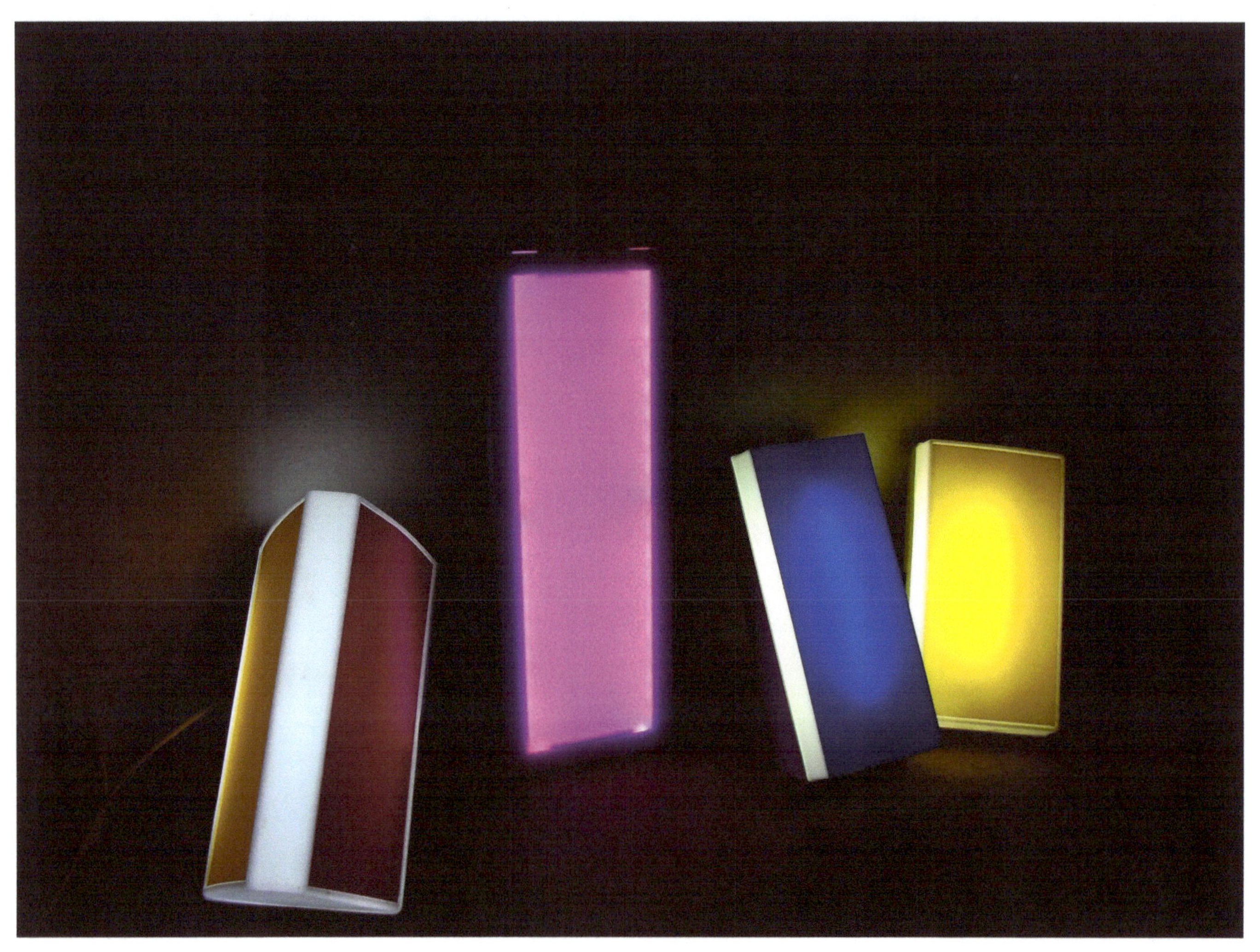

Relationship 16, 2010, recycled exit signs, vinyl and LED light box, 150 x 70 cm

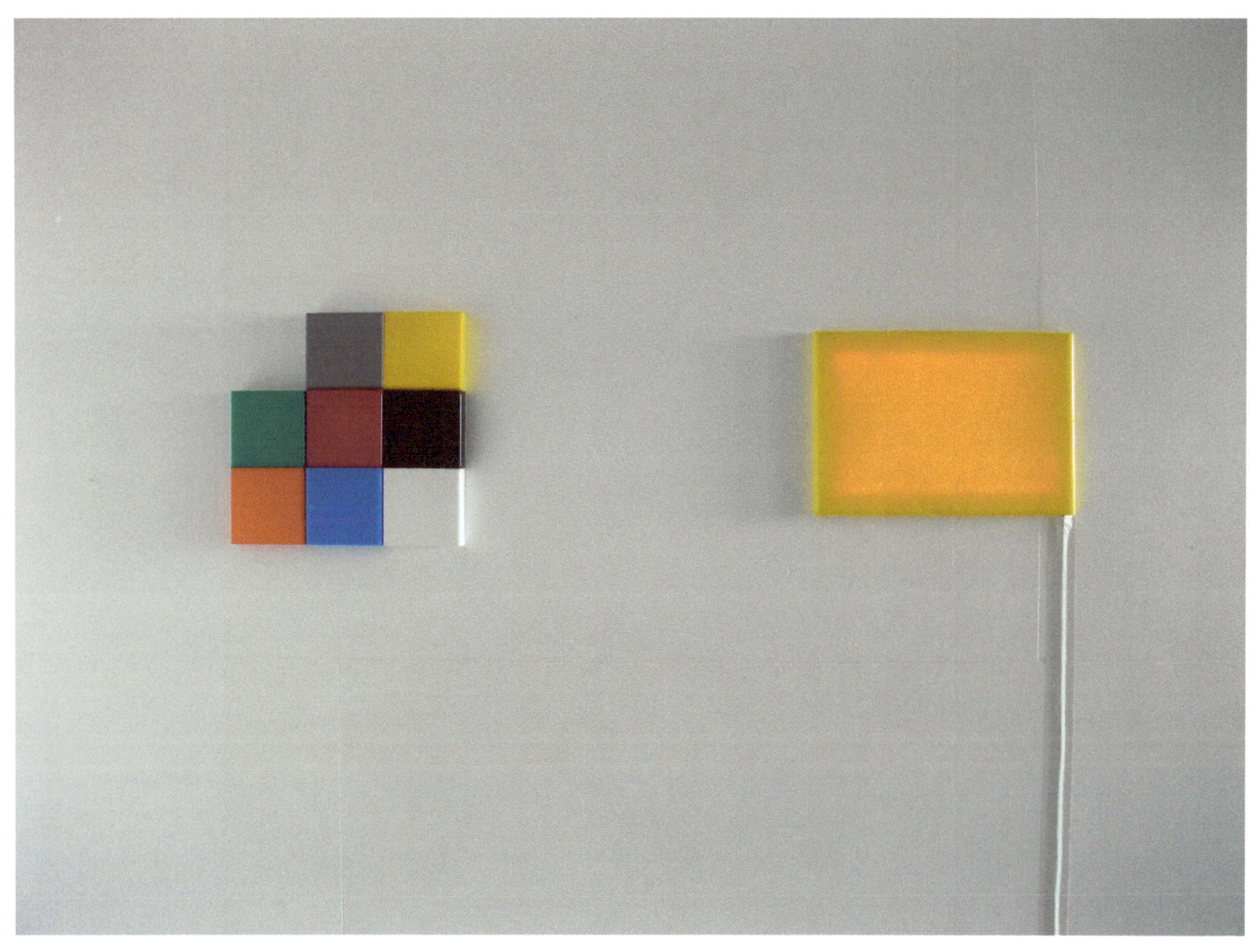

Grid and field, 2010, acrylic sheet, recycled light fittings, and LED light box, 2 x 50 x 70 cm, *Substance*, Guildford Lane Gallery, Melbourne

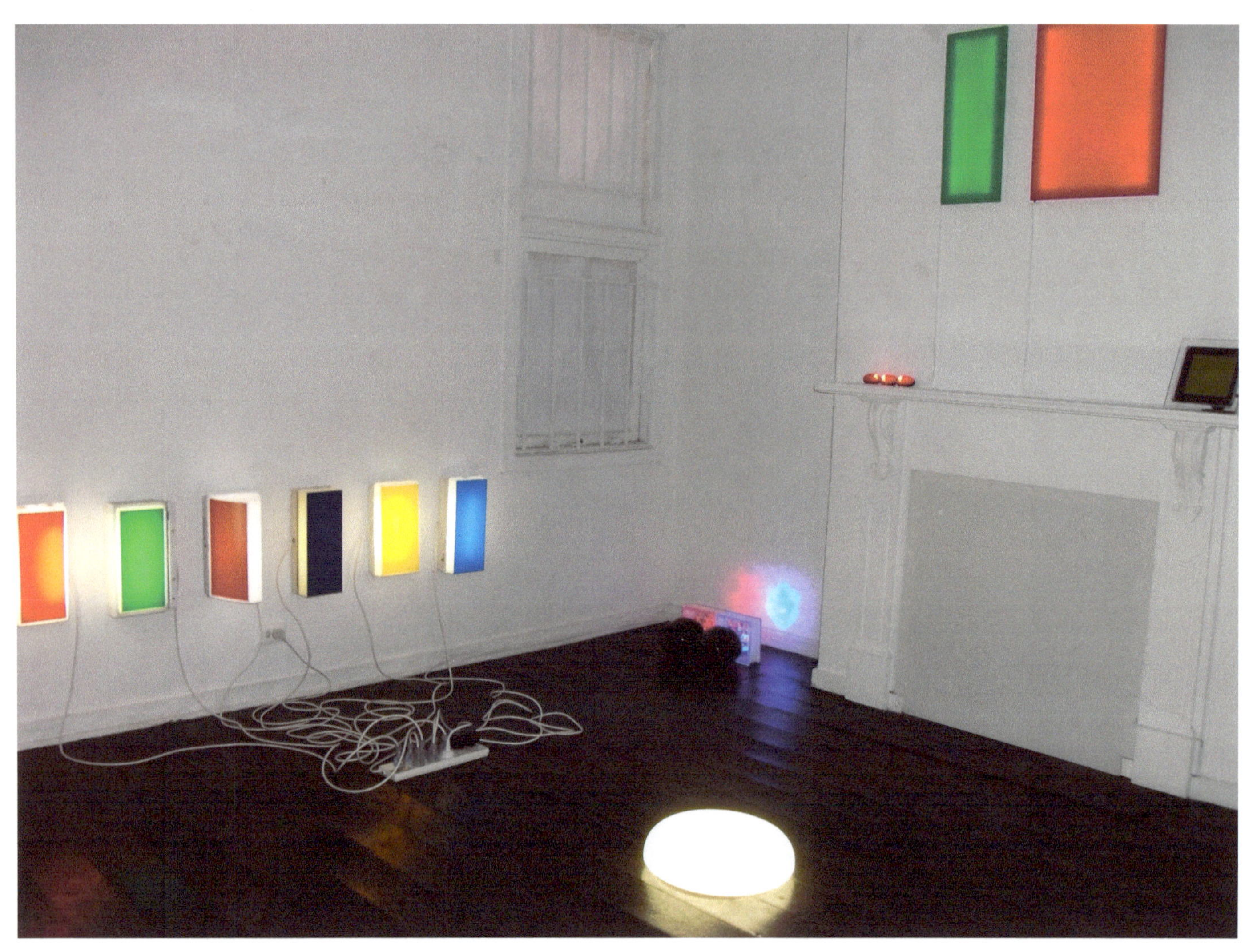

Too Much Information, part installation, 2010, Off the Kerb, Collingwood

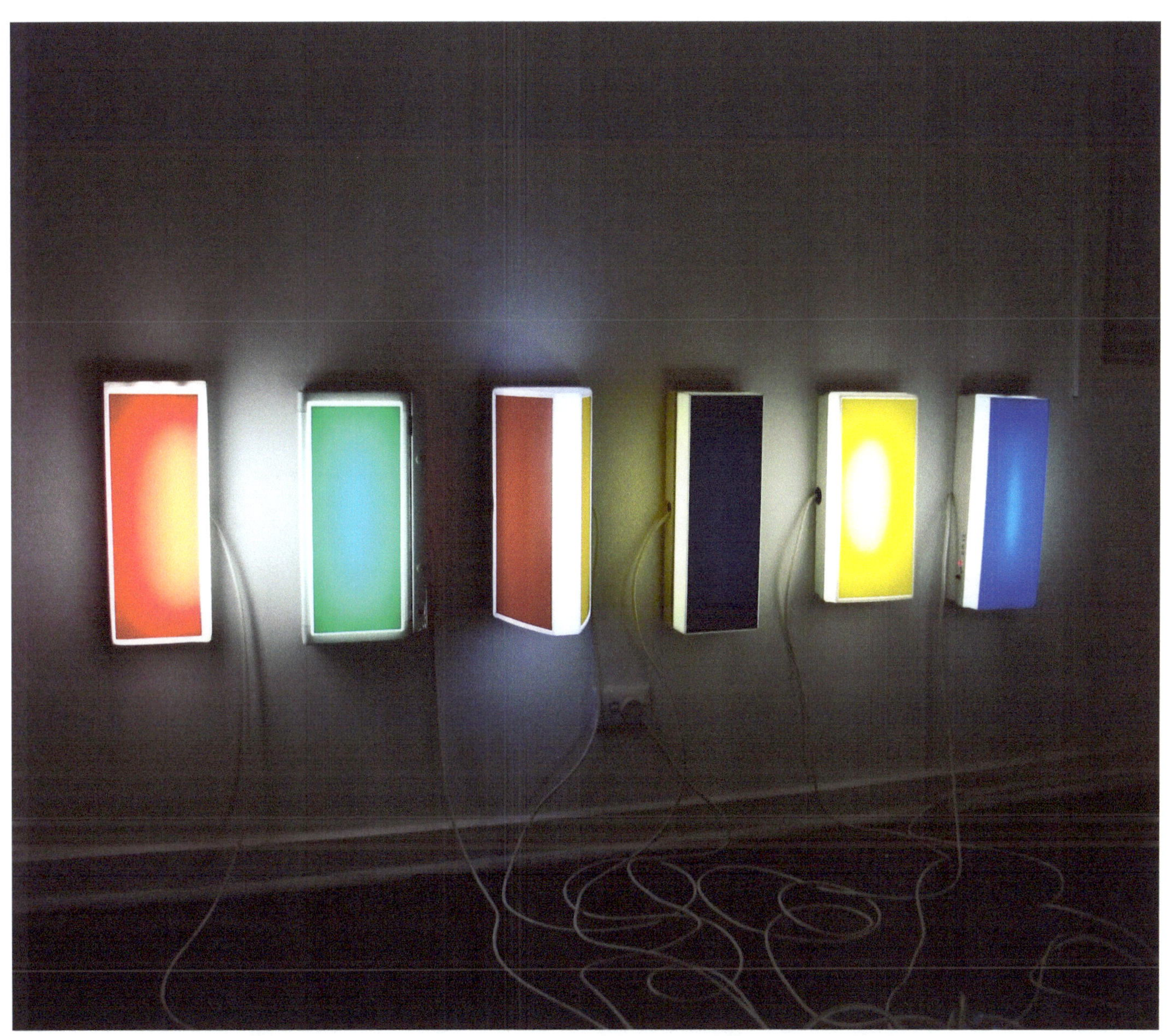

Exit signs, 2010, recycled light fittings and vinyl, 5 x 30 x 70 cm,
Too Much Information, Off the Kerb, Collingwood

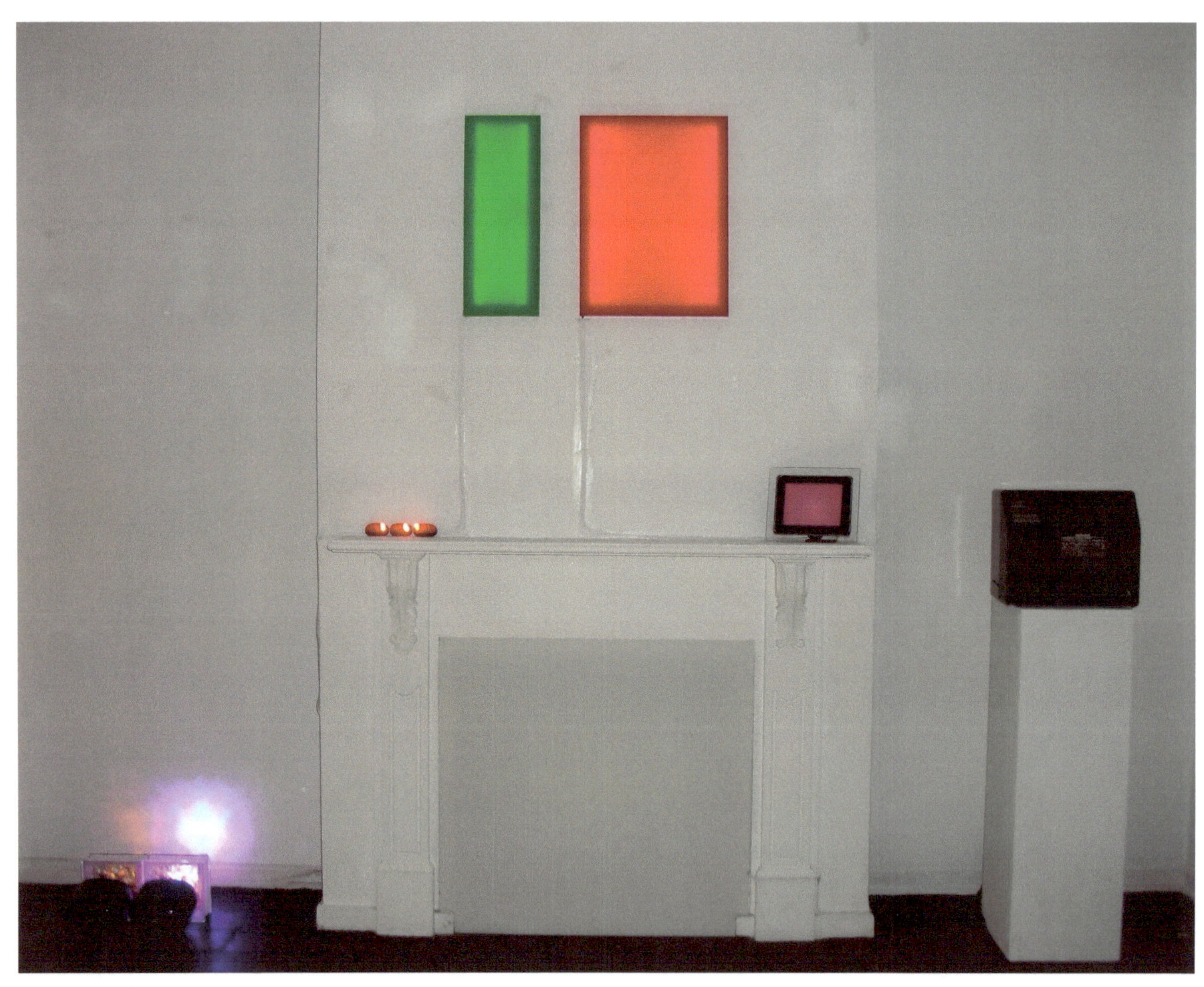

Too Much Information, part installation, 2010, Off the Kerb, Collingwood

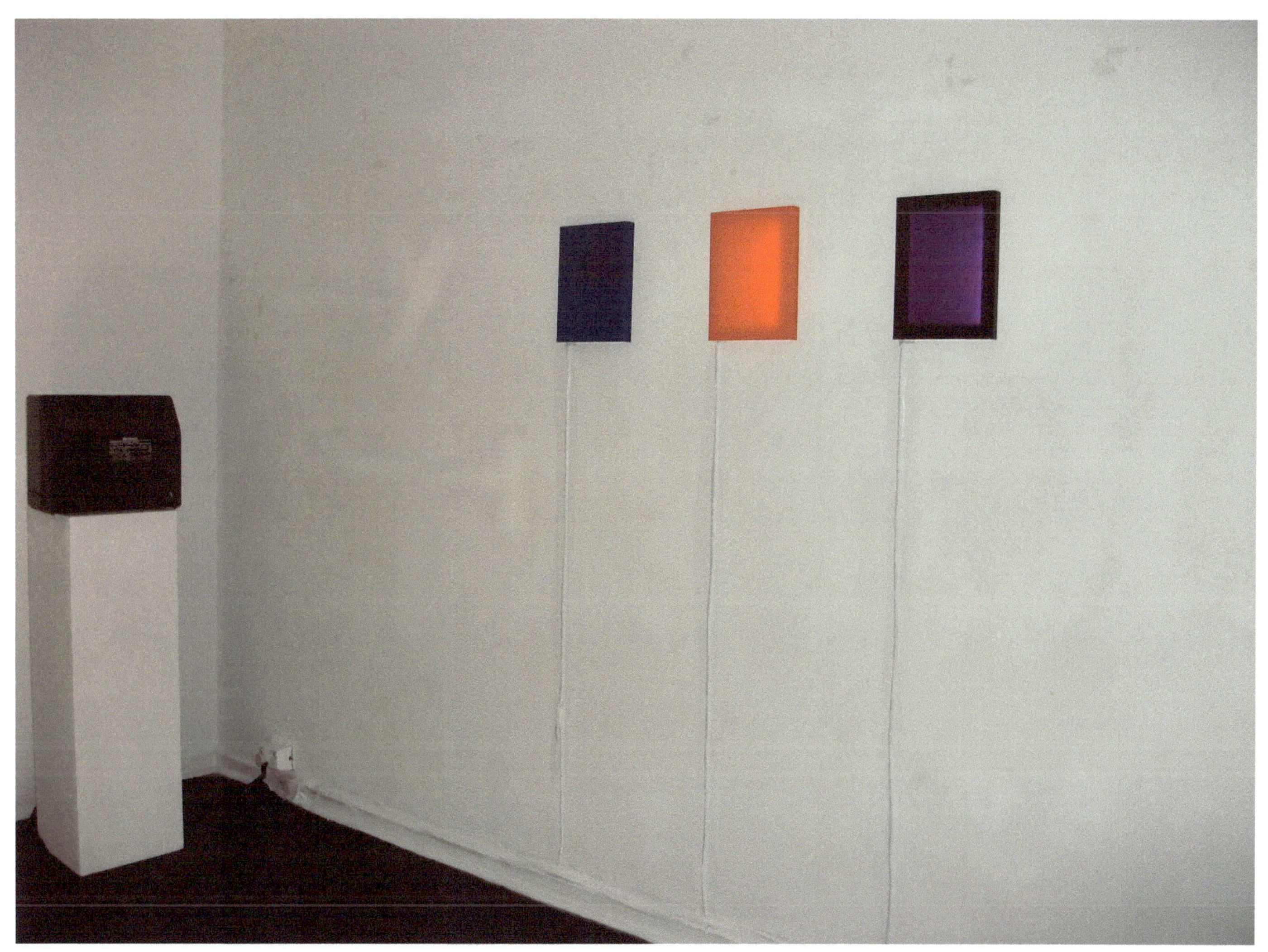

Too Much Information, part installation, 2010, Off the Kerb, Collingwood

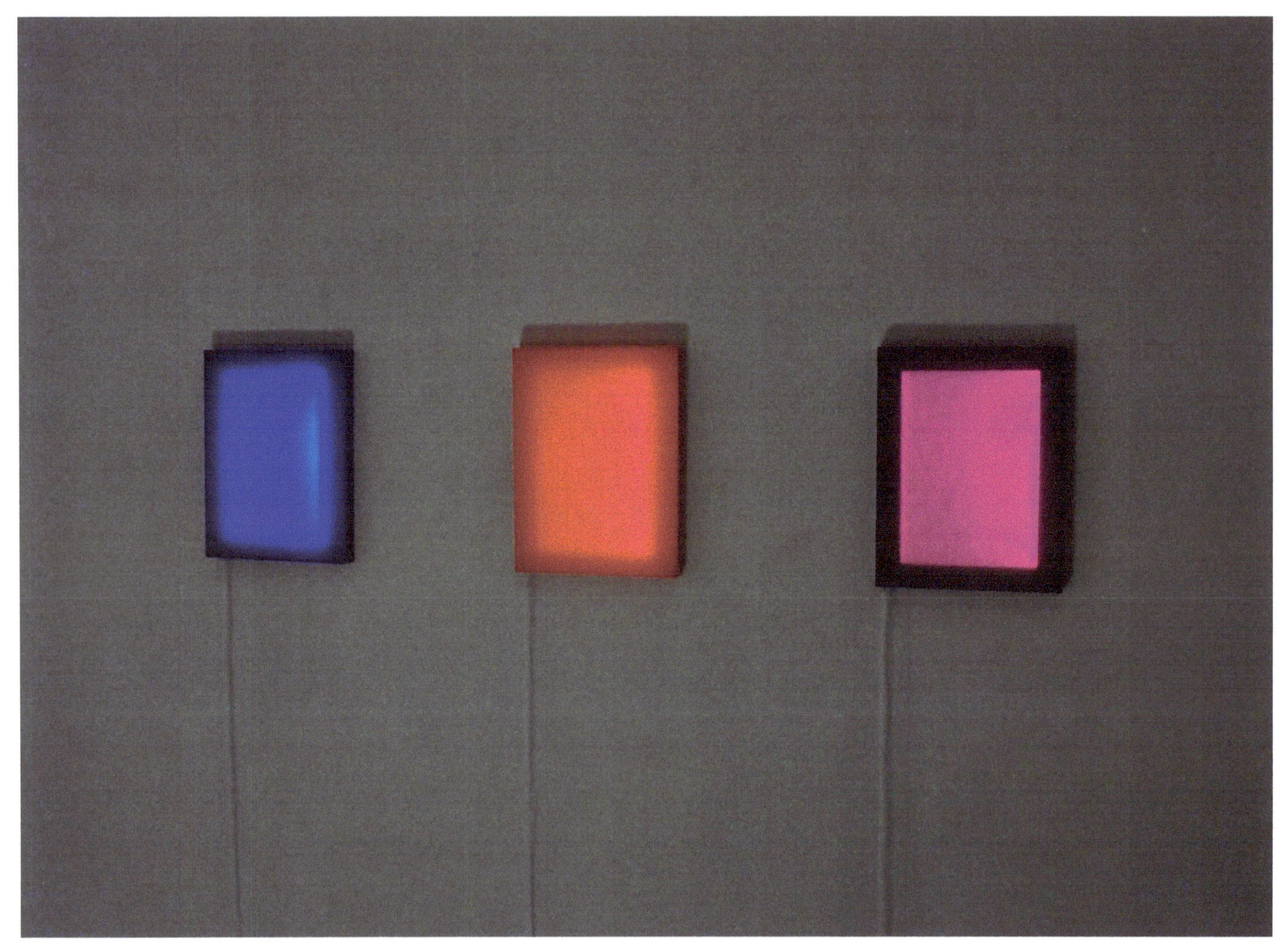

3 x A4, 2010, programmed LED light boxes and acrylic sheet, 3 x 21 x 30 cm,
Off the Kerb, Collingwood

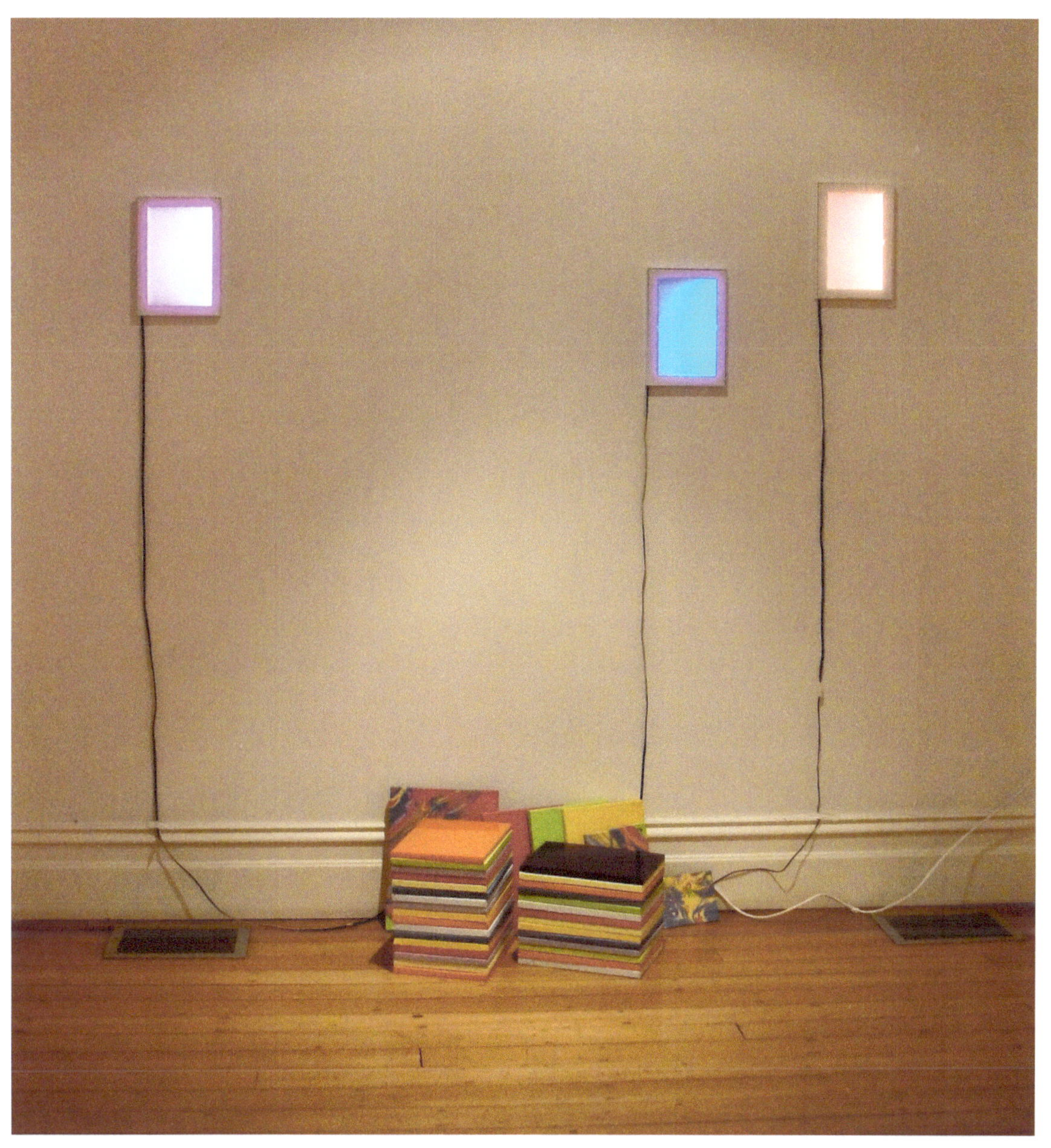

3 x A4 and painting stack, 2010, programmed LED light boxes, acrylic on canvas and acrylic sheet, 3 x 21 x 30 cm and various, *Recent Works*, Town Hall Gallery, Hawthorn

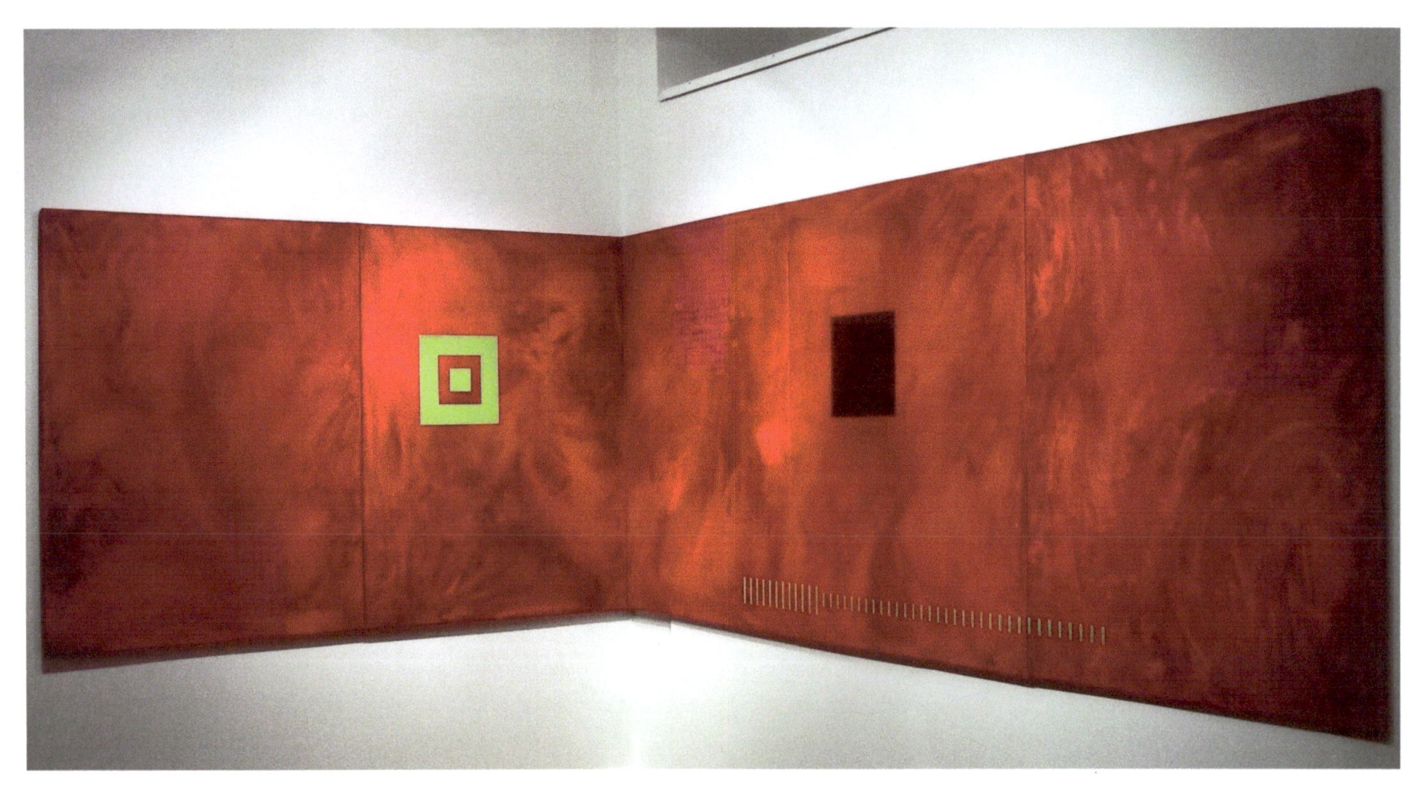

Colour field, Albers, Itten, and T.V., 2010, 5 x 70 x 121 cm,
Recent Works, Town Hall Gallery, Hawthorn

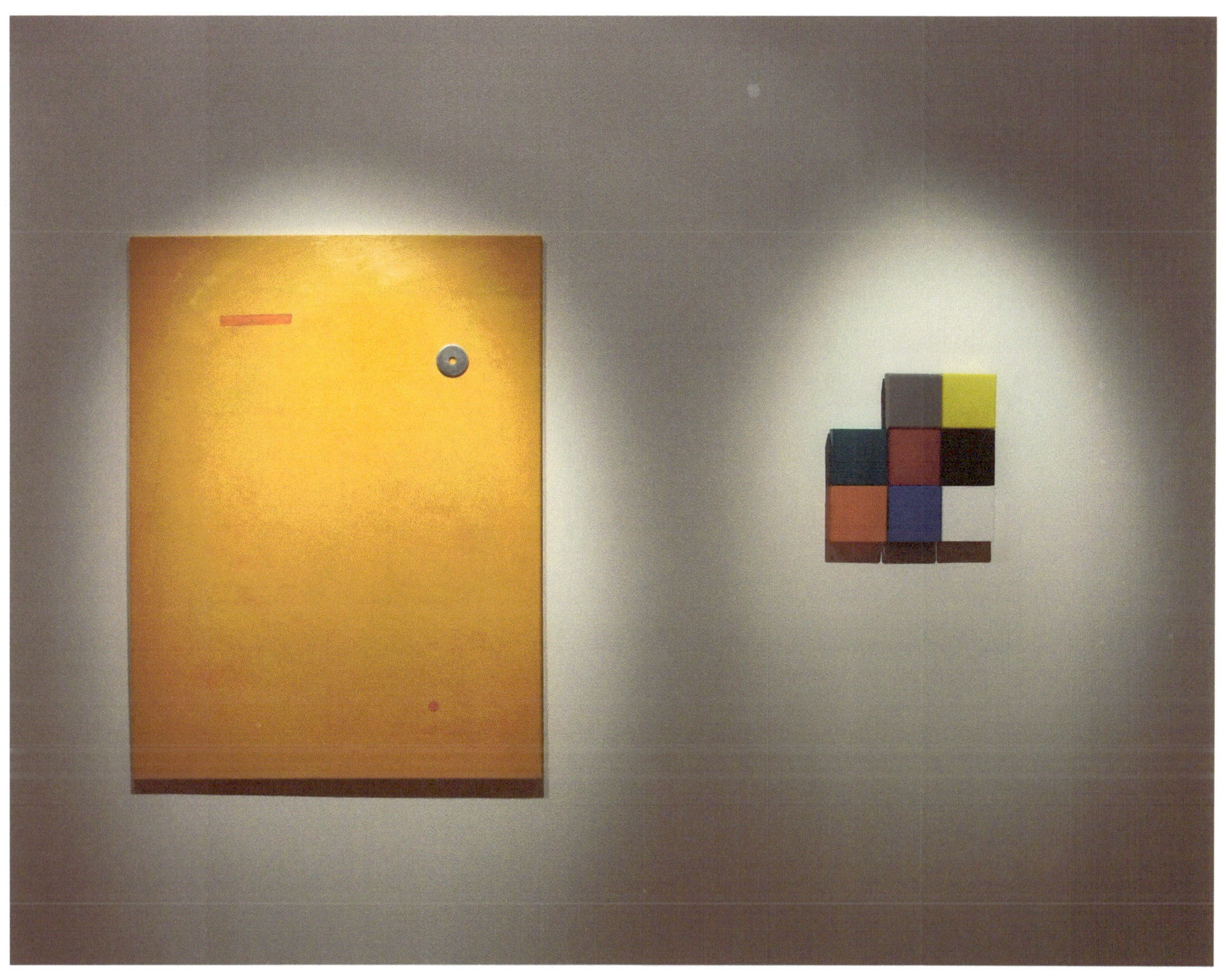

Untitled and grid, 2010, acrylic sheet, recycled light fittings, oil on canvas and aluminium, 2 x 50 x 70 cm, *Recent Works*, Town Hall Gallery, Hawthorn

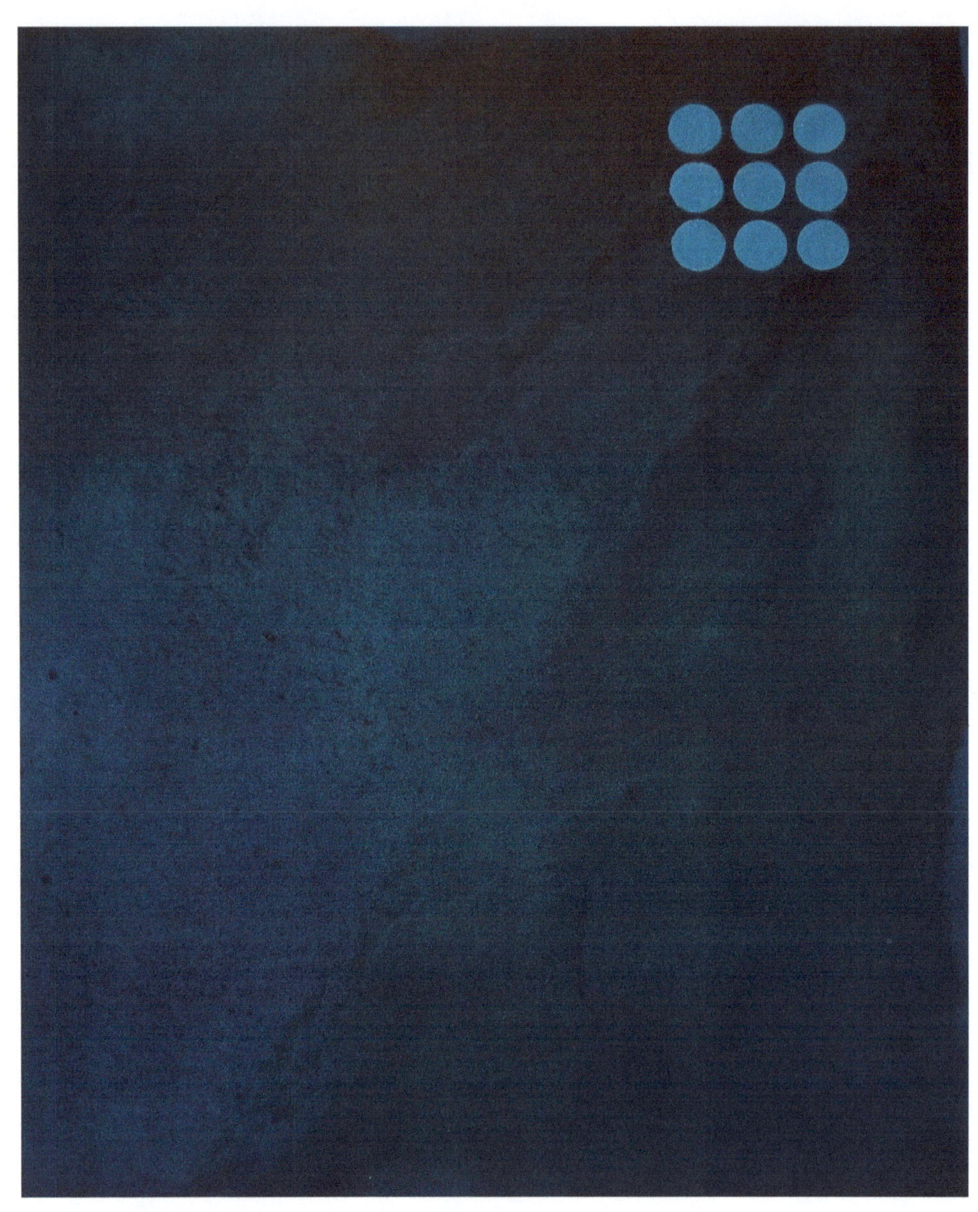

Who owns the dot, 2010, oil on canvas, 60 x 75 cm, *Recent Works*,
Town Hall Gallery, Hawthorn

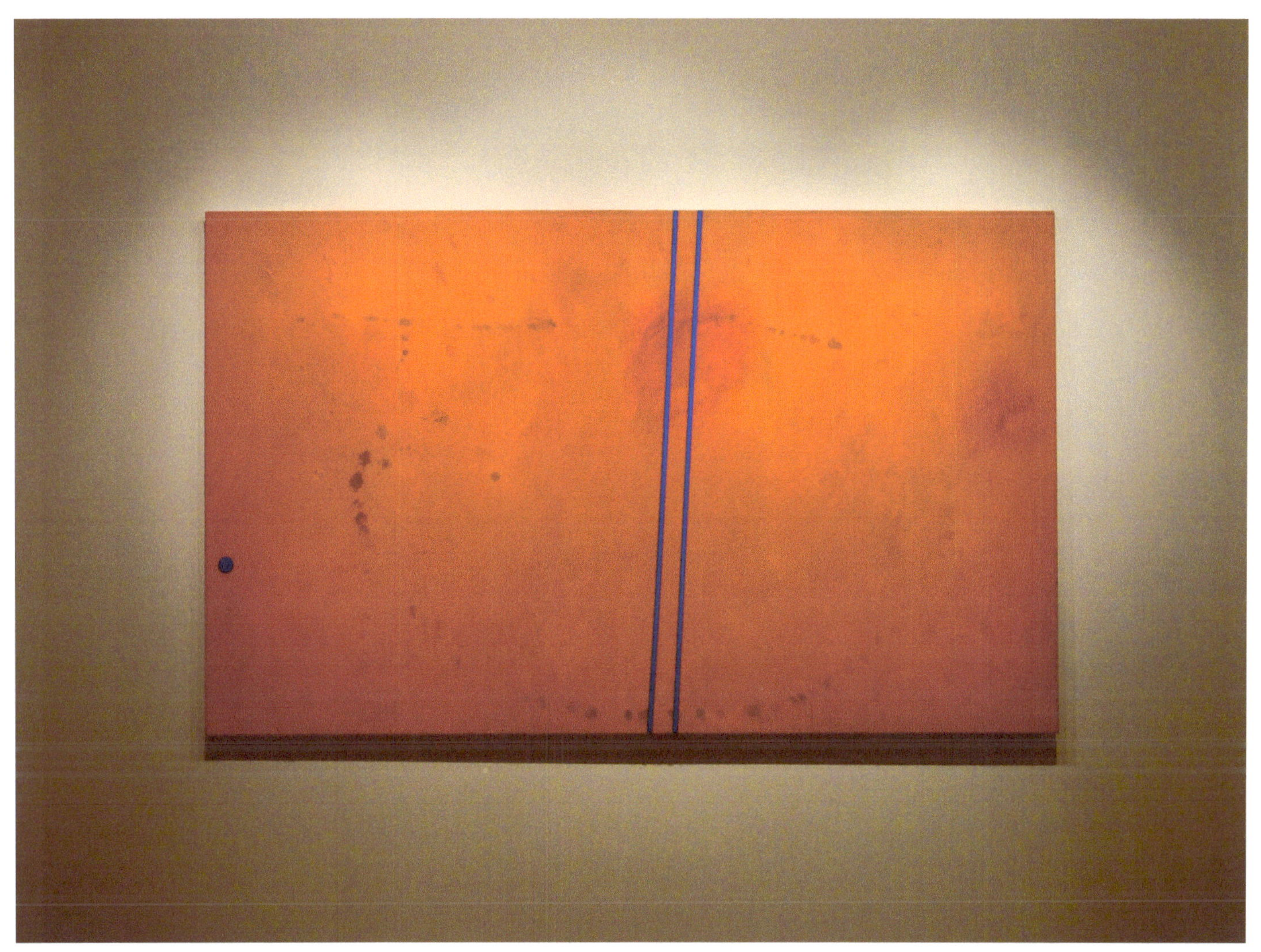

Untitled, 2010, oil on canvas, 122 x 197 cm, *Recent Works*,
Town Hall Gallery, Hawthorn

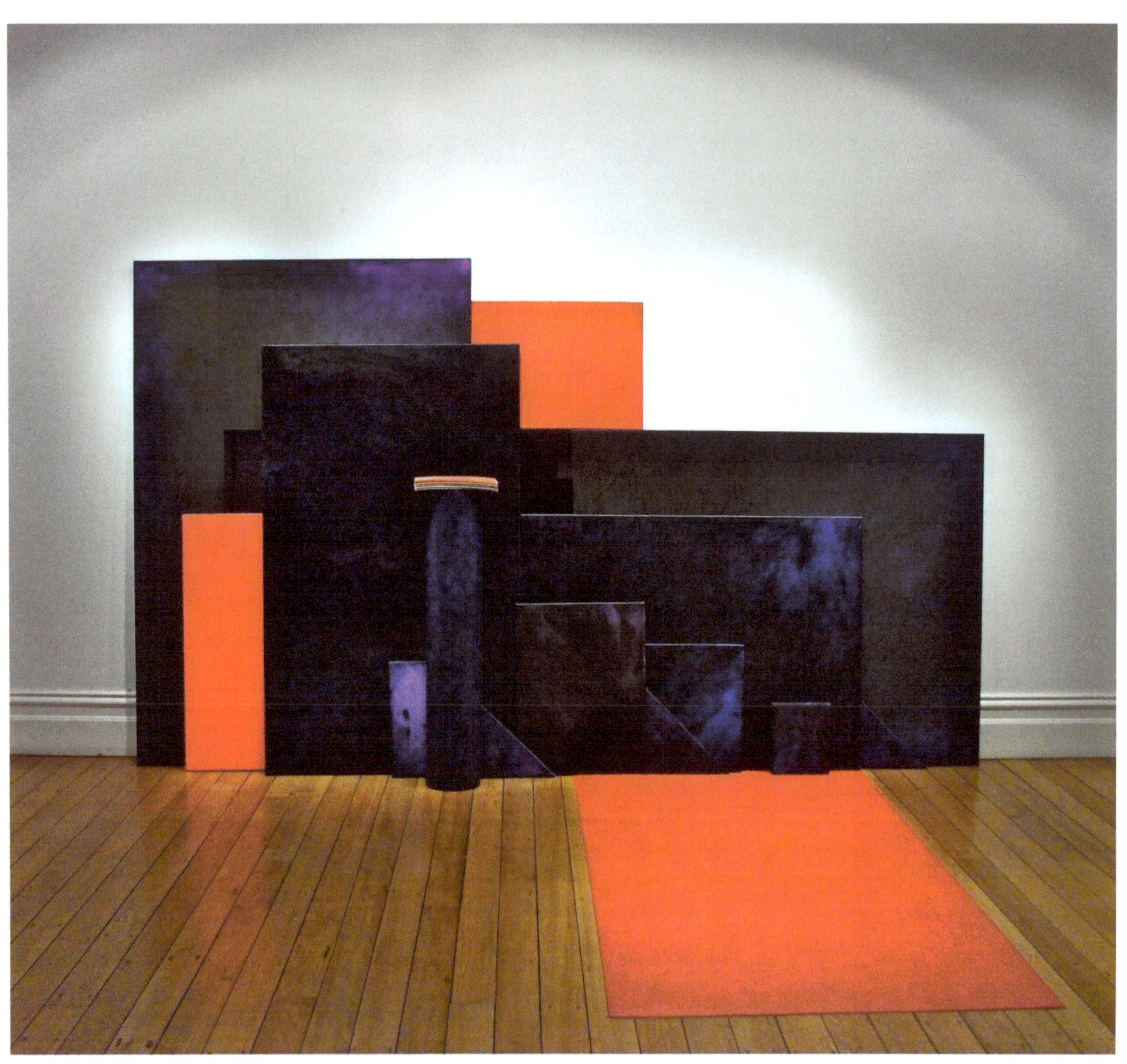

Painting stack, 2010, acrylic and oil on canvas, Marmoleum and acrylic sheet,
Recent Works, Town Hall Gallery, Hawthorn

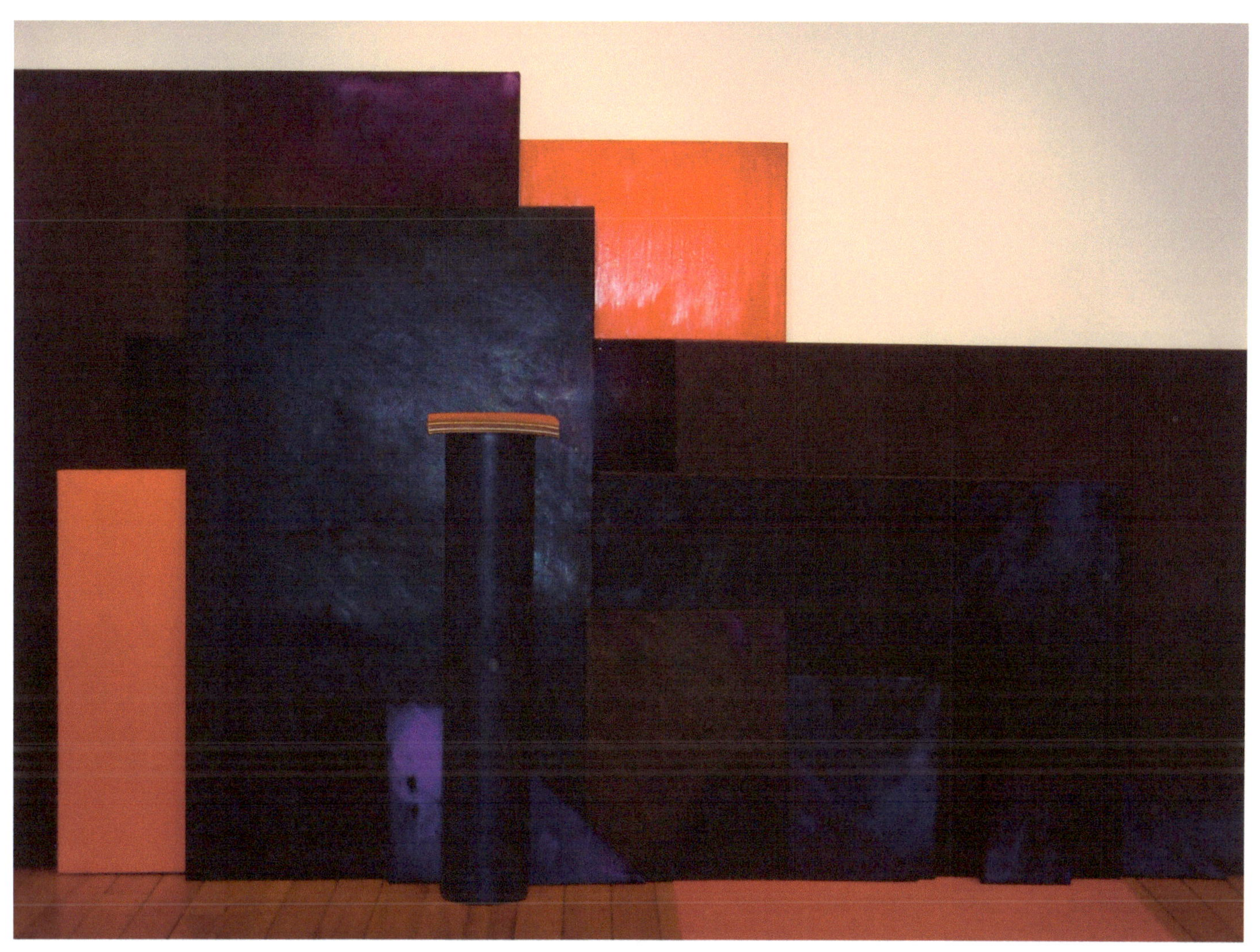

Painting stack, 2010, acrylic and oil on canvas, Marmoleum and acrylic sheet,
Recent Works, Town Hall Gallery, Hawthorn

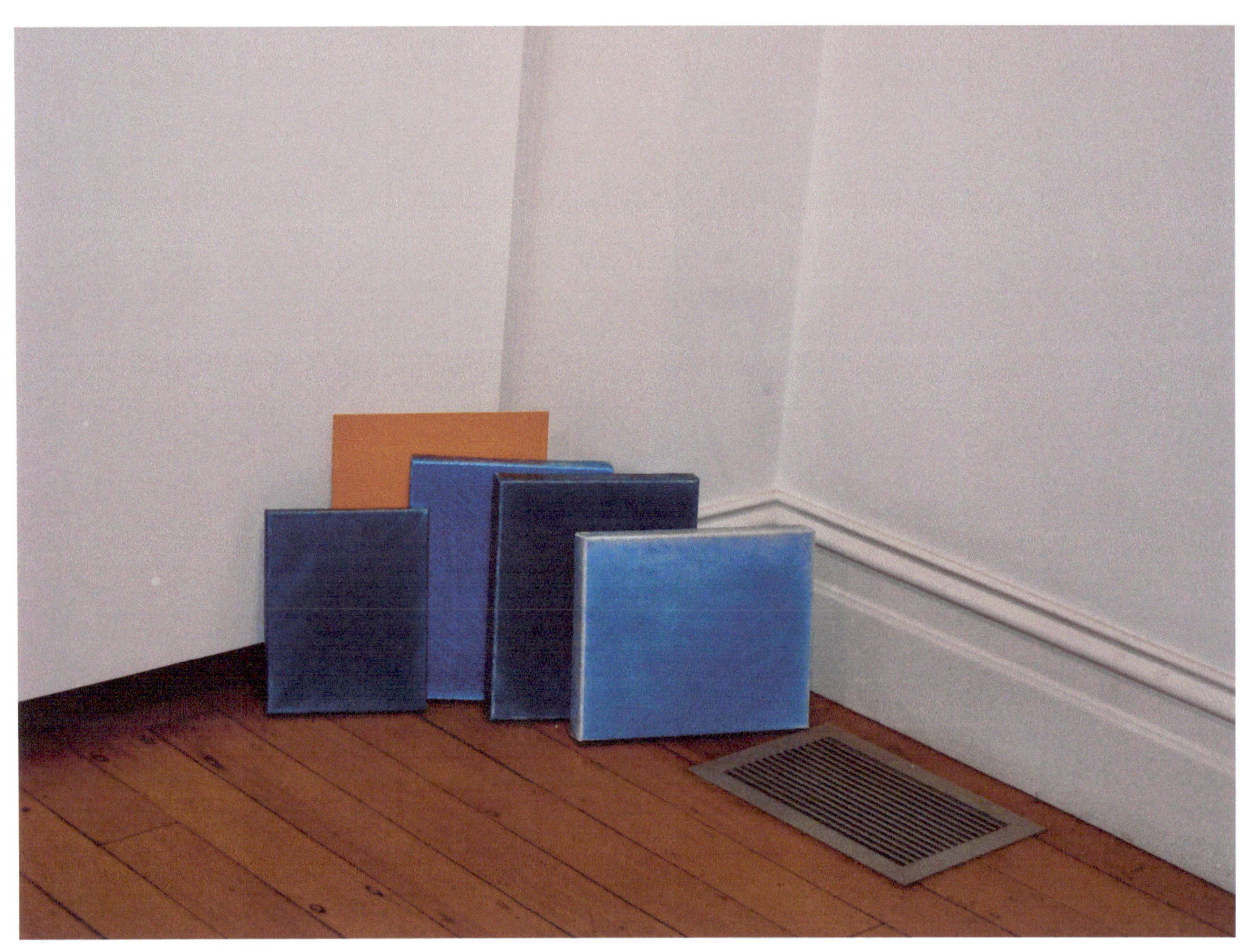

Untitled, 2010, acrylic and oil on canvas, *Recent Works*,
Town Hall Gallery, Hawthorn

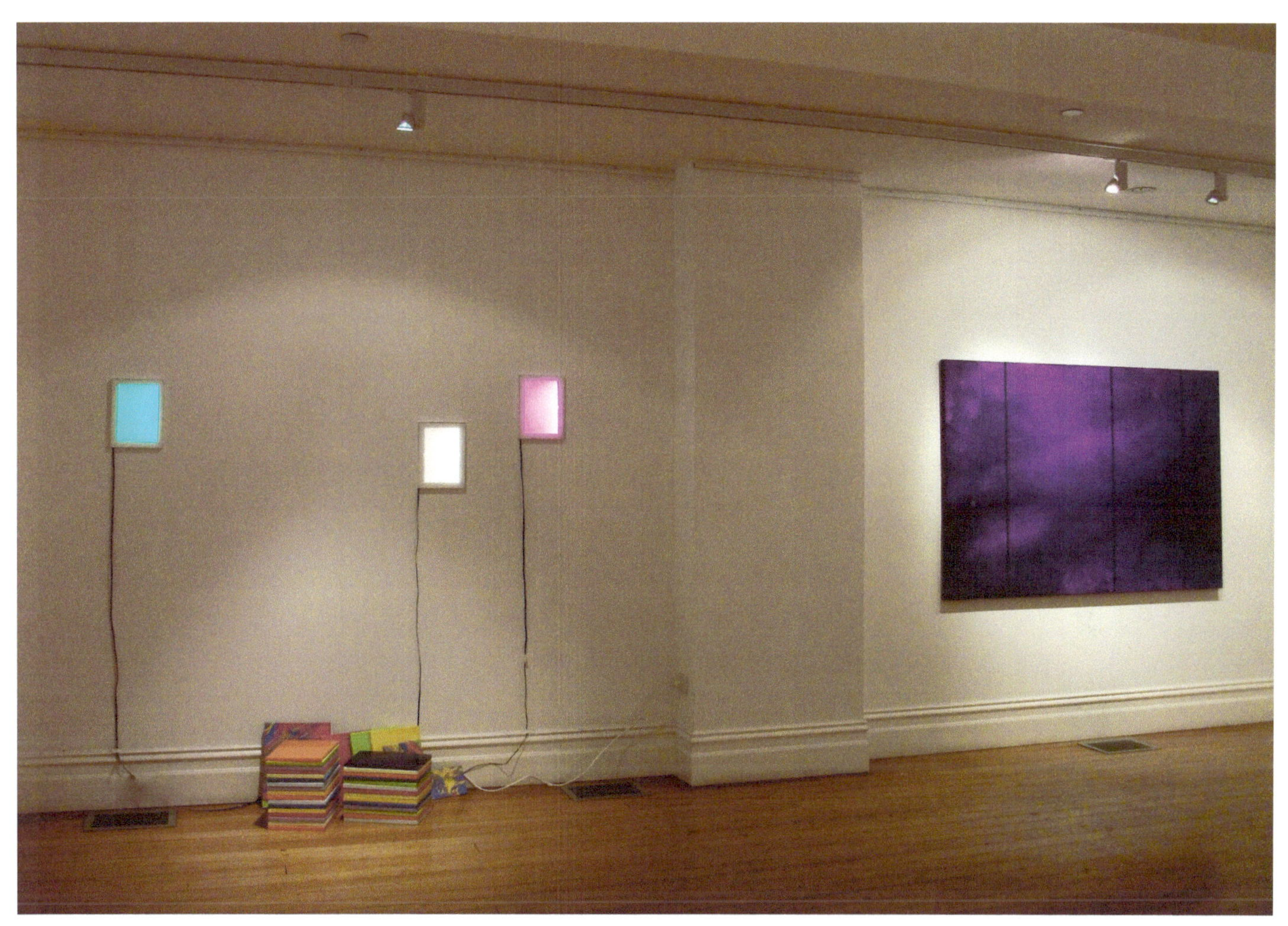

3 x A4, painting stack and untitled, 2010, programmed LED light boxes, acrylic on canvas and acrylic sheet, 3 x 21 x 30 cm and various, *Recent Works*, Town Hall Gallery, Hawthorn

2011

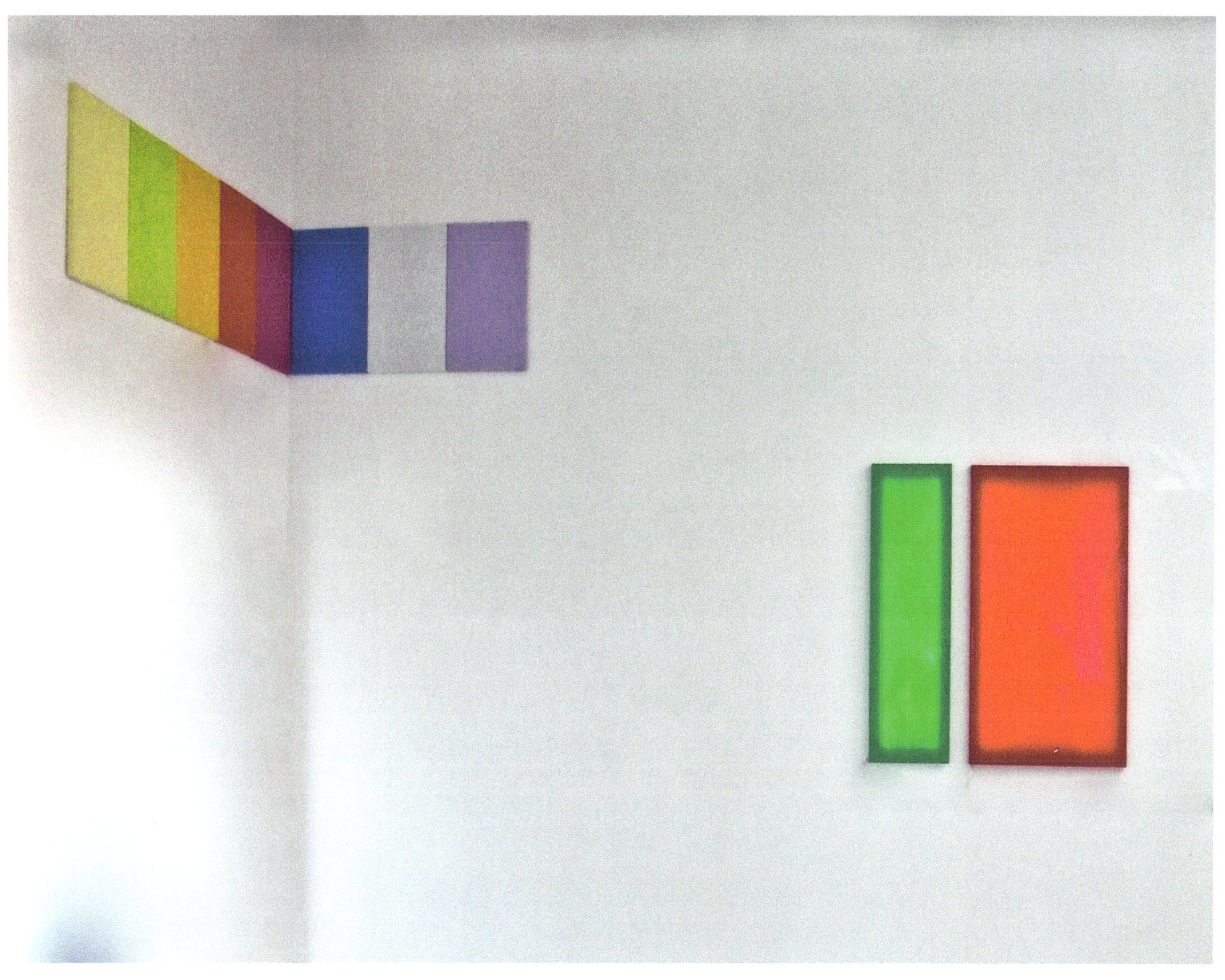

Colour screens, 2011, acrylic on canvas, programmed LED light boxes and acrylic sheet,
8 x A4 canvases, 2 x A4 and 4 x A4 screens

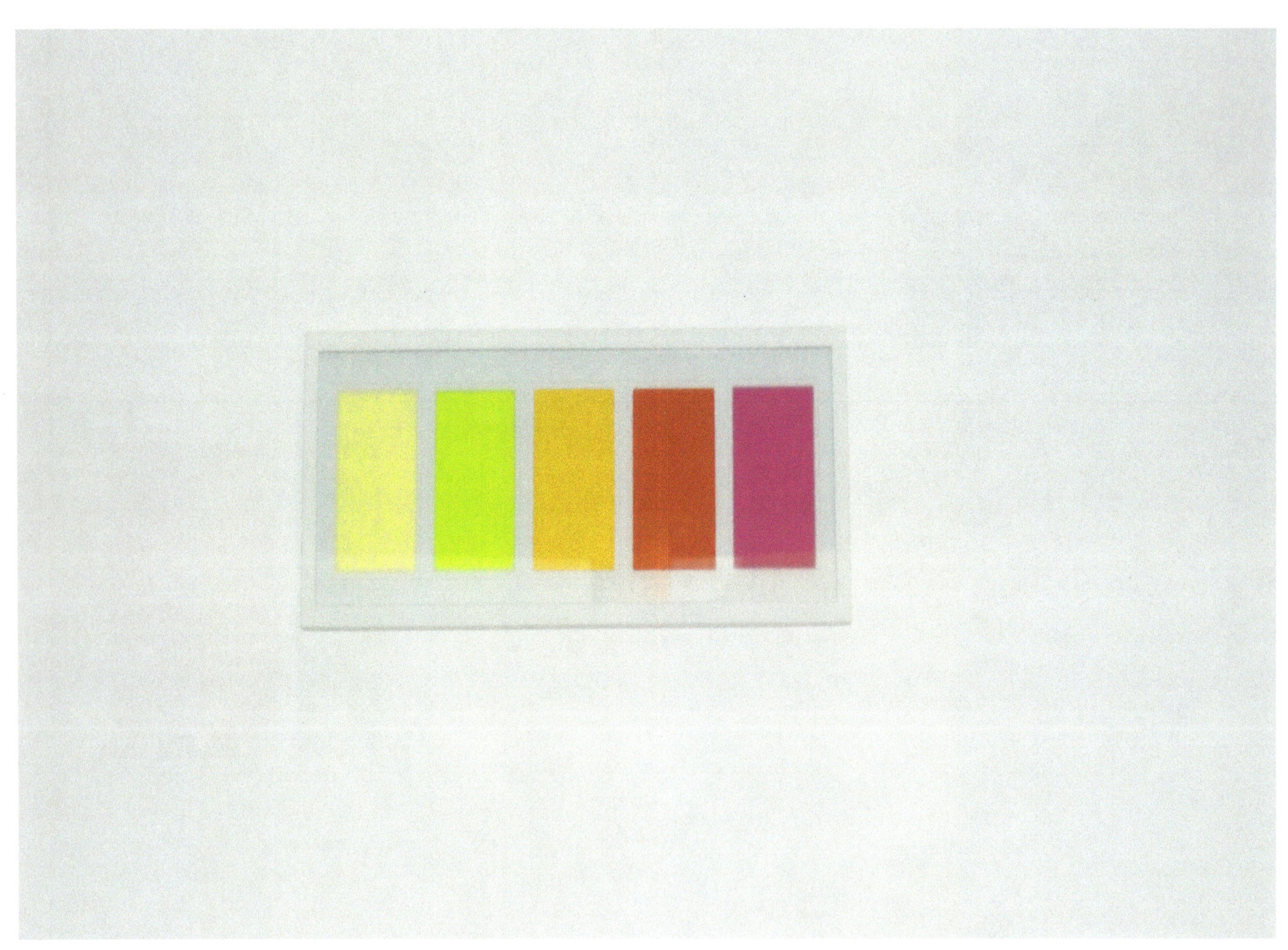

Colour fields, 2011, acrylic on paper, programmed, 23 x 61 cm

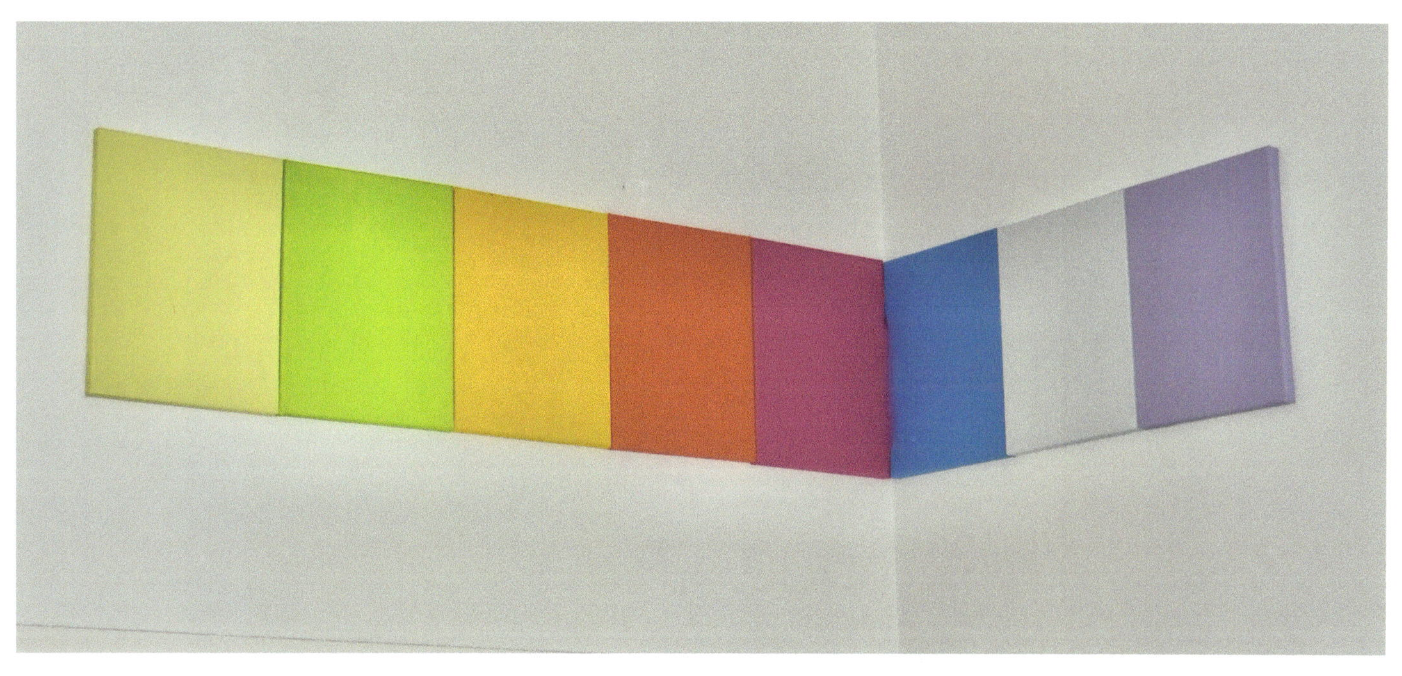

Colour screens, 2011, acrylic on canvas, 8 x A4 canvases,
Ramp Gallery, Monash Gallery of Art, Wheelers Hill

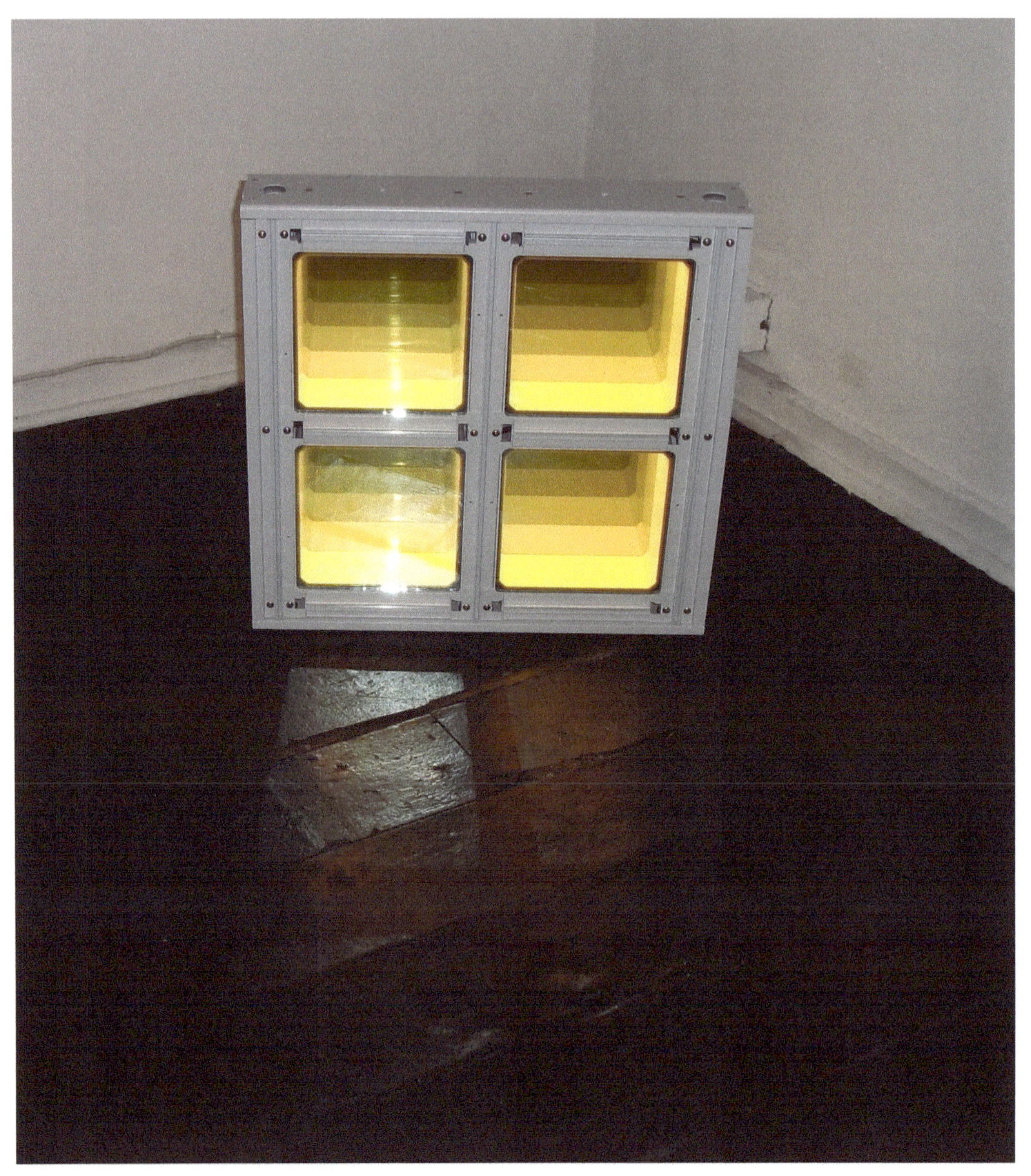

2 x 2, 2011, programmed LED light boxes, 51 x 51 cm
Intoxication, Off the Kerb, Collingwood

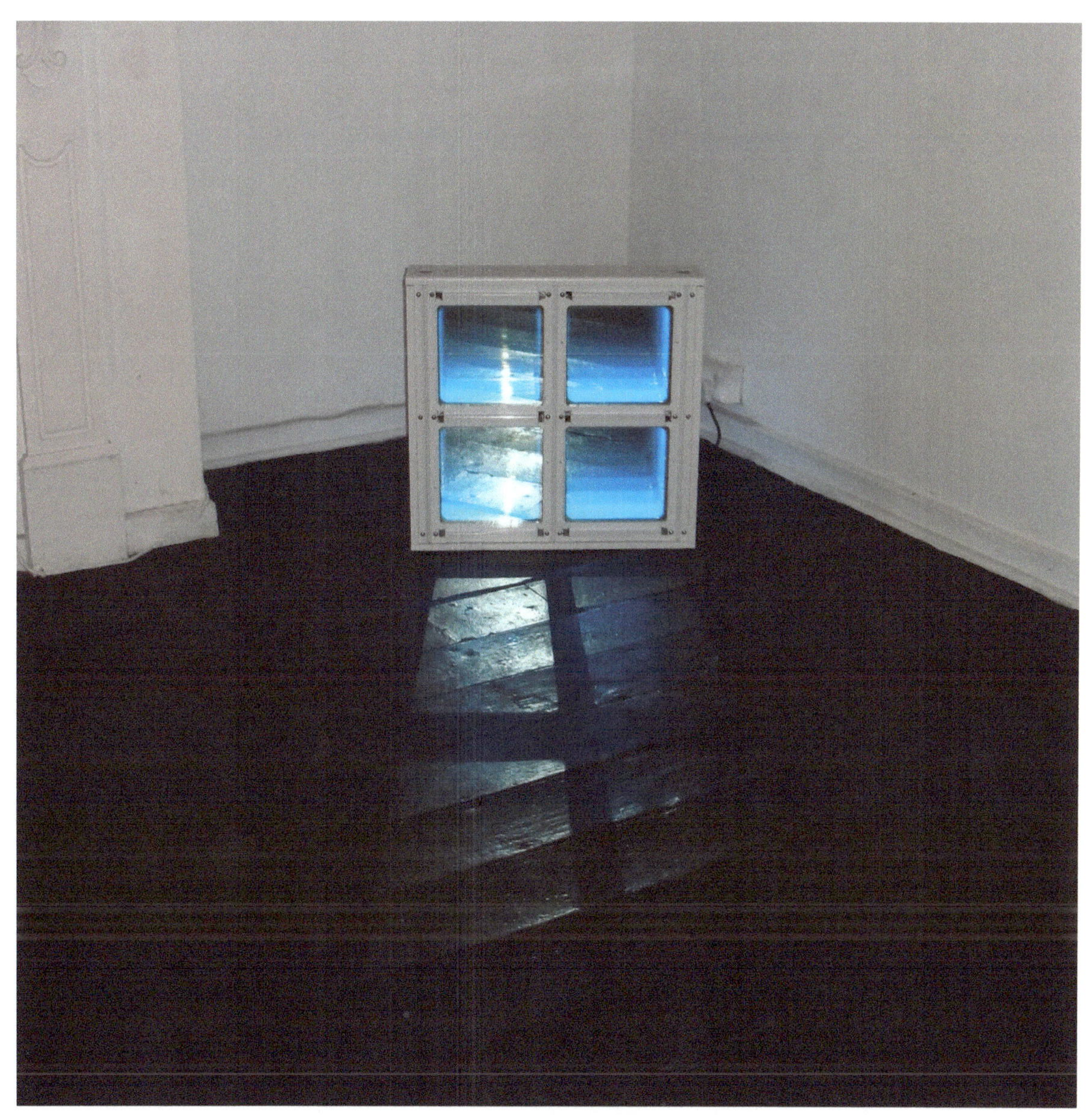

2 x 2, 2011, programmed LED light boxes, 51 x 51 cm
Intoxication, Off the Kerb, Collingwood

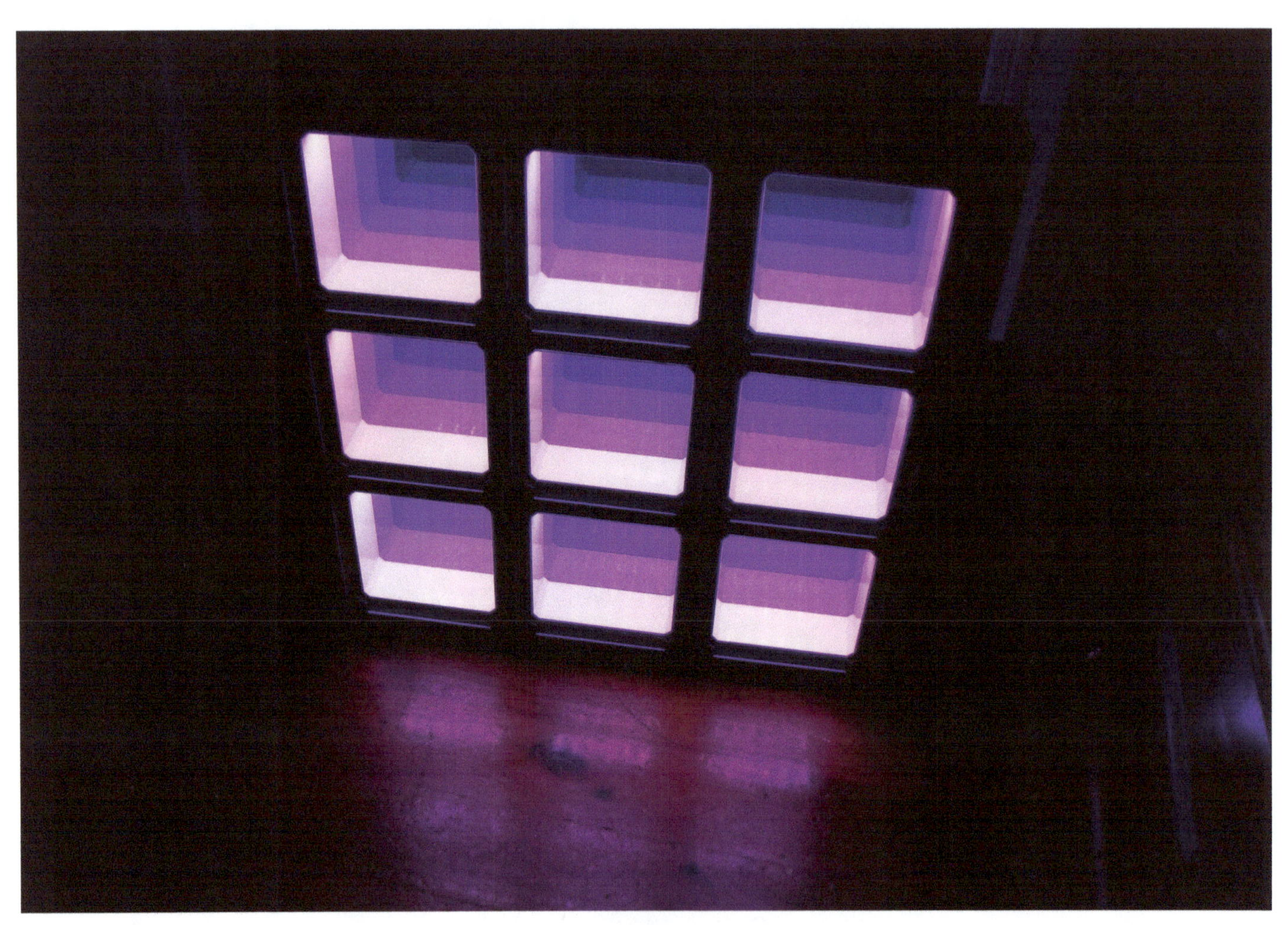

3 x 3, 2011, programmed LED light boxes, 74 x 74 cm

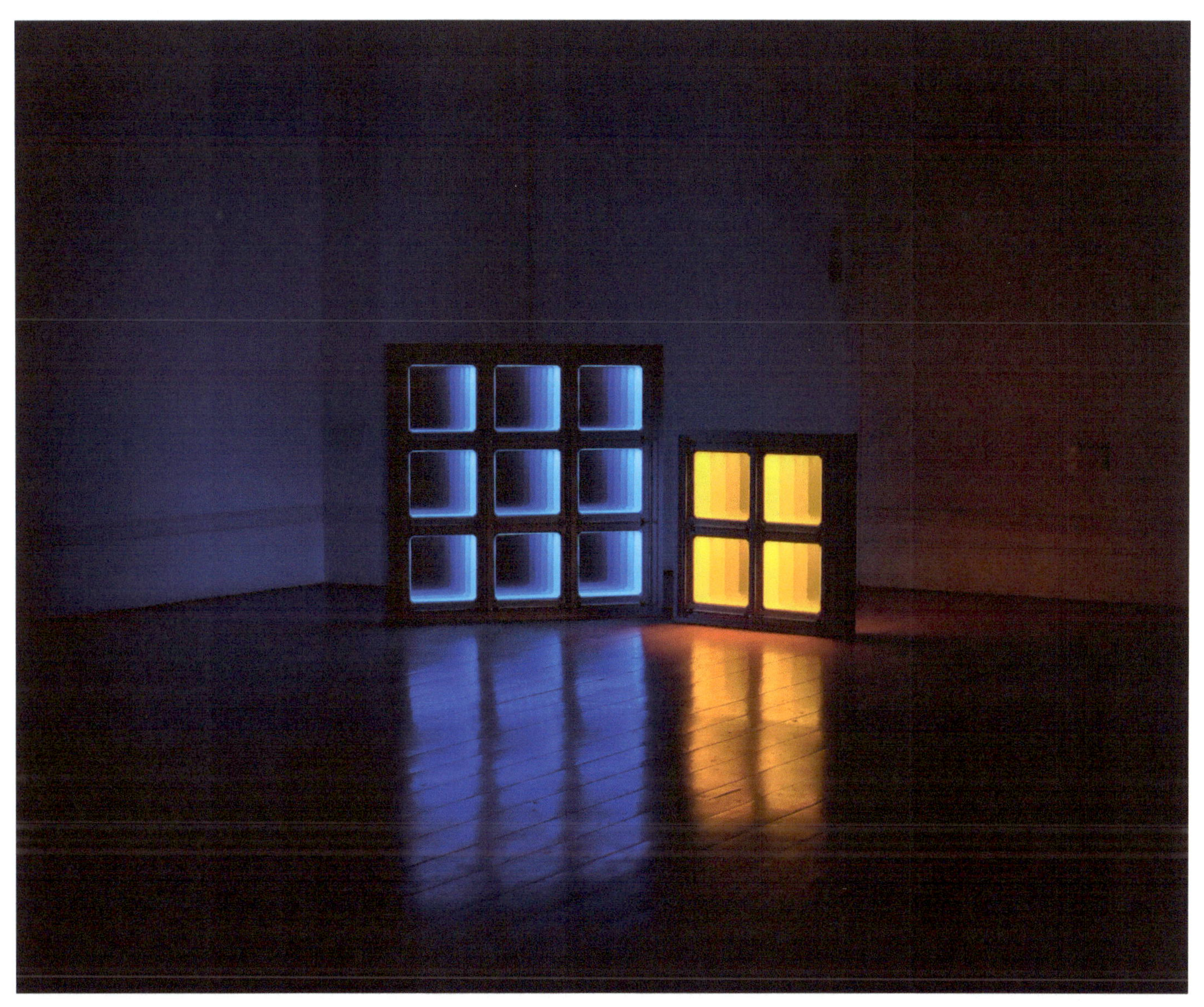

3 x 3 and 2 x 2, 2011, programmed LED light boxes, 74 x 74 cm and 51 x 51 cm,
PRE-FAB, Town Hall Gallery, Hawthorn

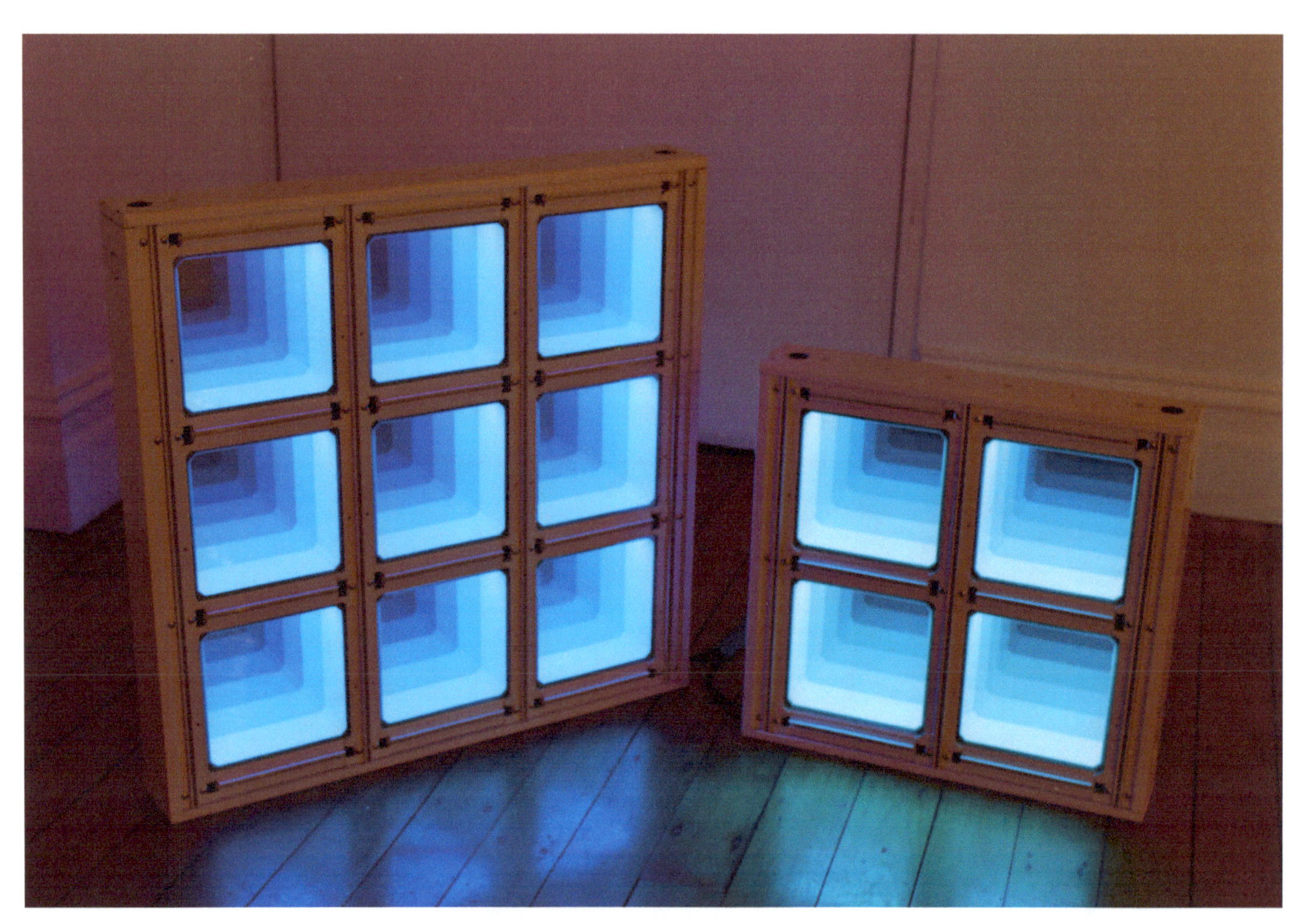

3 x 3 and 2 x 2, 2011, programmed LED light boxes, 74 x 74 cm and 51 x 51 cm

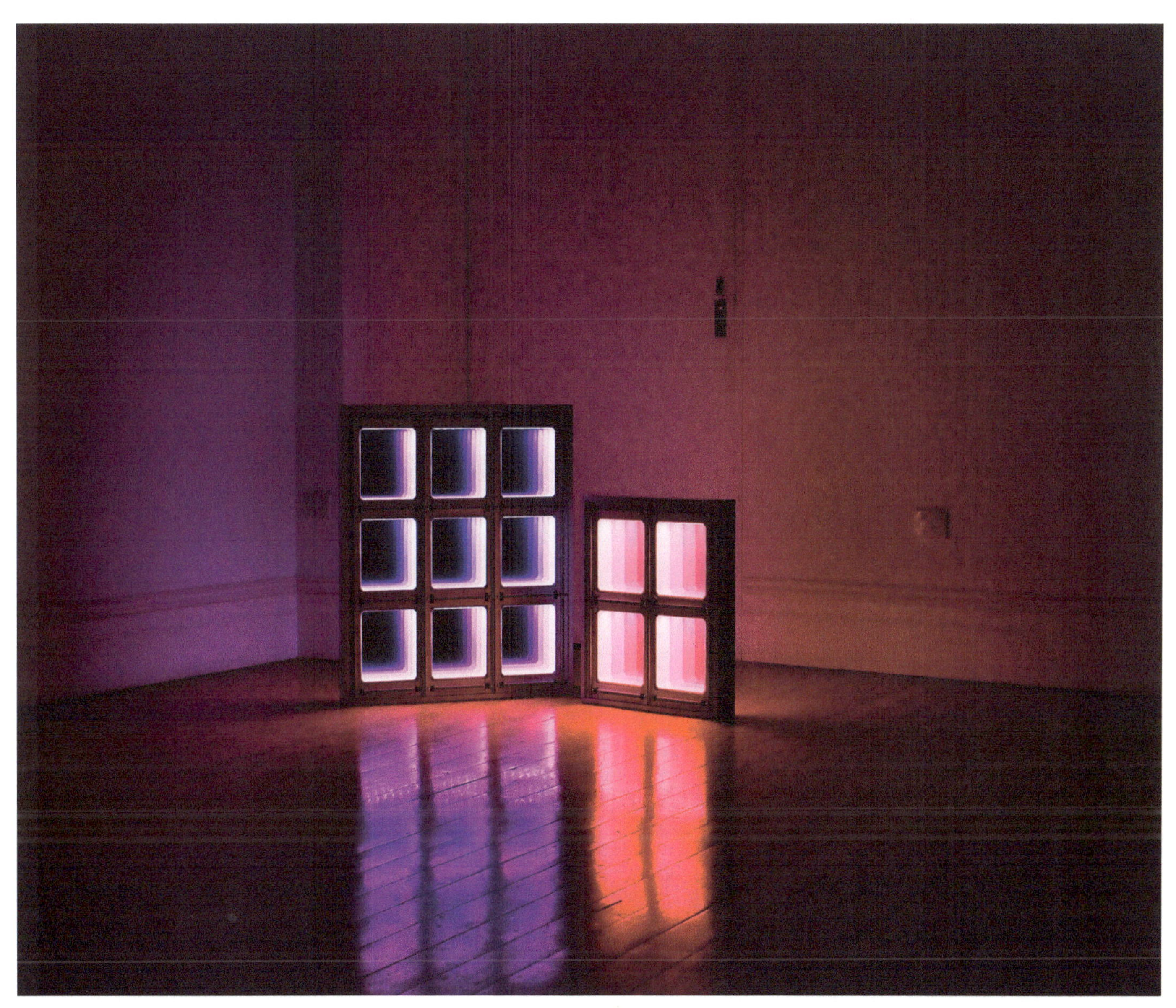

3 x 3 and 2 x 2, 2011, programmed LED light boxes, 74 x 74 cm and 51 x 51 cm

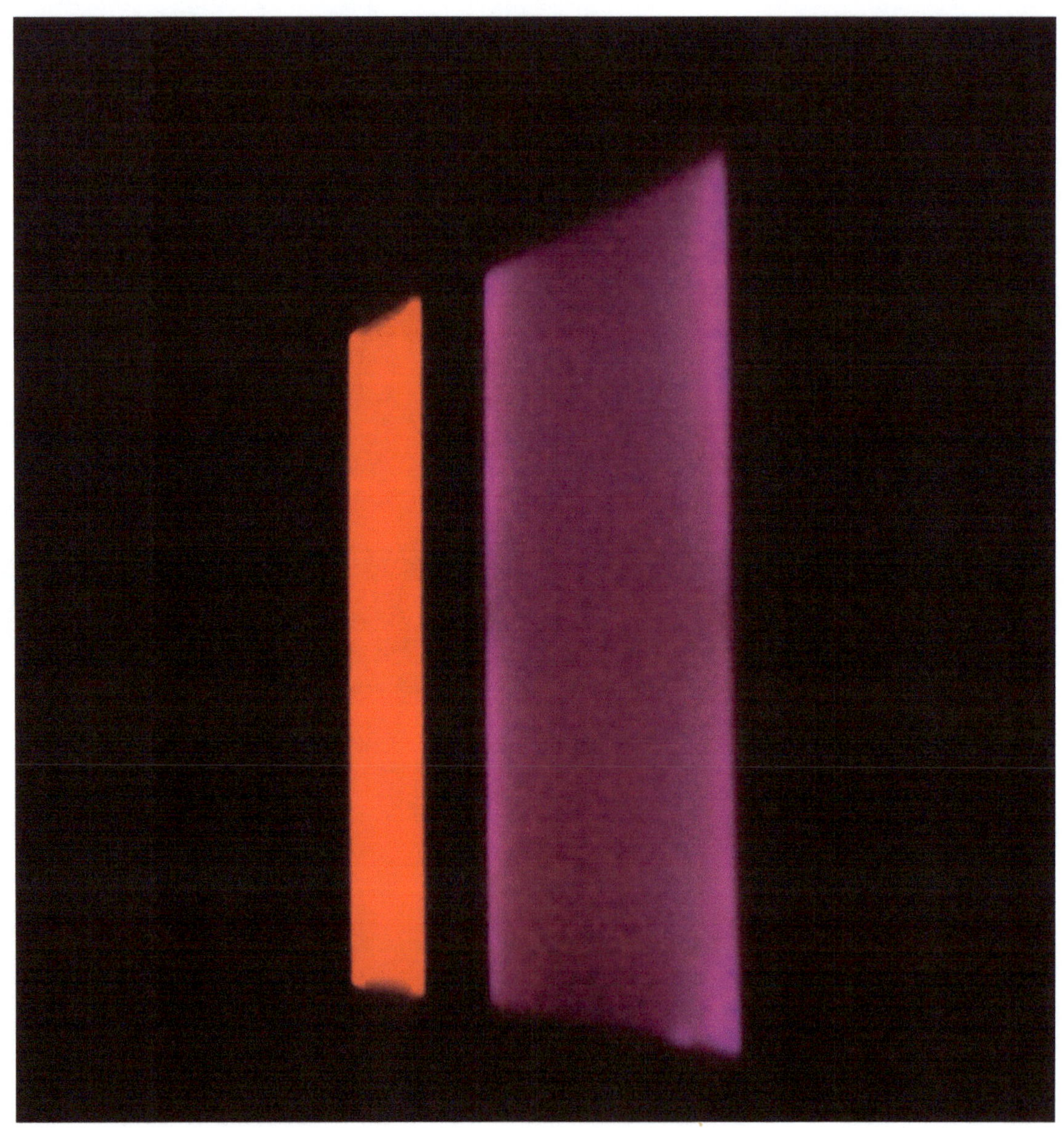

Colour screens, 2011, programmed LED light boxes and acrylic sheet,
2 x A4 and 4 x A4 screens, Monash University, Caulfield

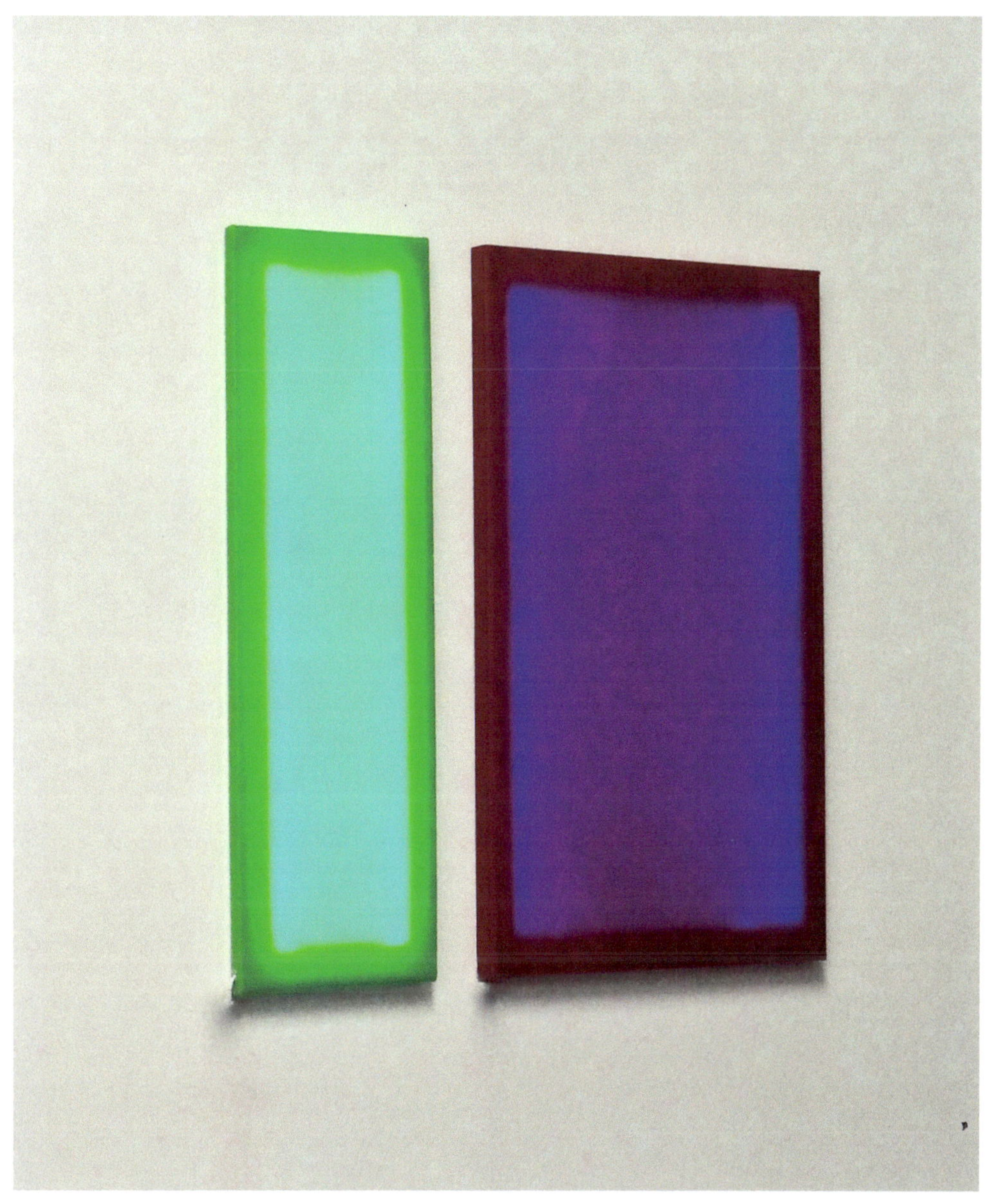

Colour screens, 2011, programmed LED light boxes and acrylic sheet,
2 x A4 and 4 x A4 screens, Monash University, Caulfield

2012

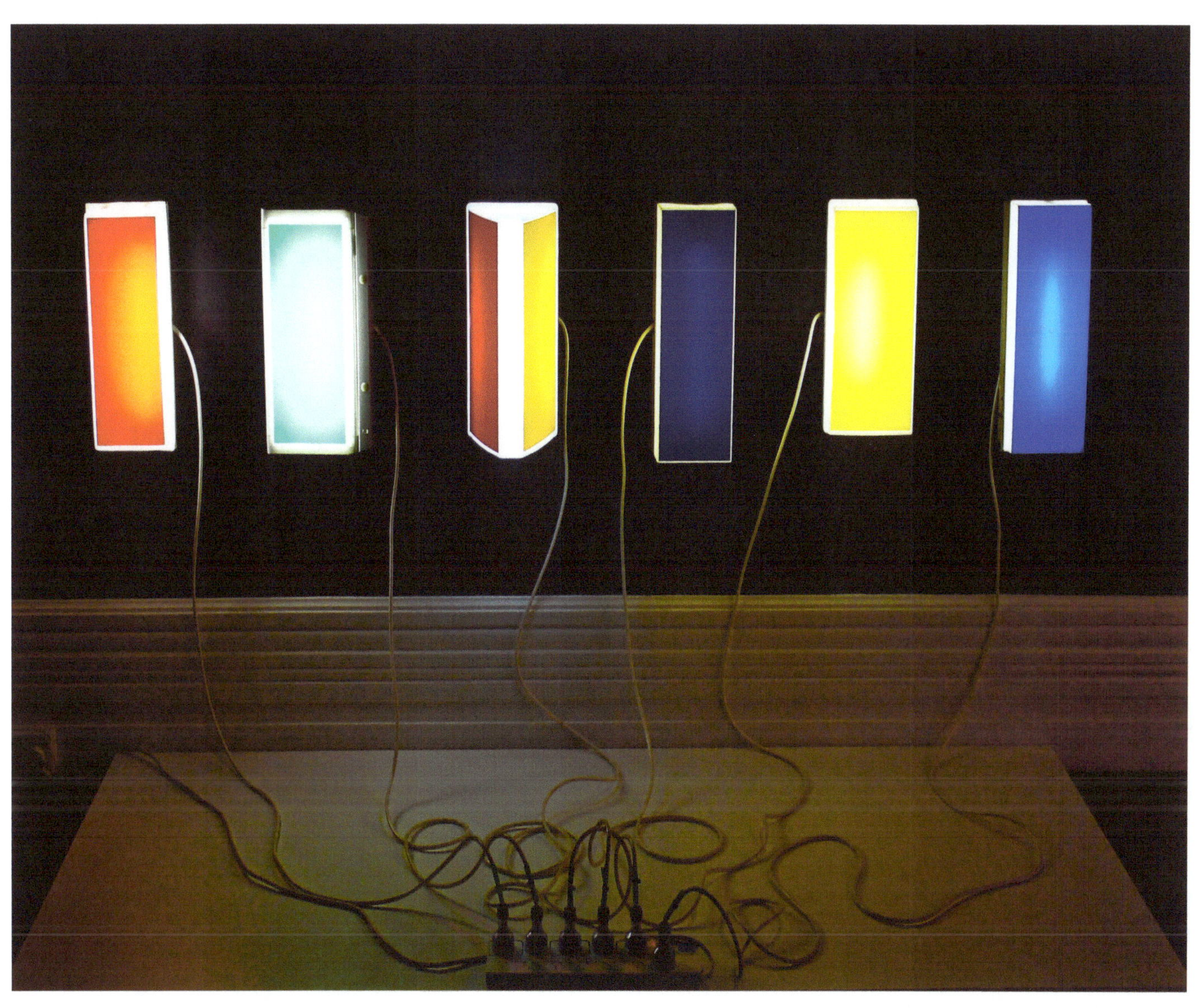

Exit signs, 2012, reworked exit signs, LEDs and vinyl, *Albury Art Prize*, MAMA, Albury

Untitled, 2012, programmed LED light box, 27 x 27 cm

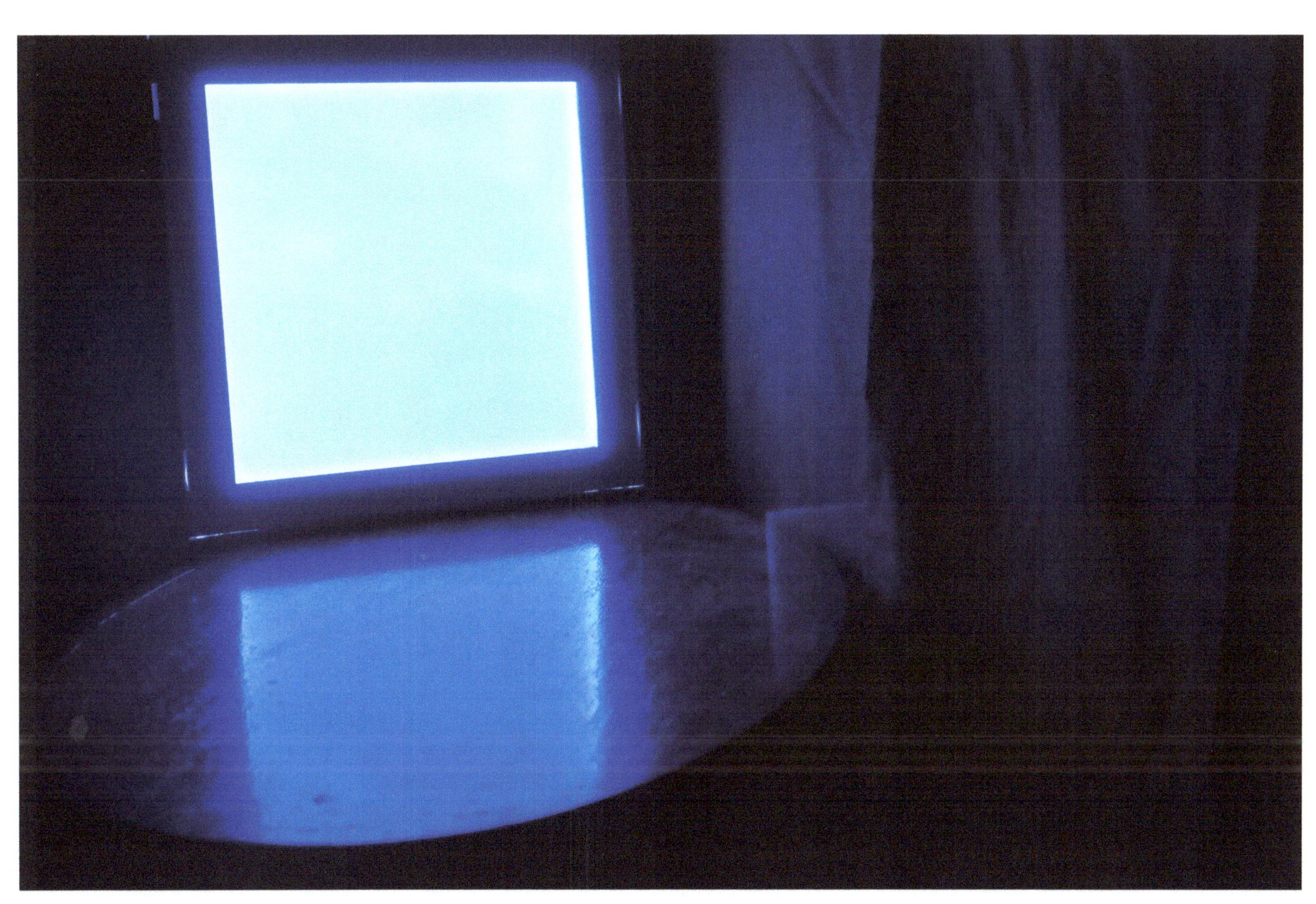

Untitled, 2012, programmed LED light box, 27 x 27 cm

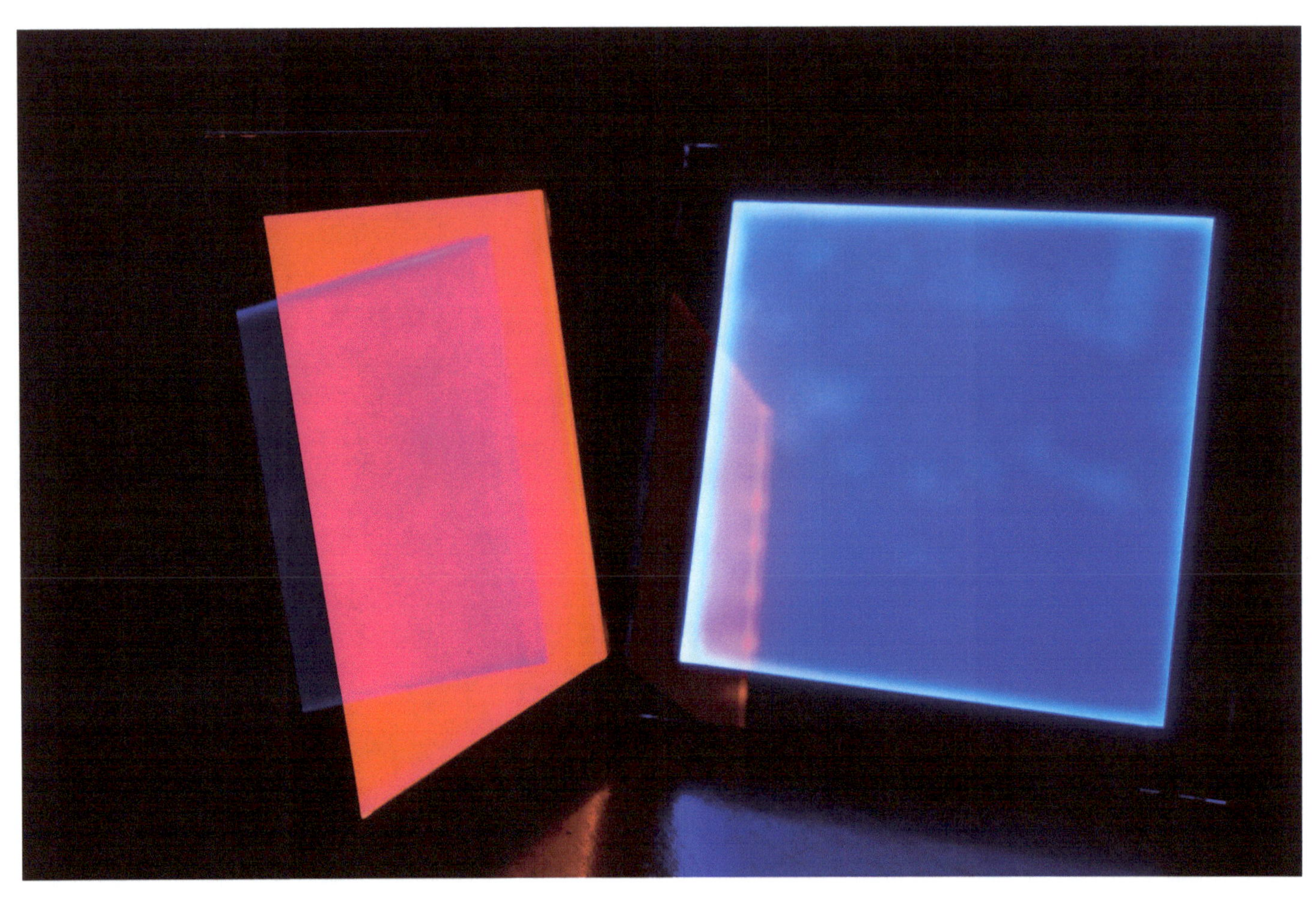

Untitled, 2012, programmed LED light boxes, 2 x 27 x 27 cm

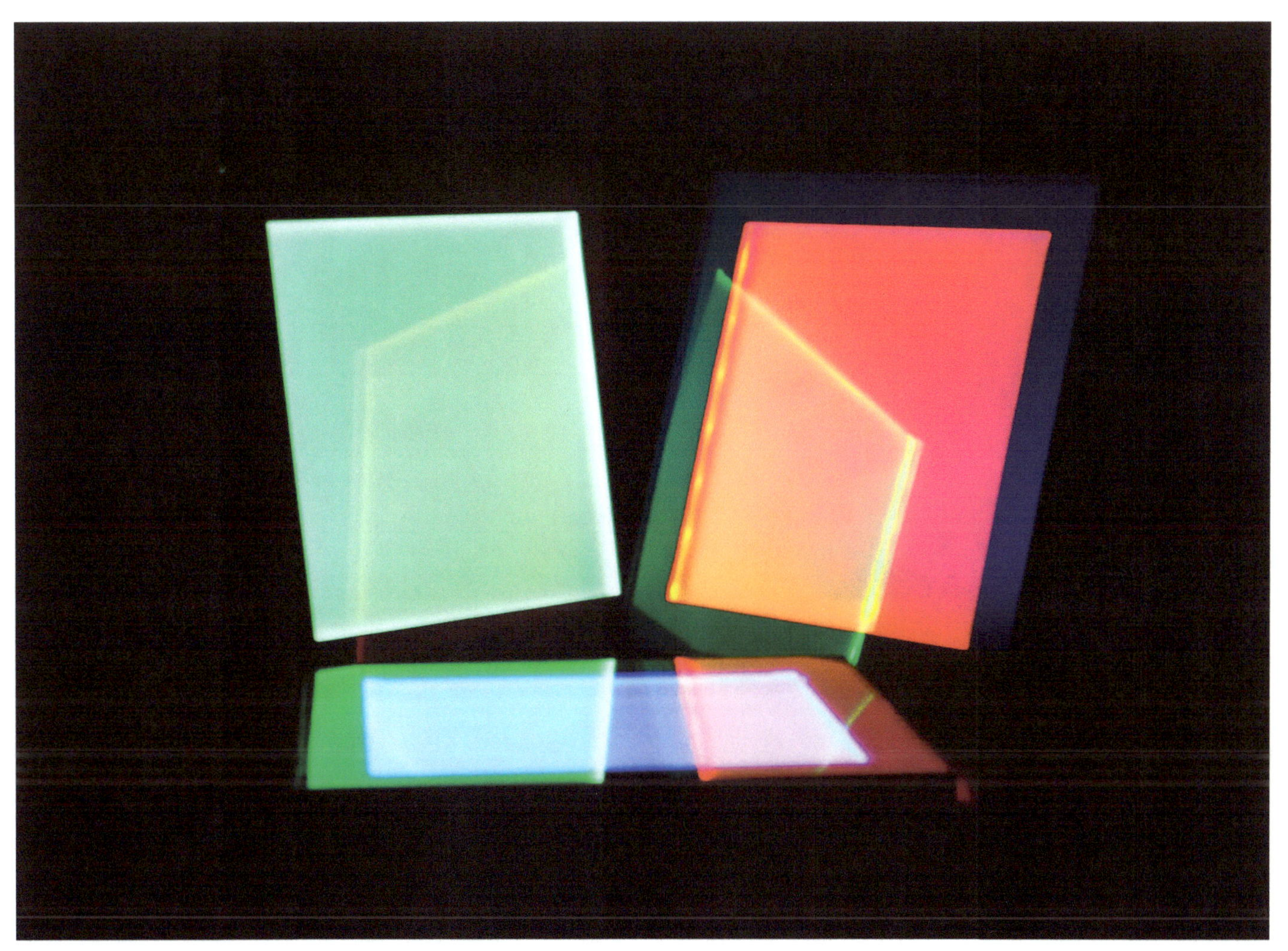

Untitled, 2012, programmed LED light boxes, 2 x 27 x 27 cm

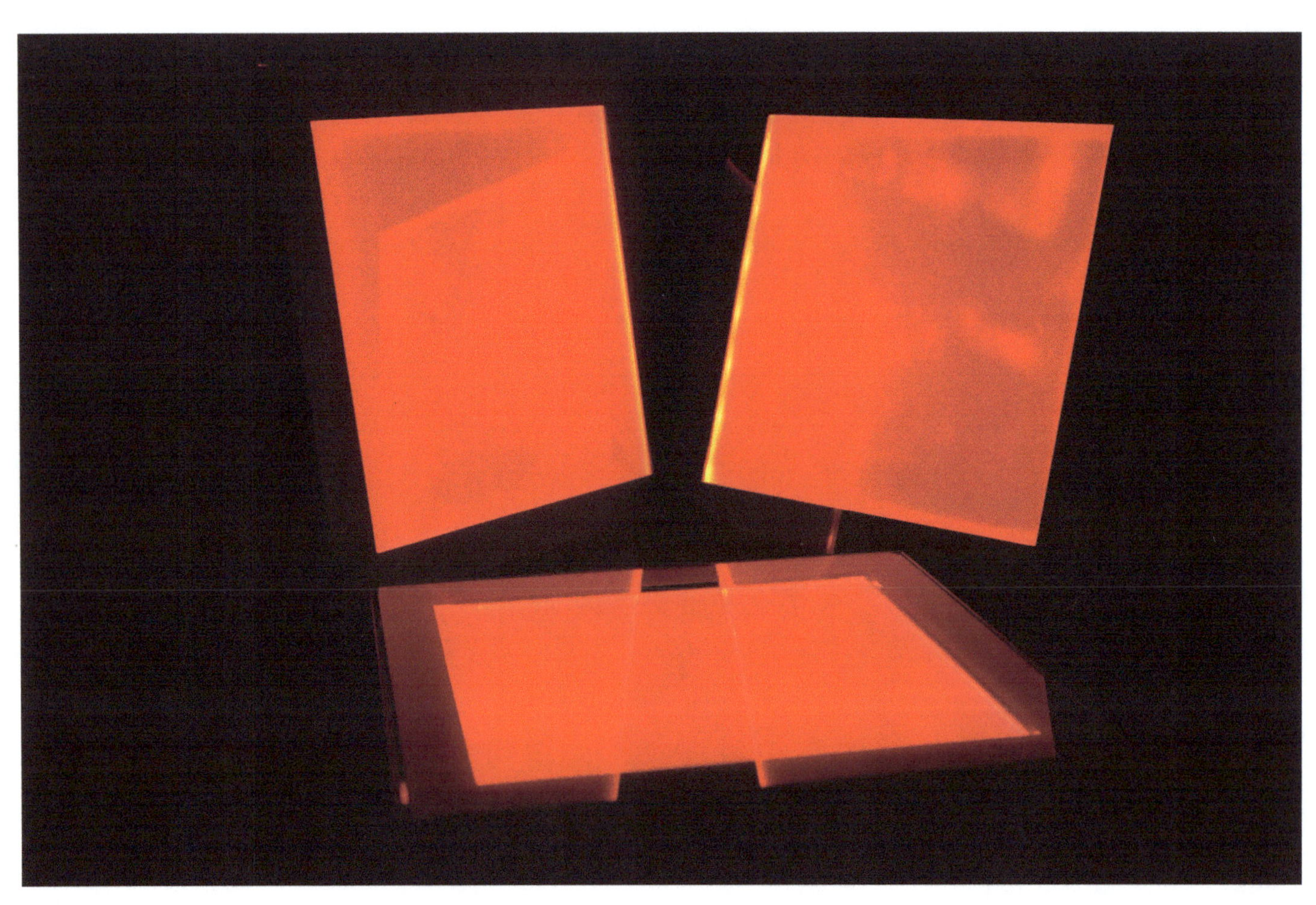

Untitled, 2012, programmed LED light boxes, 3 x 27 x 27 cm

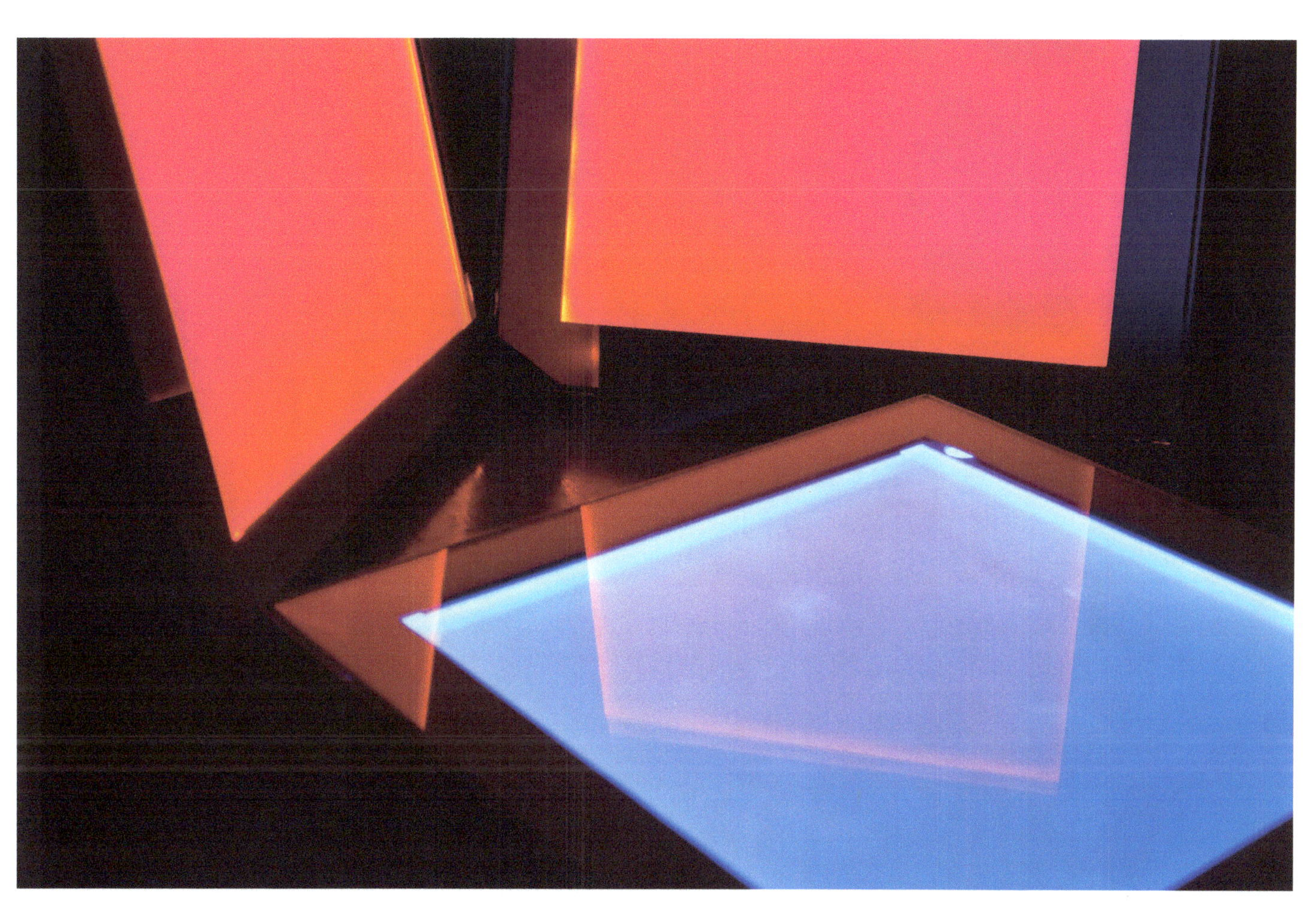

Untitled, 2012, programmed LED light boxes, 3 x 27 x 27 cm

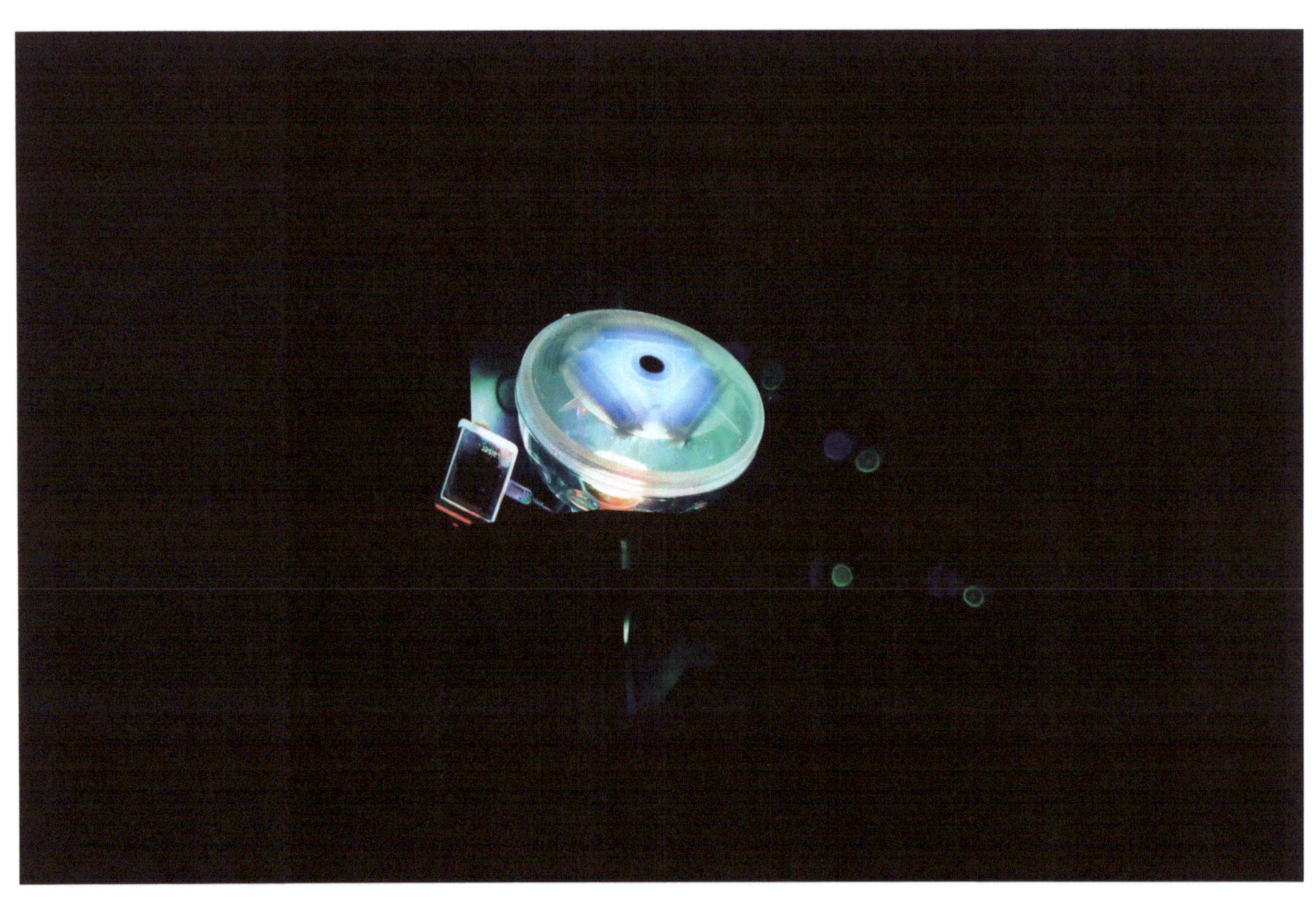

Untitled, 2012, various LED lights, 20 x 20 cm

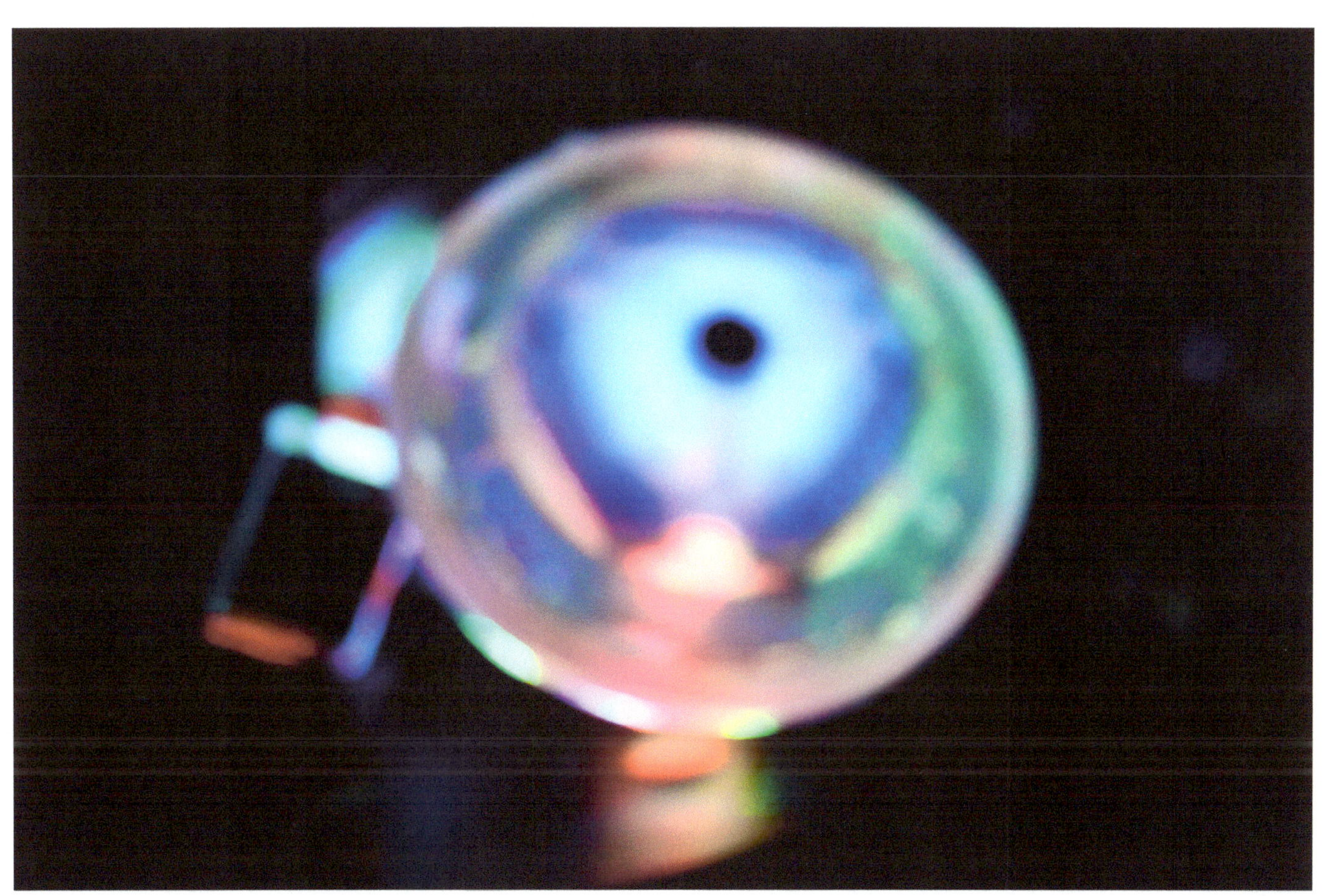

Untitled, 2012, various LED lights, 20 x 20 cm

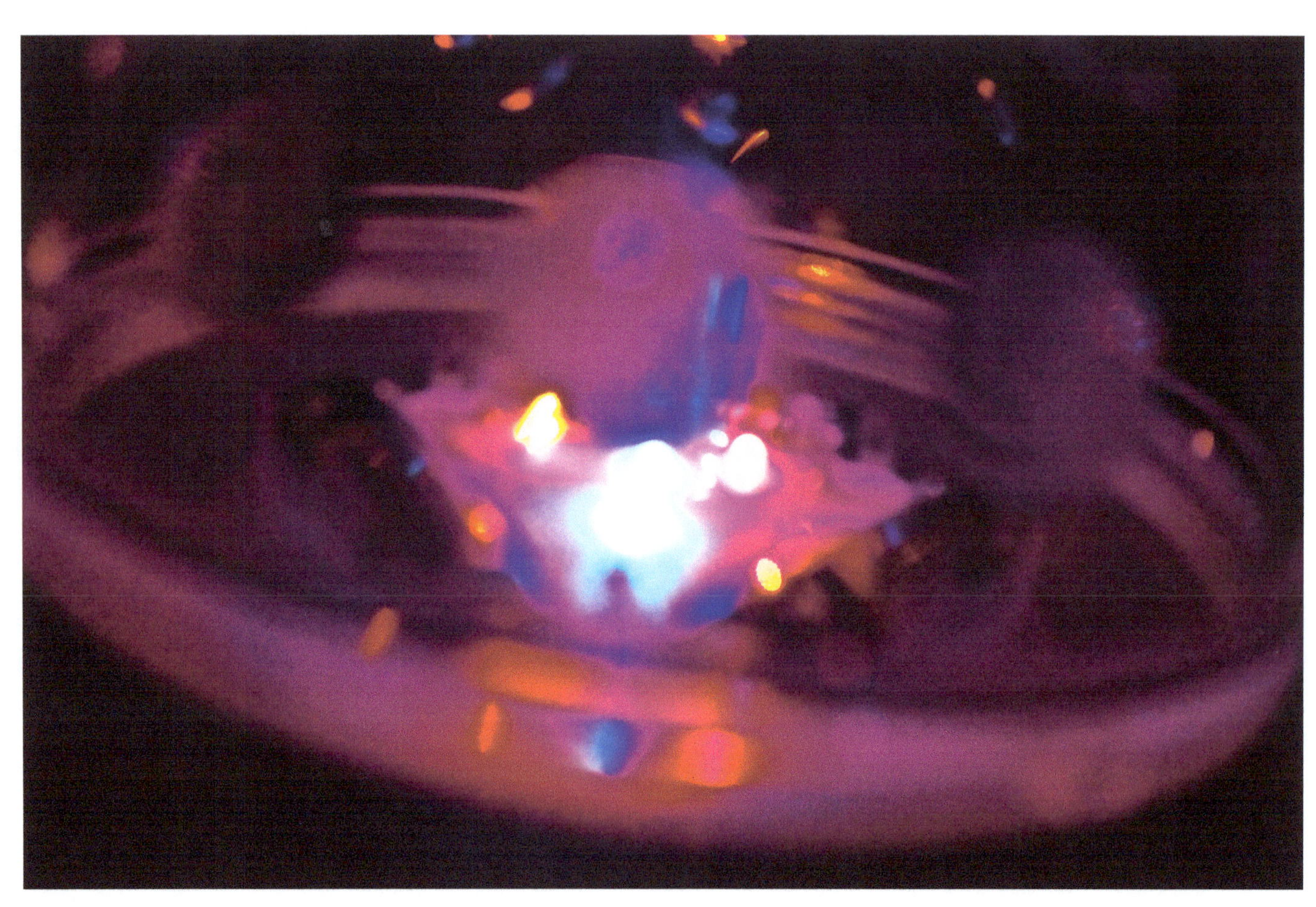

Untitled, 2012, various LED lights, 22 x 22 cm

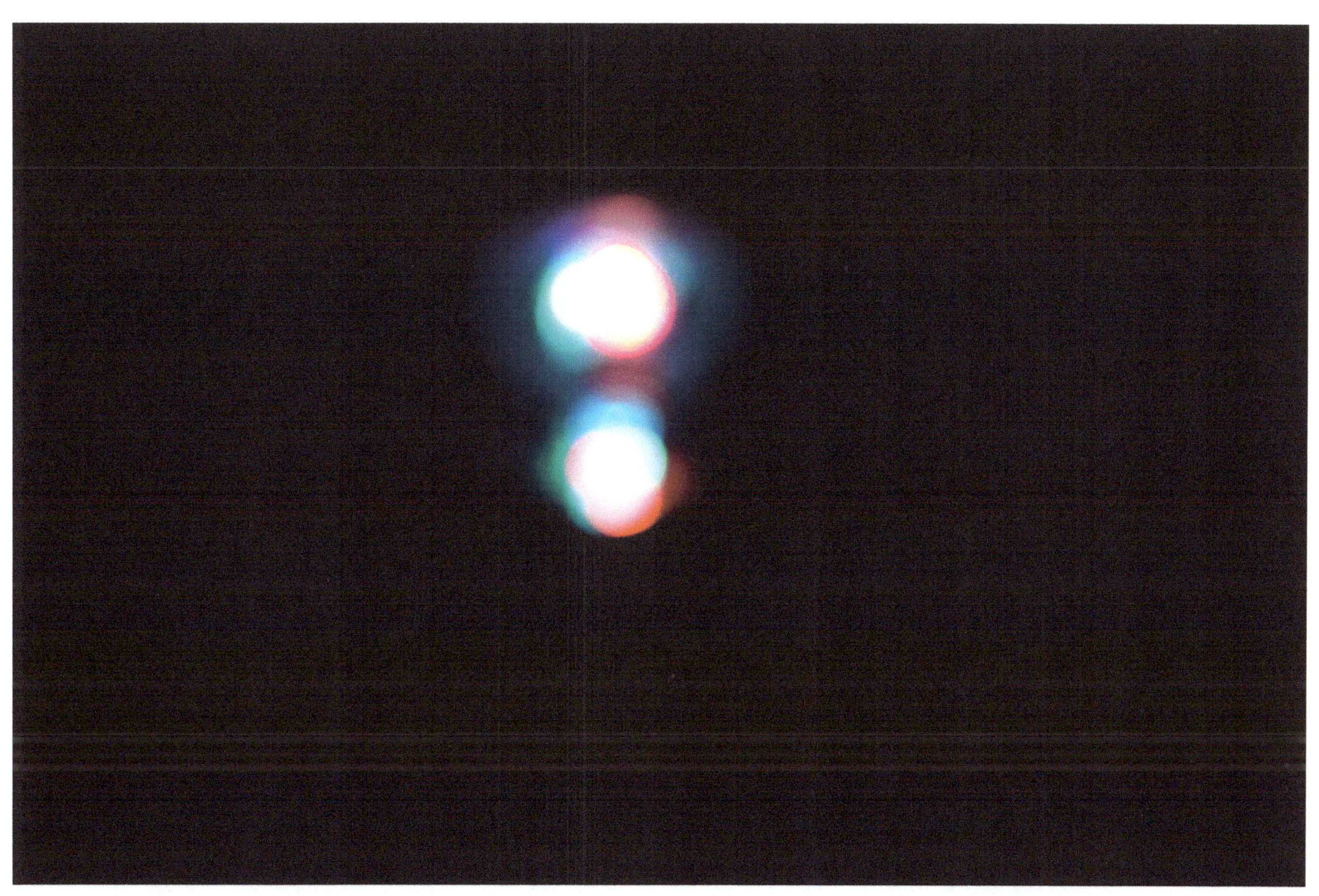

Untitled, 2012, various LED lights, 10 x 15 cm

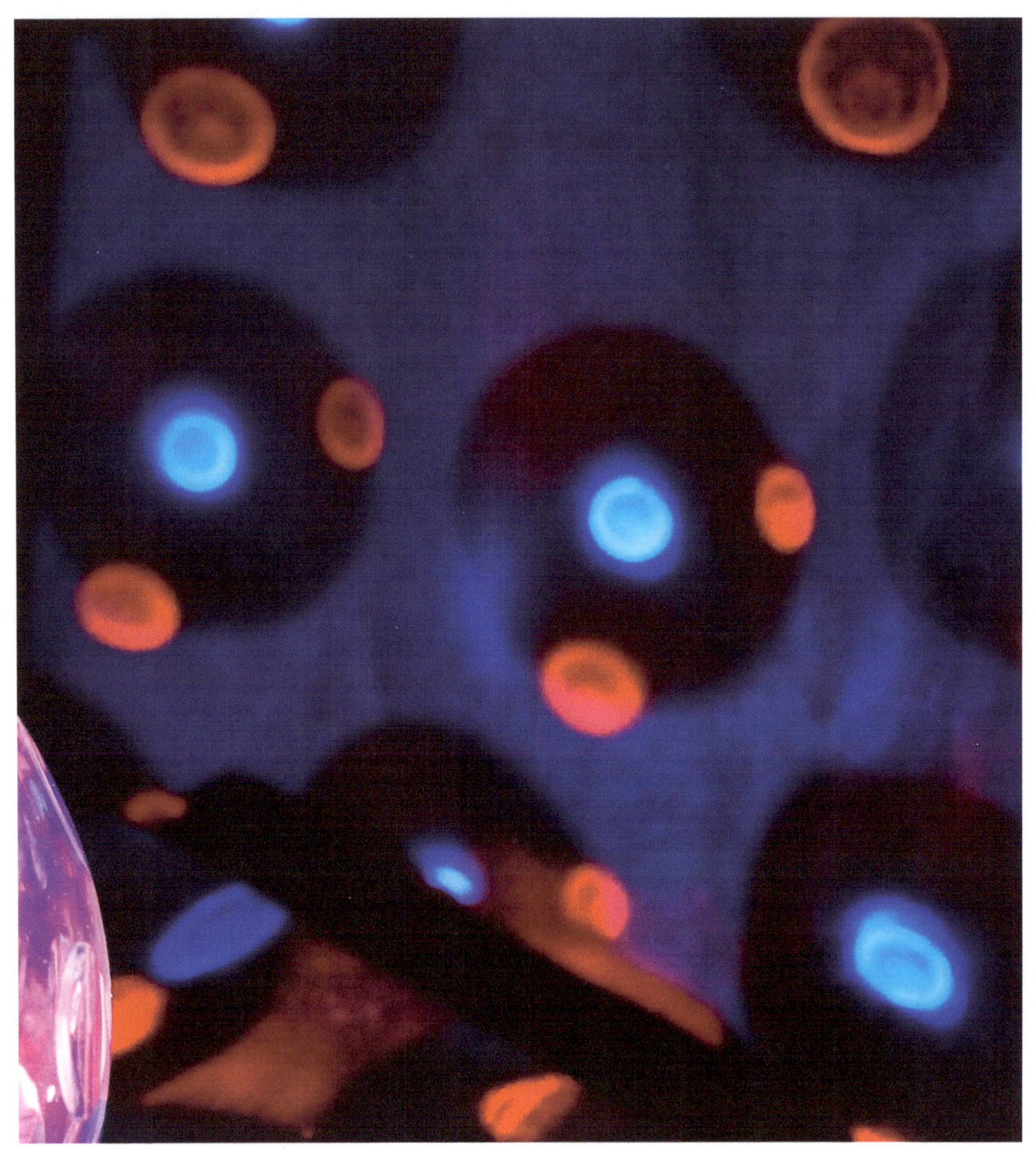

Untitled, 2012, various LED lights, 25 x 25 cm

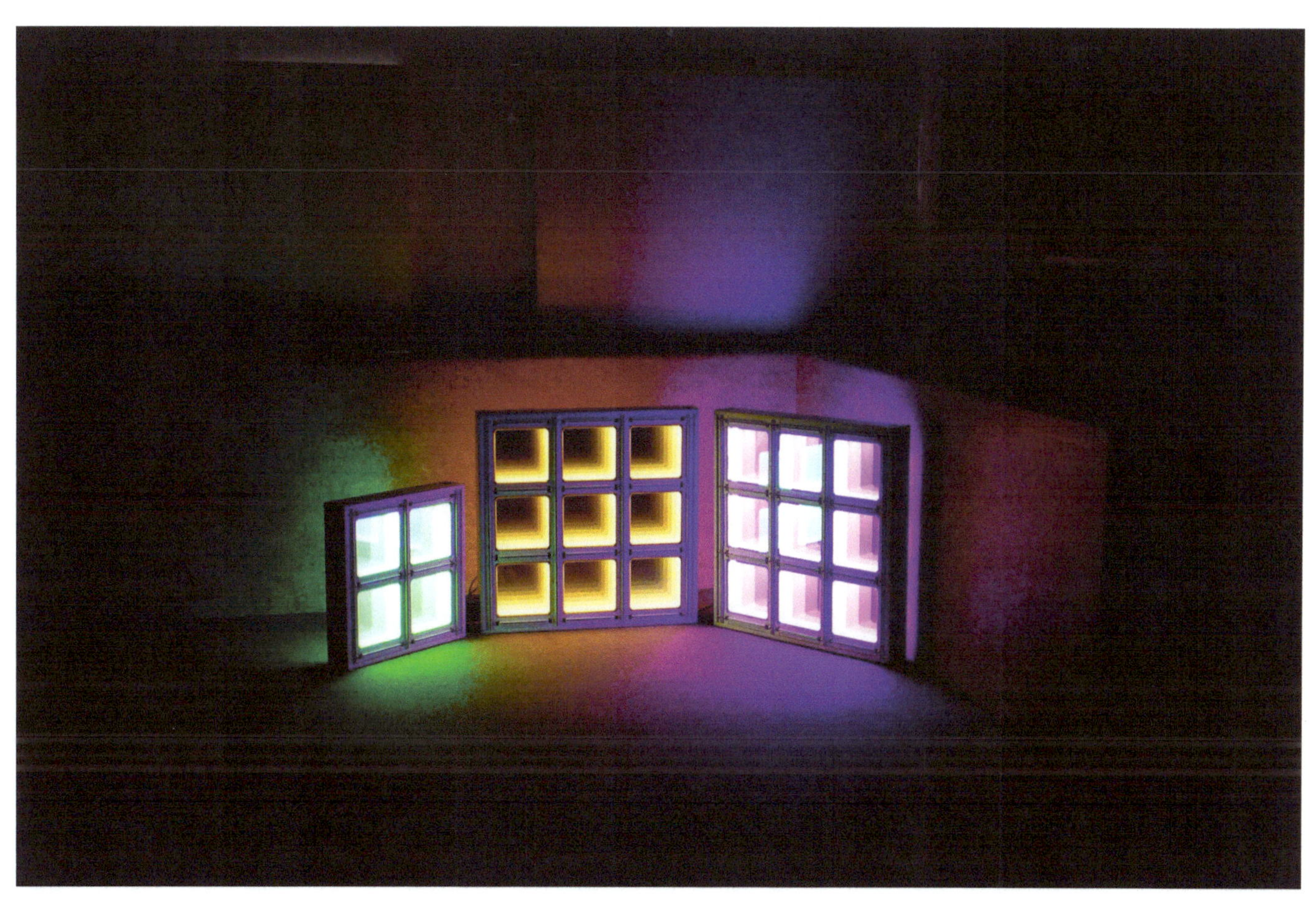

Light in space 2, 2012, programmed LED light boxes, and 1 x 51 x 51 cm and 2 x 74 x 74cm,
Light in Space, Stephen McLaughlin Gallery, Melbourne

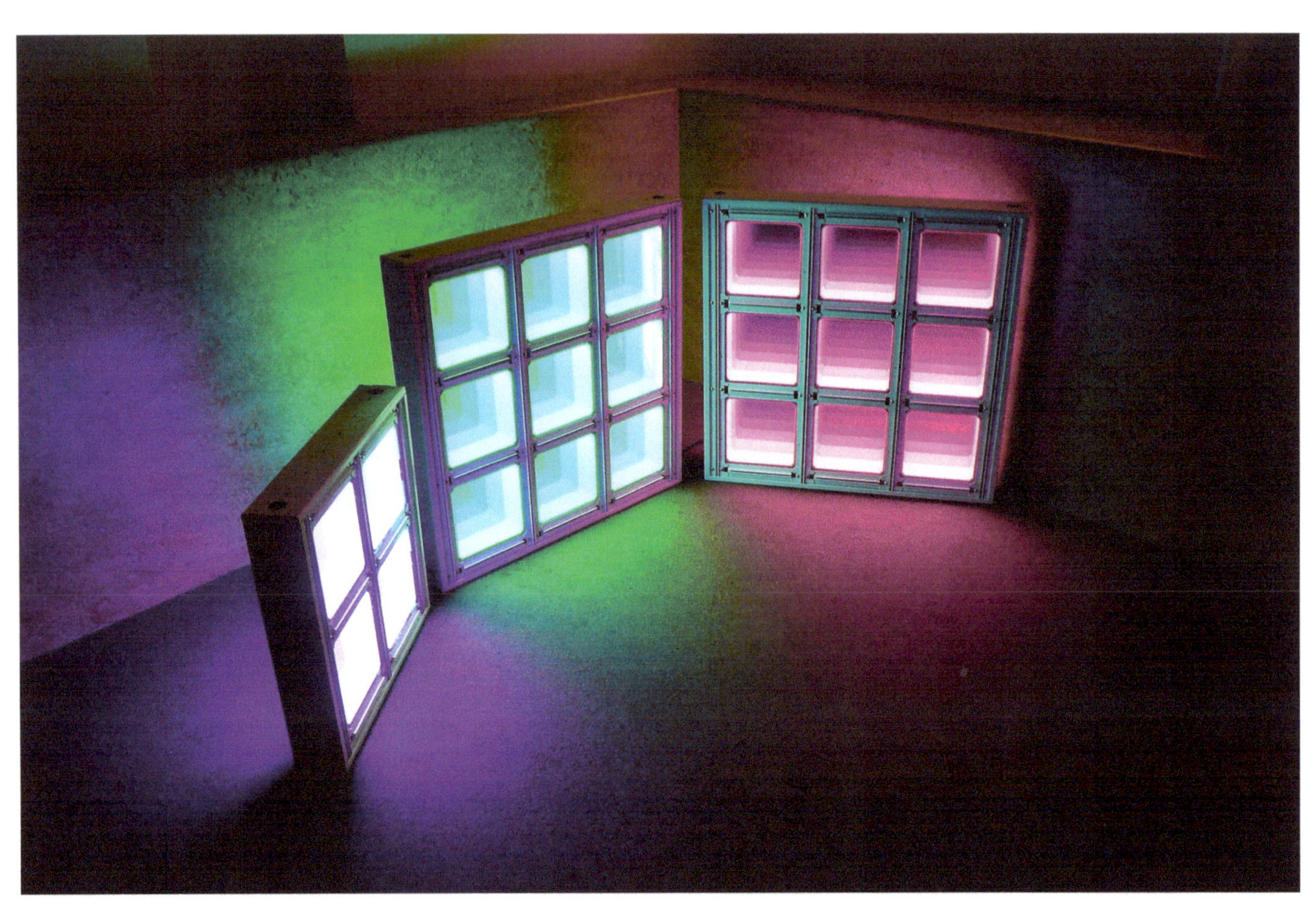

Light in space 2, 2012, programmed LED light boxes, and 1 x 51 x 51 cm and 2 x 74 x 74 cm,
Light in Space, Stephen McLaughlin Gallery, Melbourne

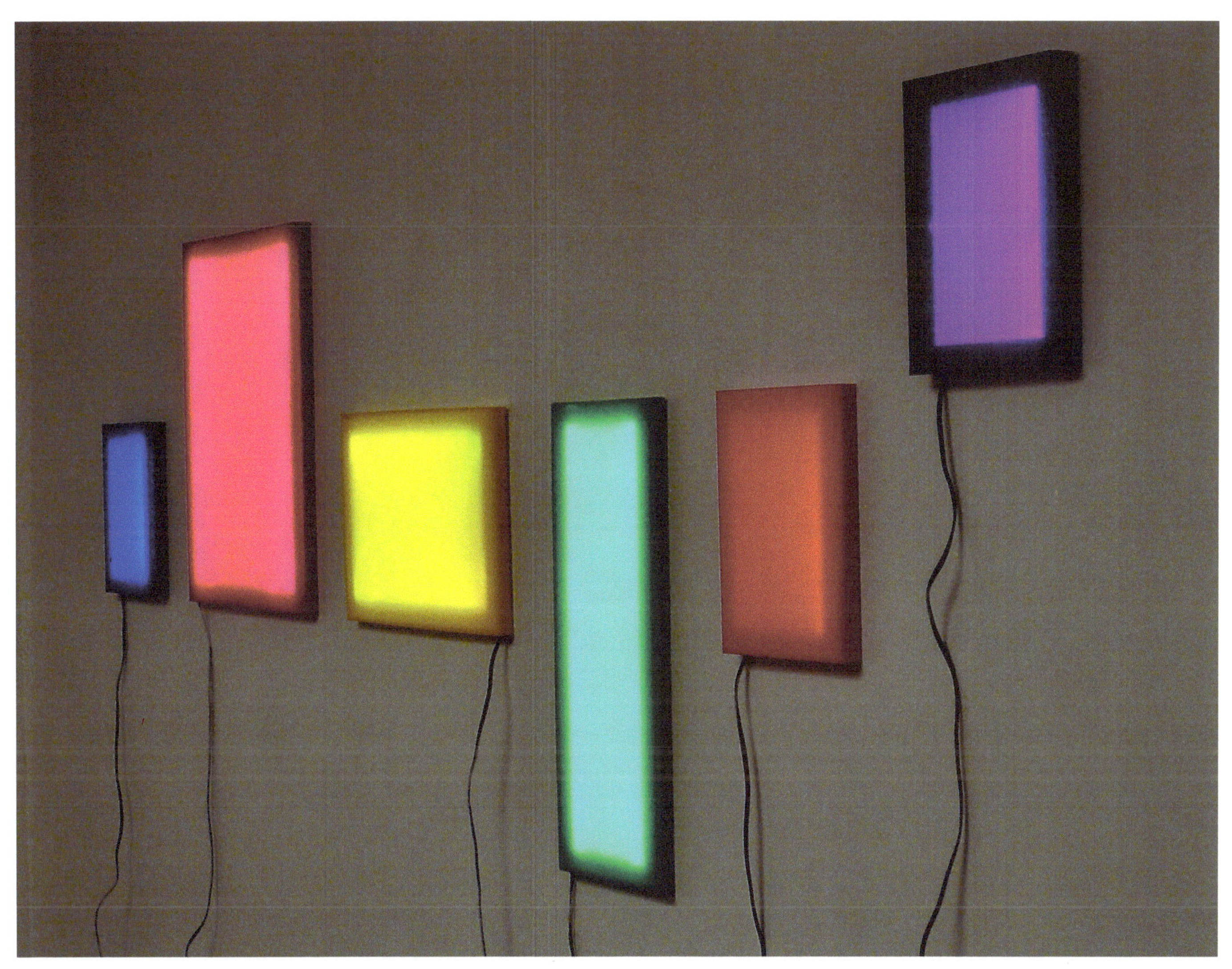

Light in space 2, 2012, programmed LED light boxes, A4 and multiples of A4 sized screens,
Light in Space, Stephen McLaughlin Gallery, Melbourne

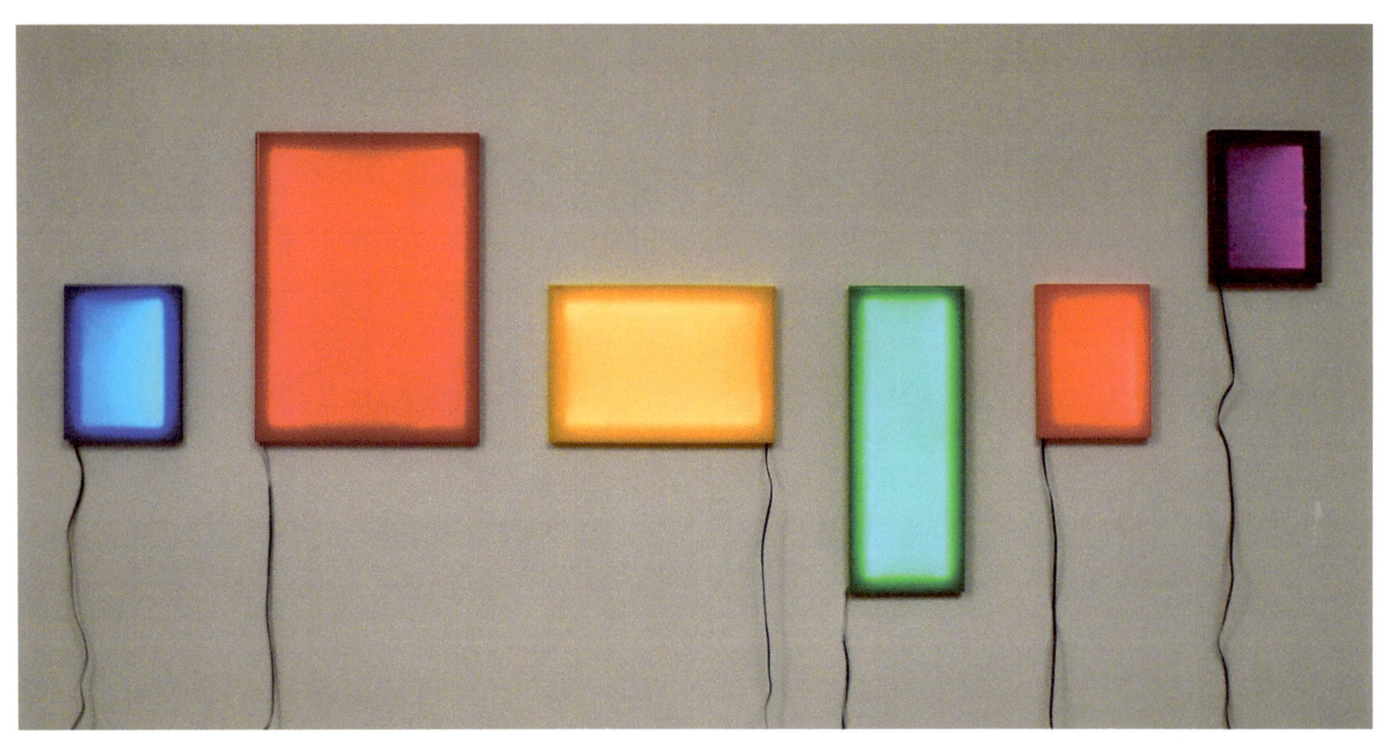

Light in space 2, 2012, programmed LED light boxes, A4 and multiples of A4 sized screens,
Light in Space, Stephen McLaughlin Gallery, Melbourne

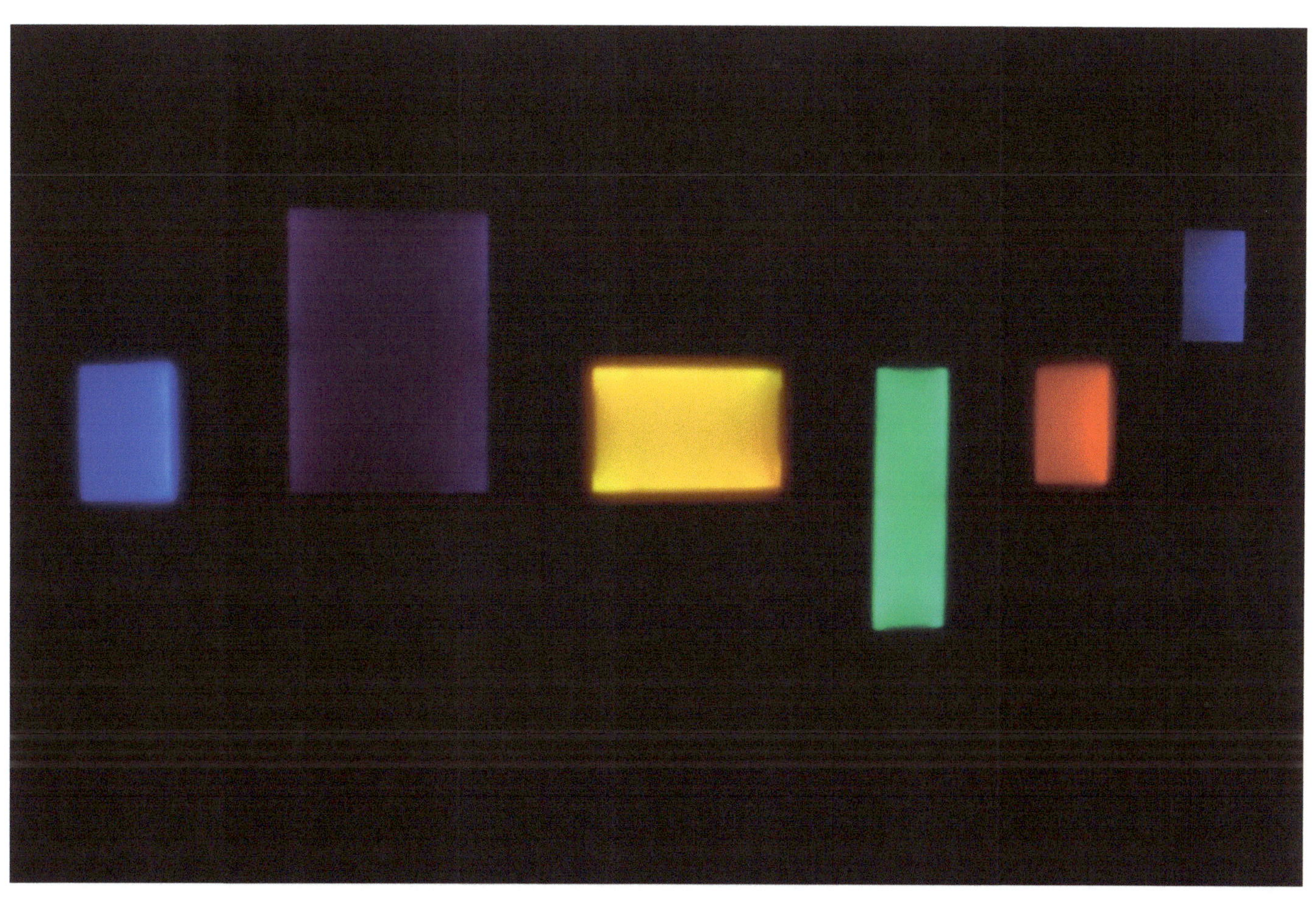

Light in space 2, 2012, programmed LED light boxes, A4 and multiples of A4 sized screens, *Light in Space*, Stephen McLaughlin Gallery, Melbourne

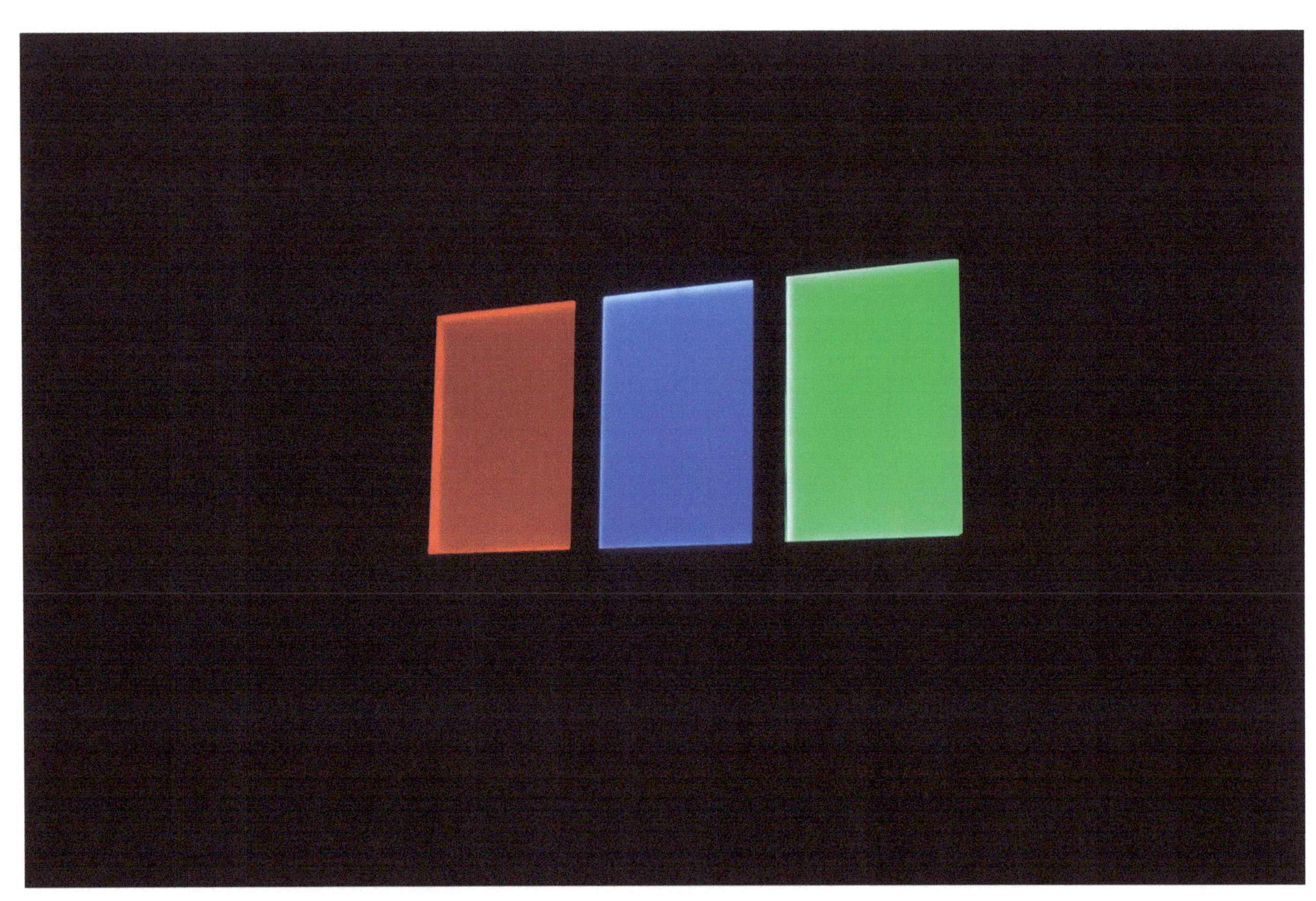

Triple screen, 2012, programmed LED light boxes, 3 x A4 sized screen panel

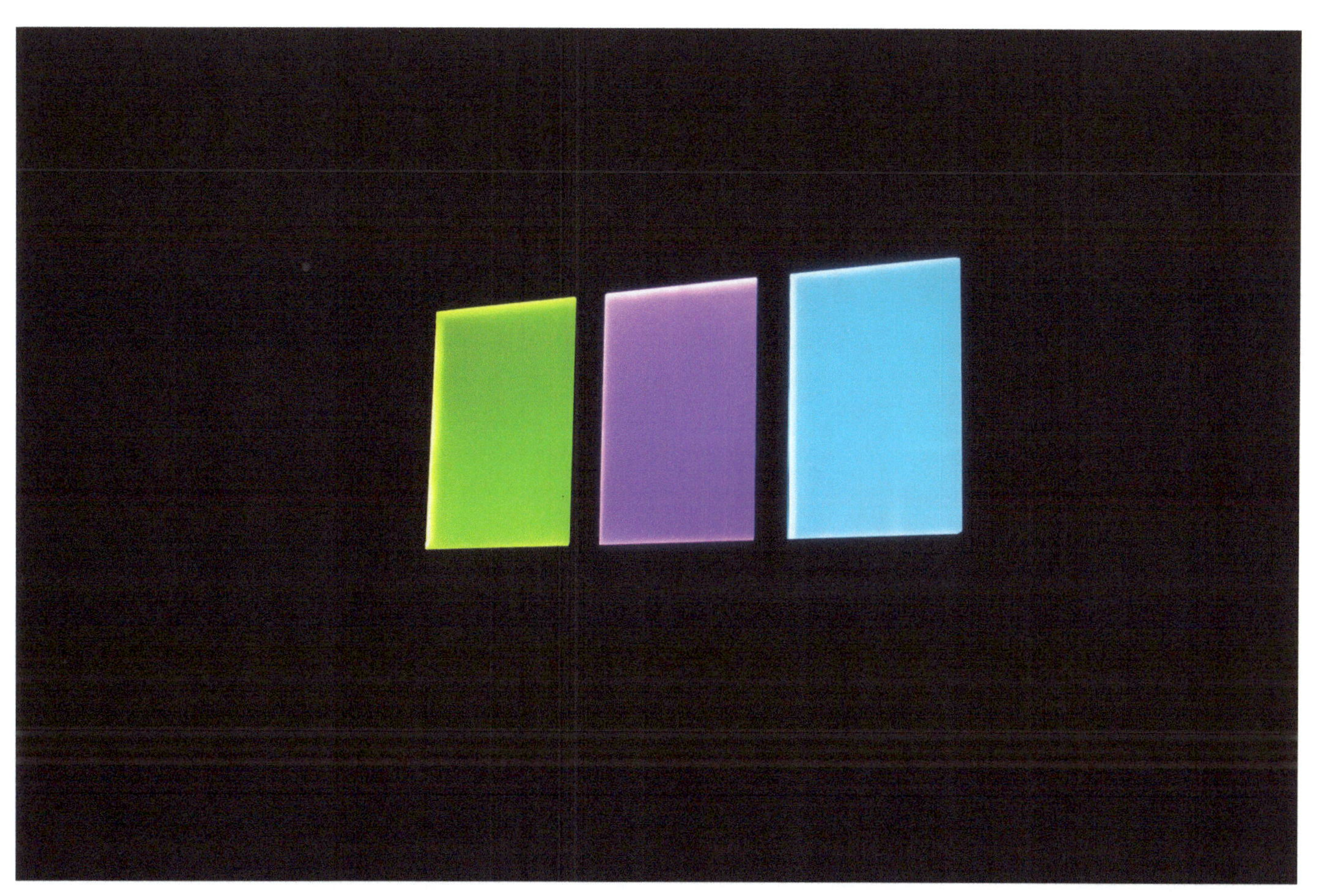

Triple screen, 2012, programmed LED light boxes, 3 x A4 sized screen panel

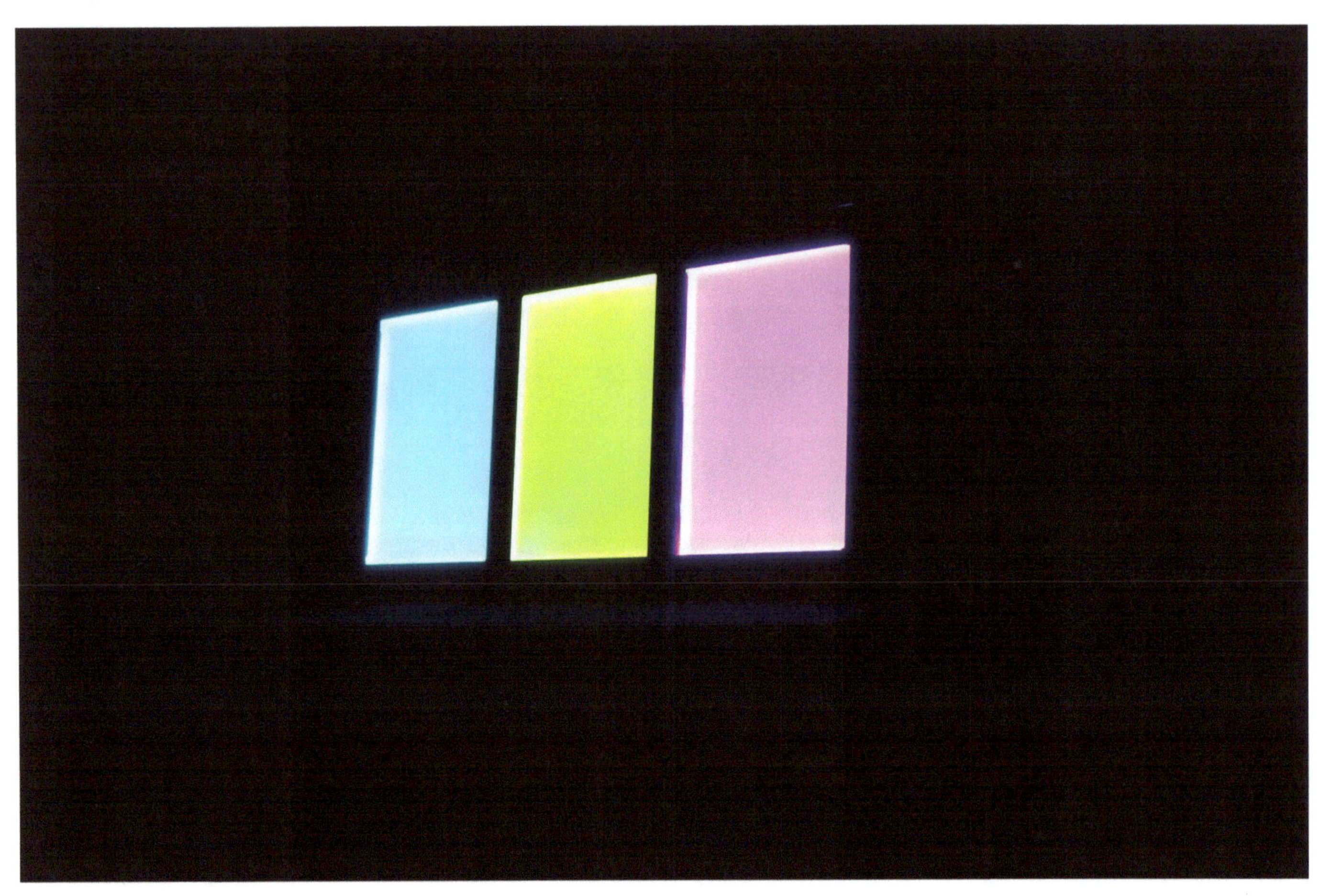

Triple screen, 2012, programmed LED light boxes, 3 x A4 sized screen panel

Triple screen, 2012, programmed LED light boxes, 3 x A4 sized screen panel

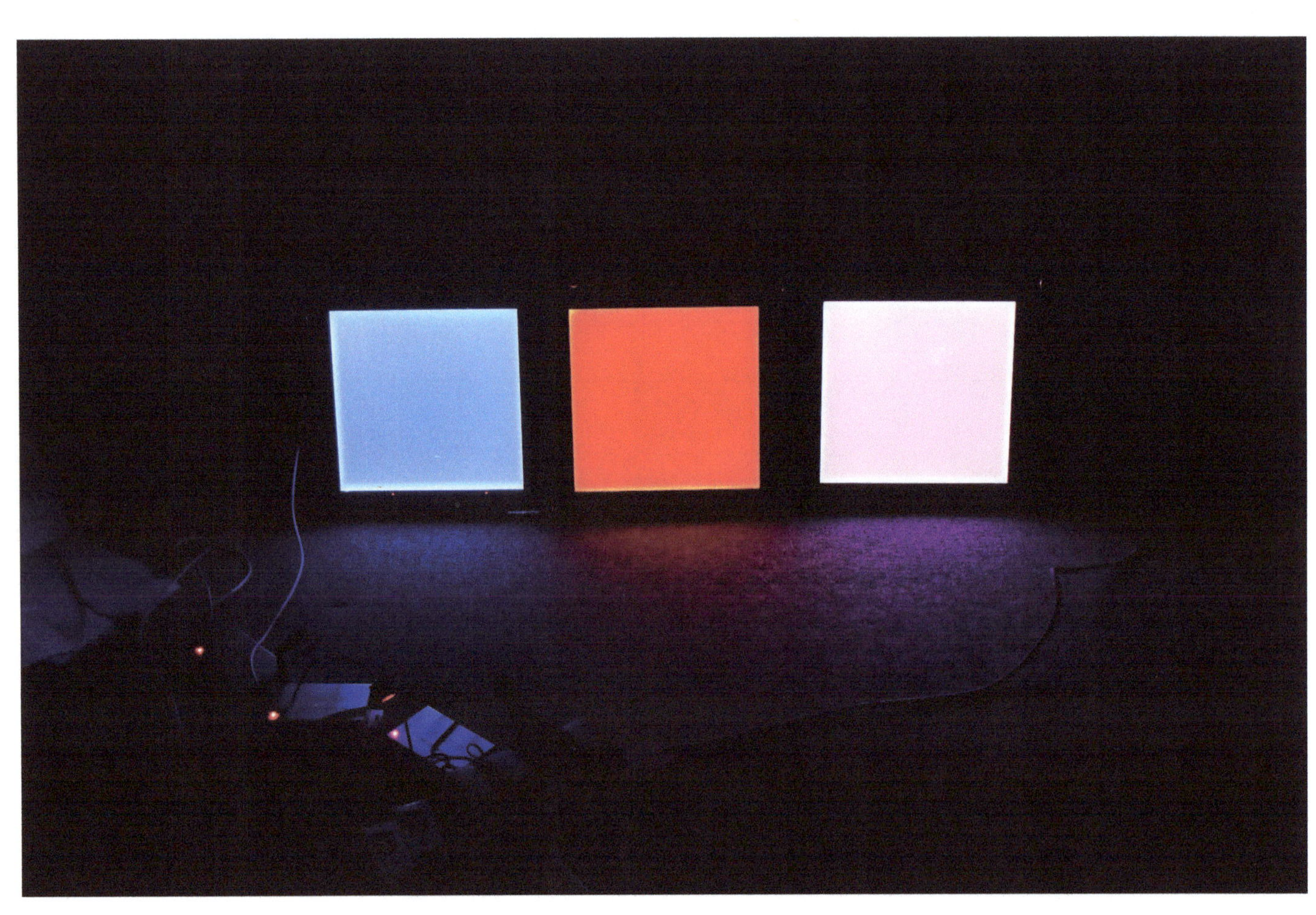

Untitled, 2012, programmed LED light boxes, 3 x 24 x 24 cm

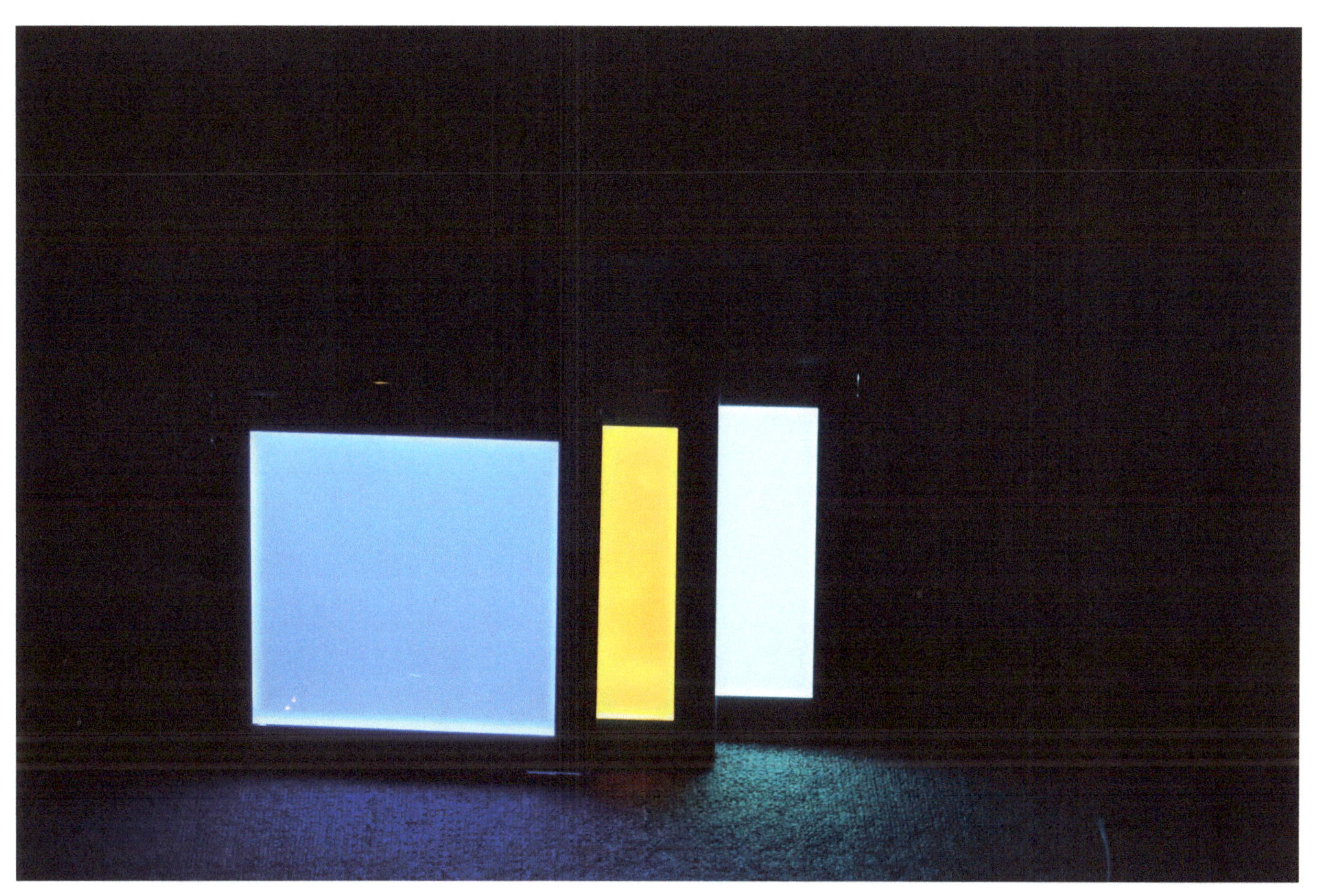

Untitled, 2012, programmed LED light boxes, 3 x 24 x 24 cm

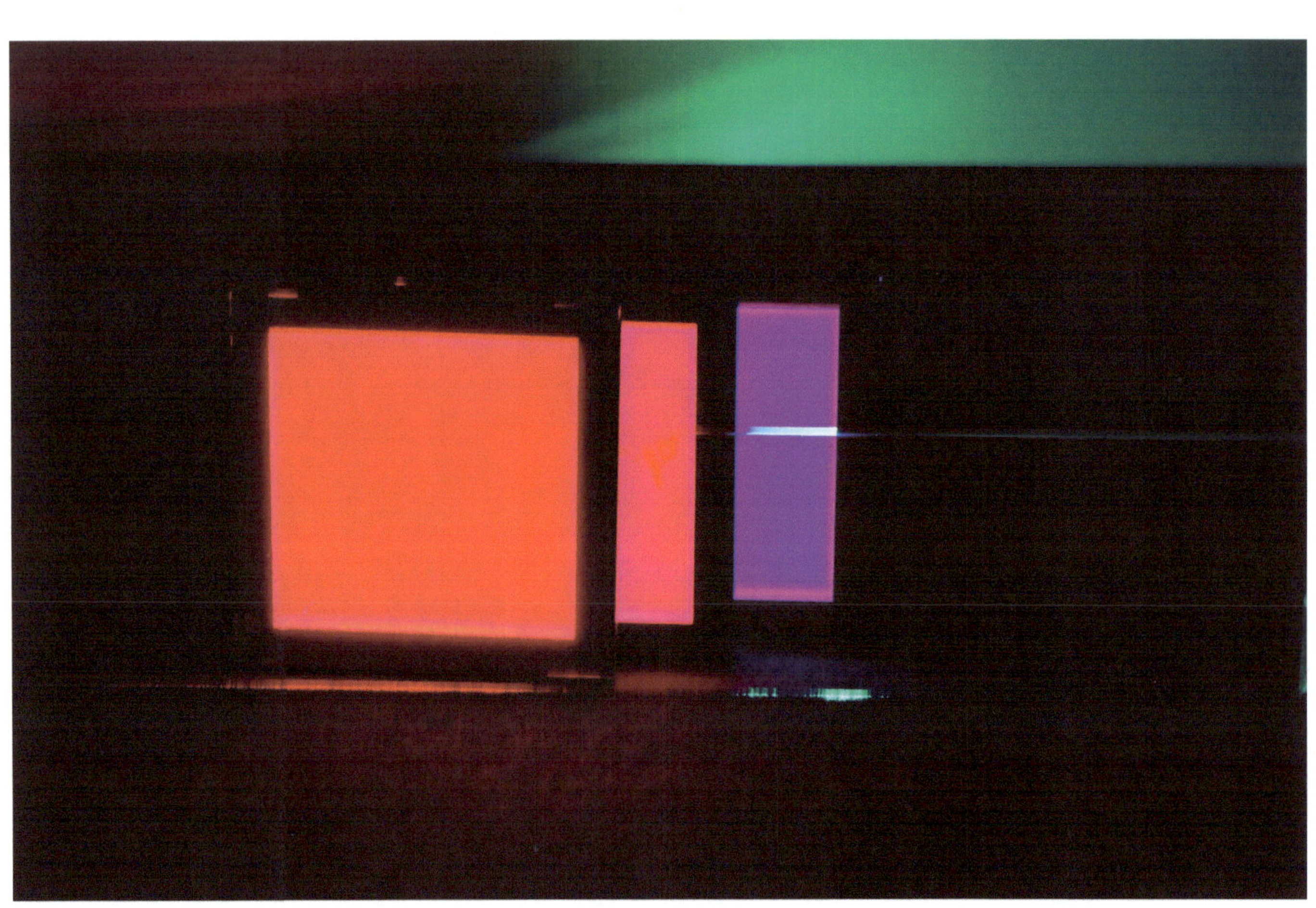

Untitled, 2012, programmed LED light boxes, 3 x 24 x 24 cm

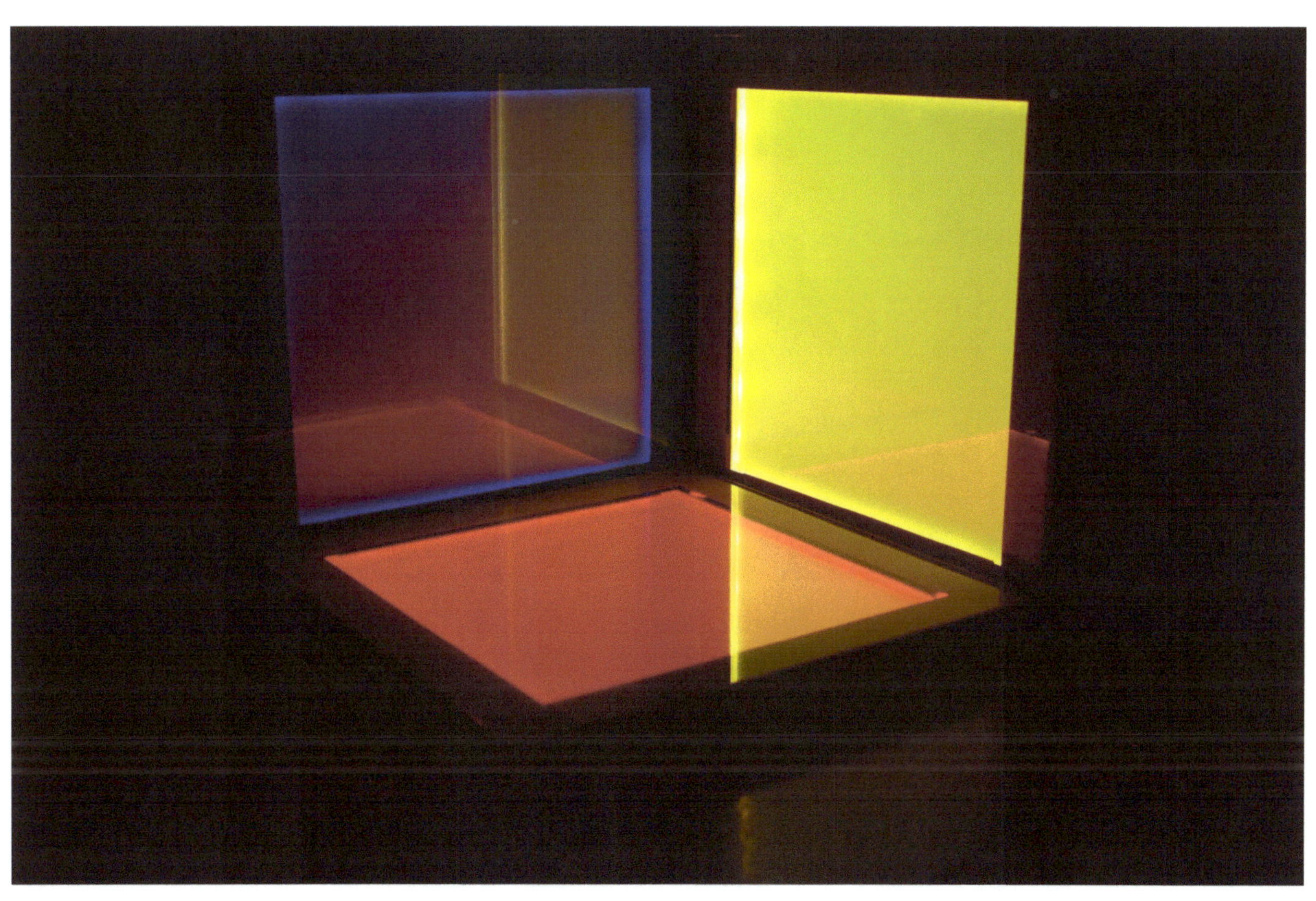

Untitled, 2012, programmed LED light boxes, 3 x 27 x 27 cm

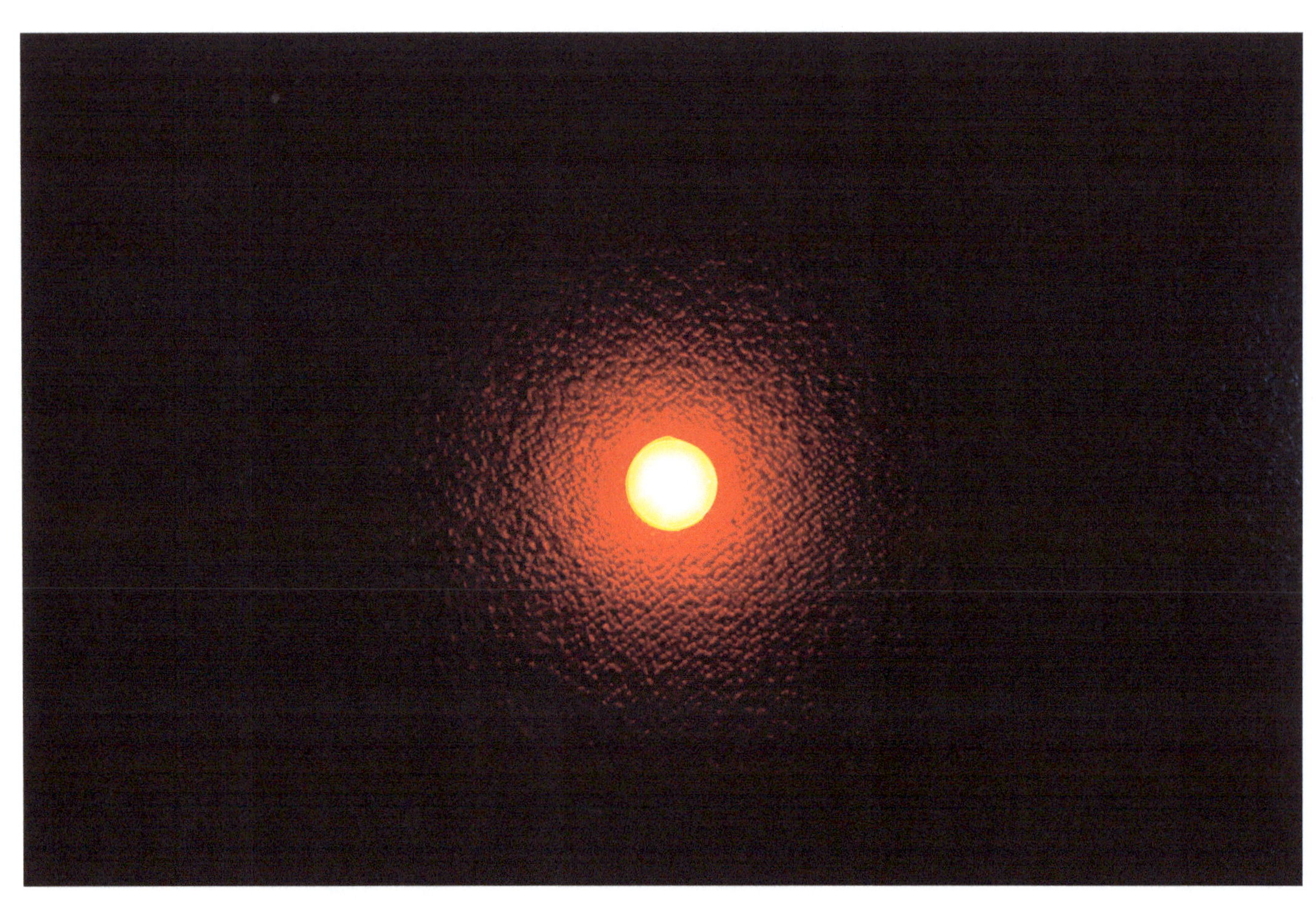

Untitled, 2012, programmed LED fitting, 5 cm diameter

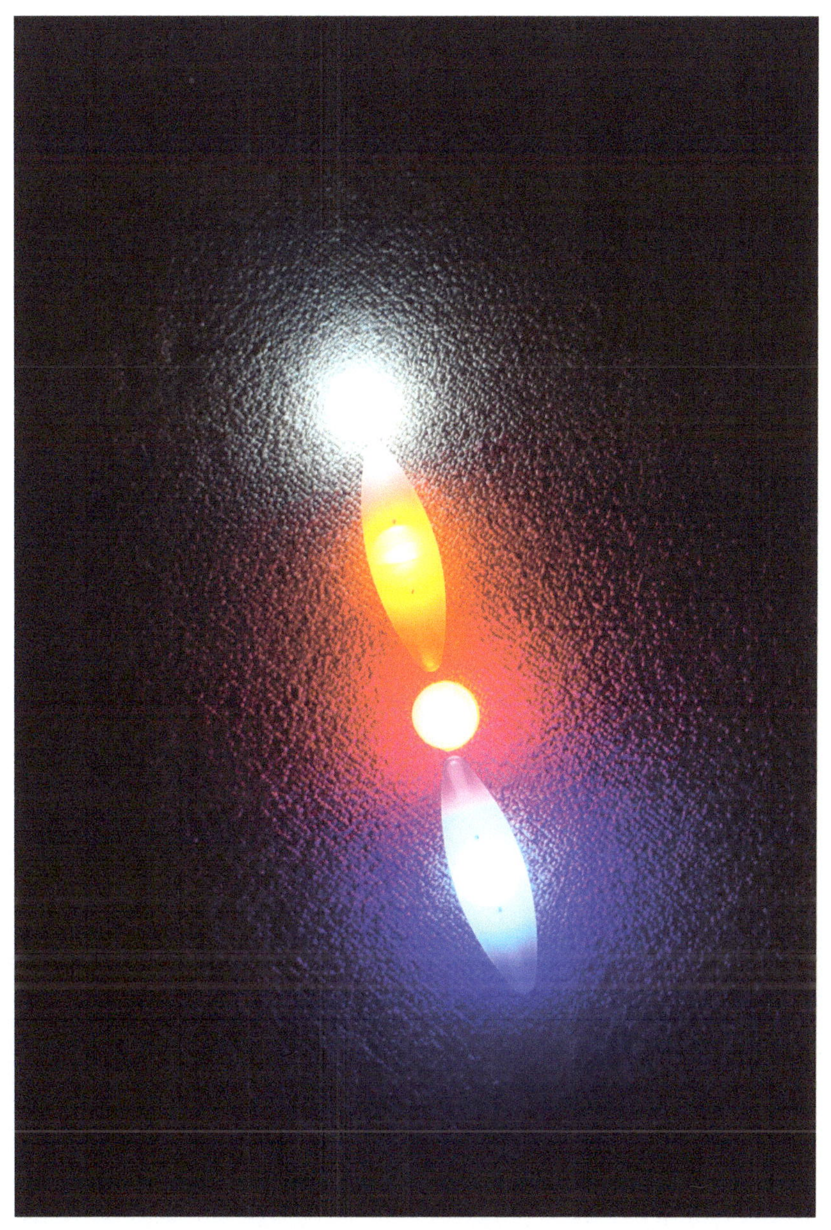

Untitled, 2012, programmed LED fittings and bike lights, 5 x 25 cm

Psychedelic sun, 2012, video still, 1 minute

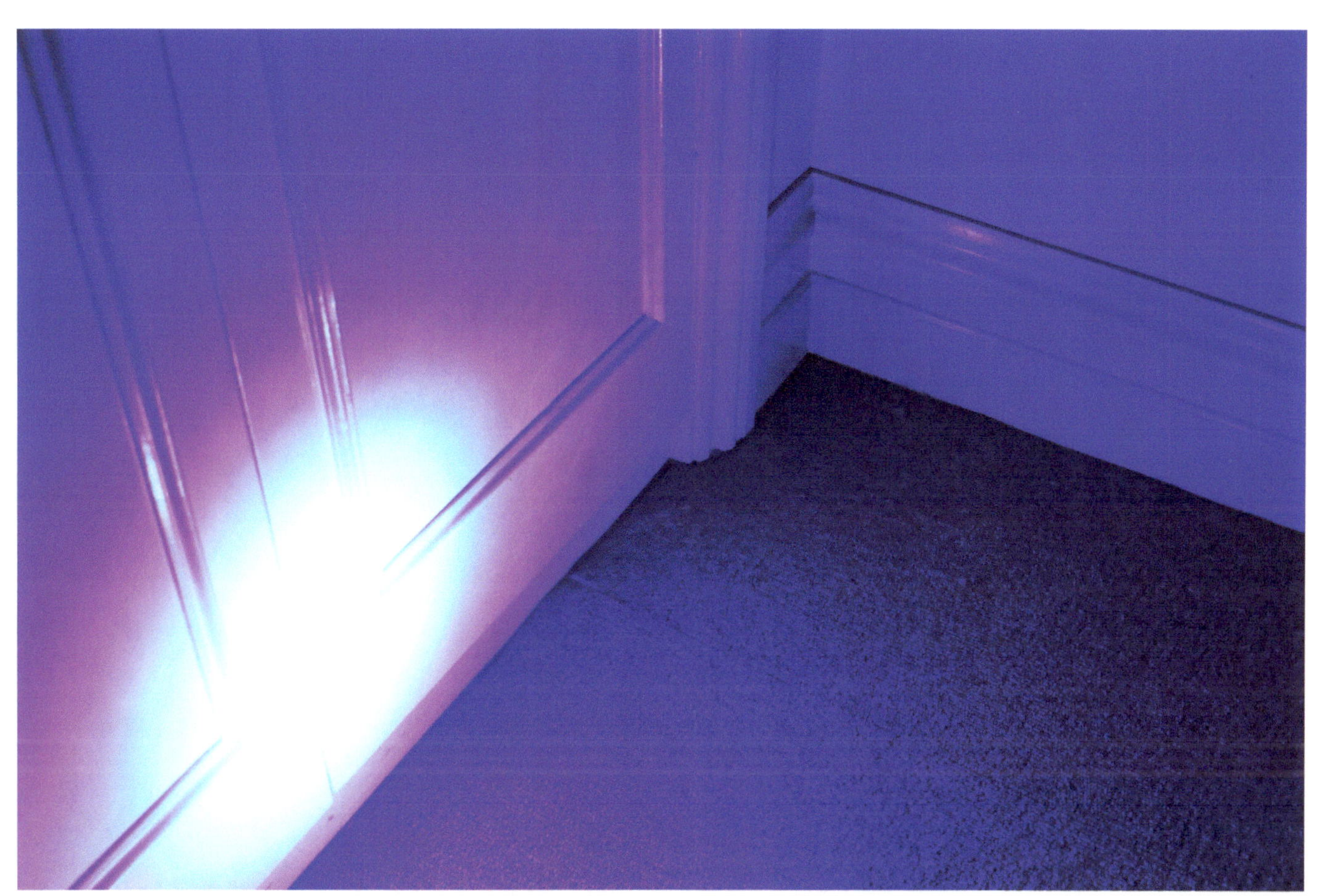

Psychedelic sun 2, 2012, video still, 1 minute

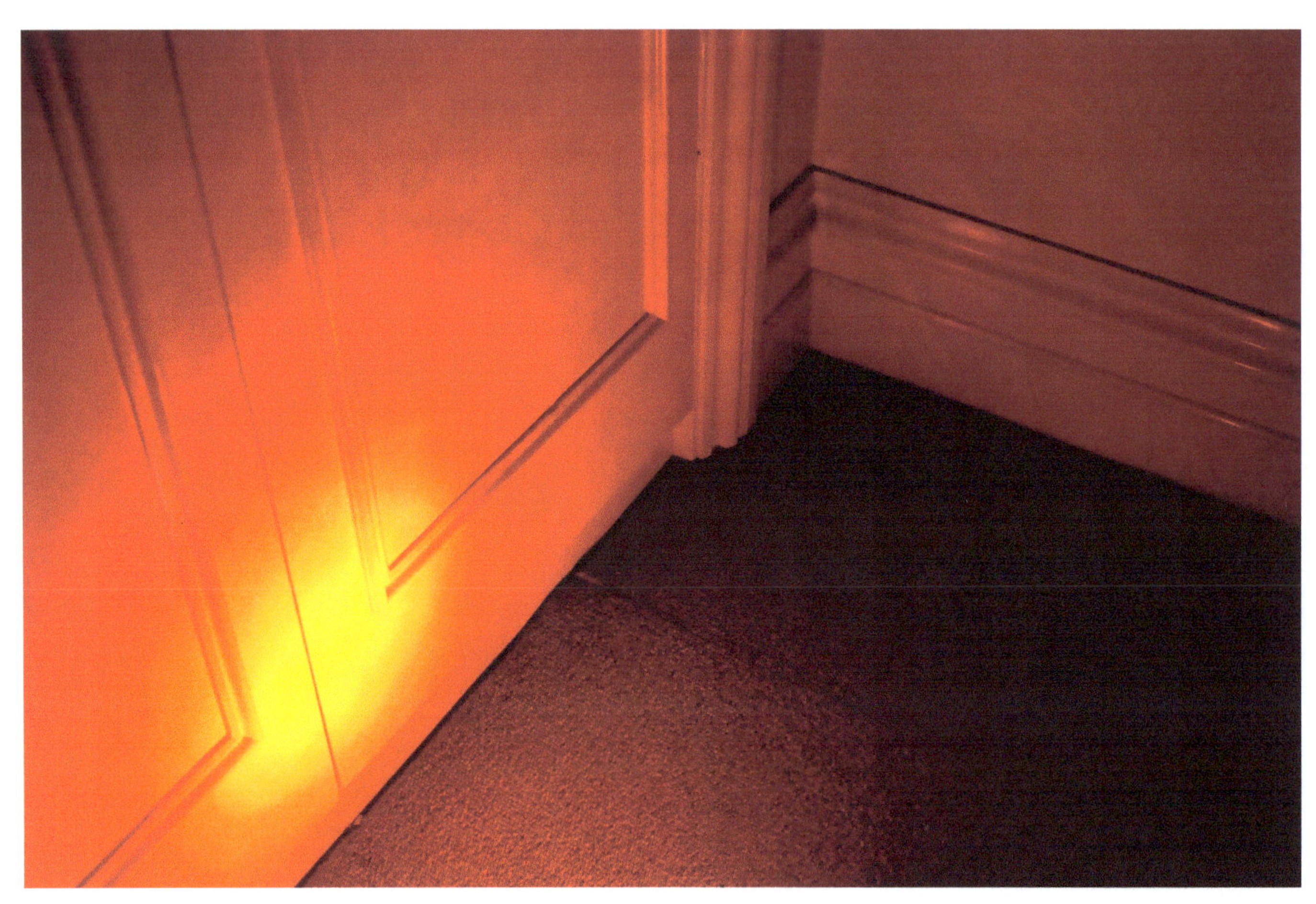

Psychedelic sun 2, 2012, video still, 1 minute

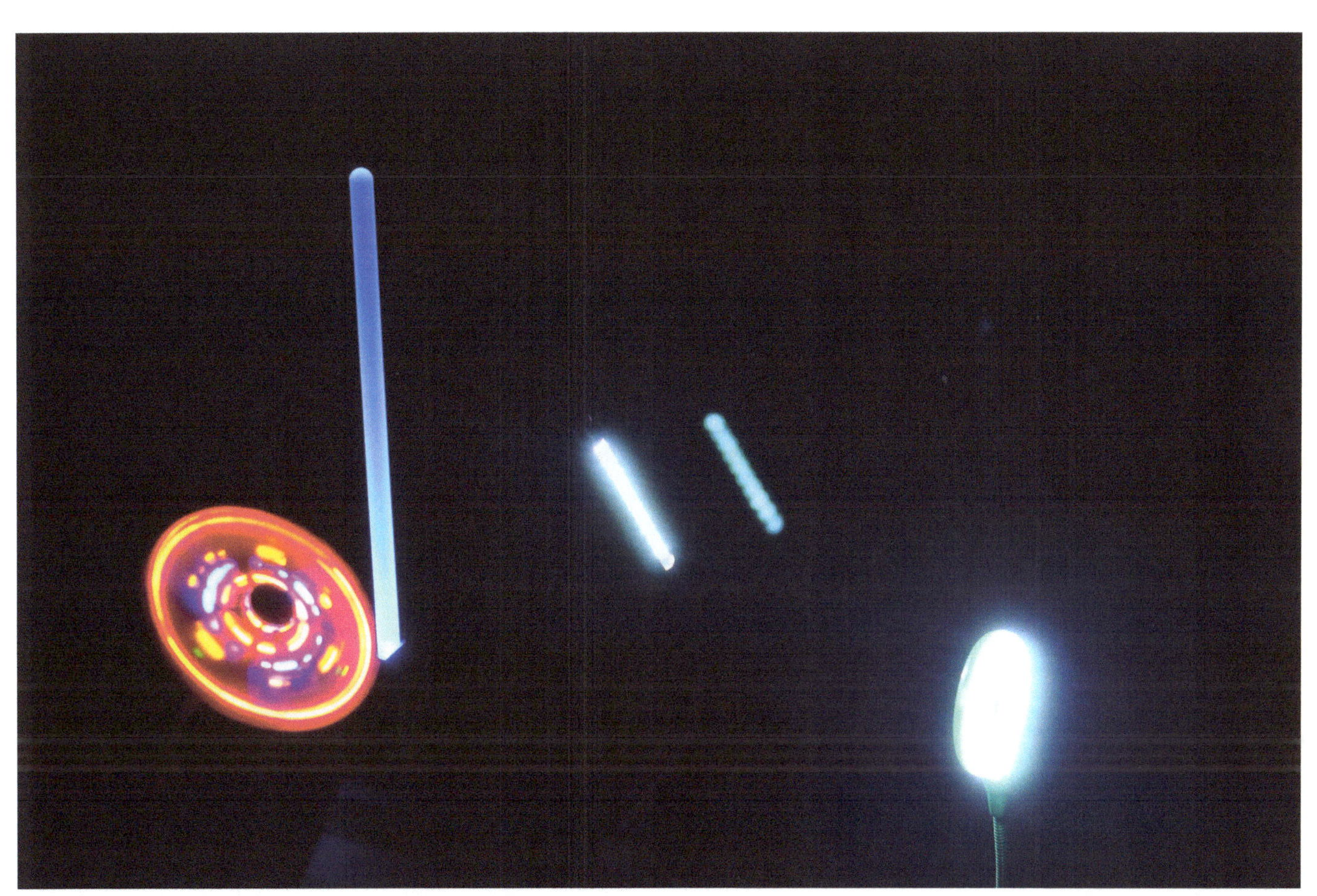

Untitled, 2012, various LED lights

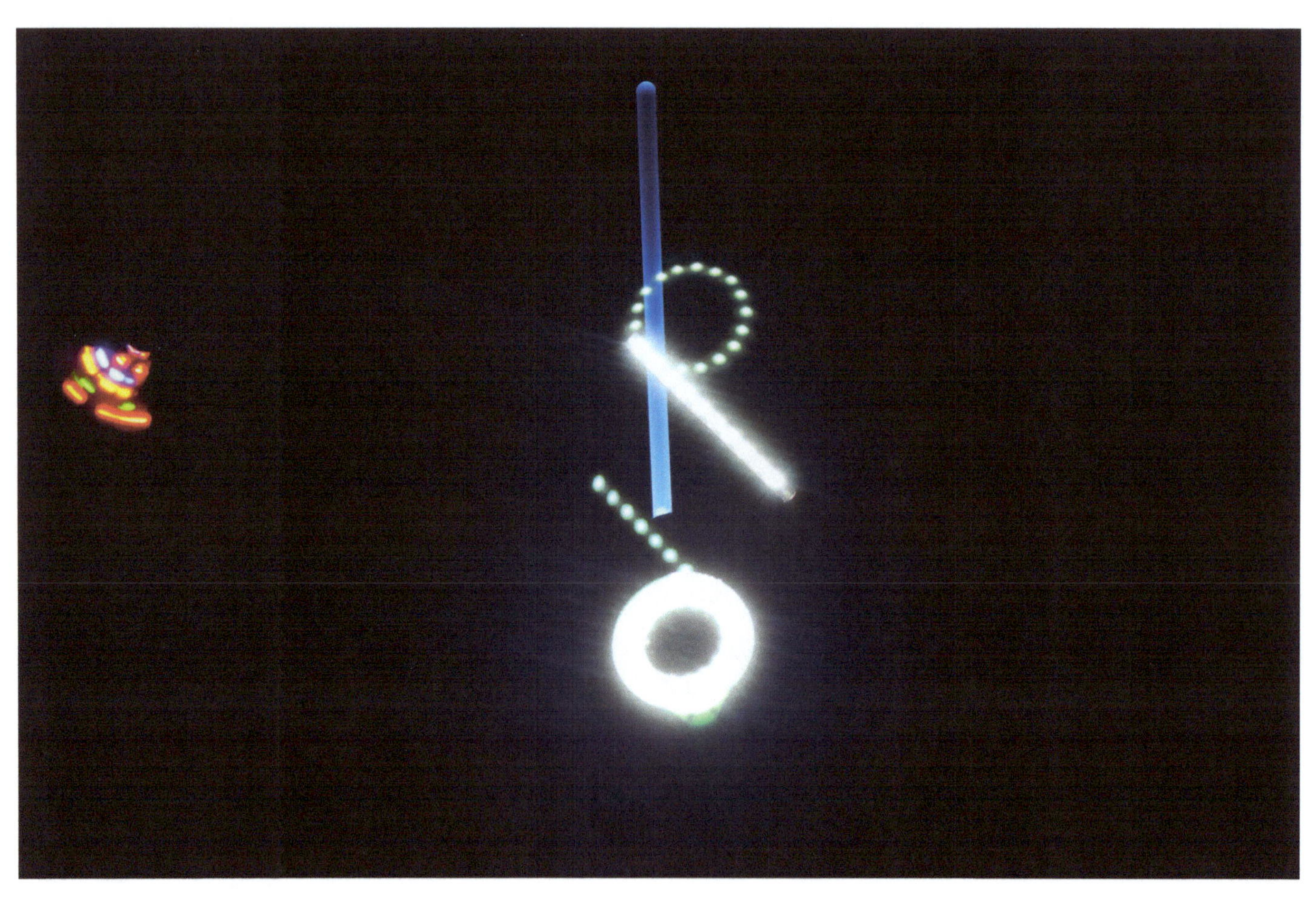

Untitled, 2012, various LED lights

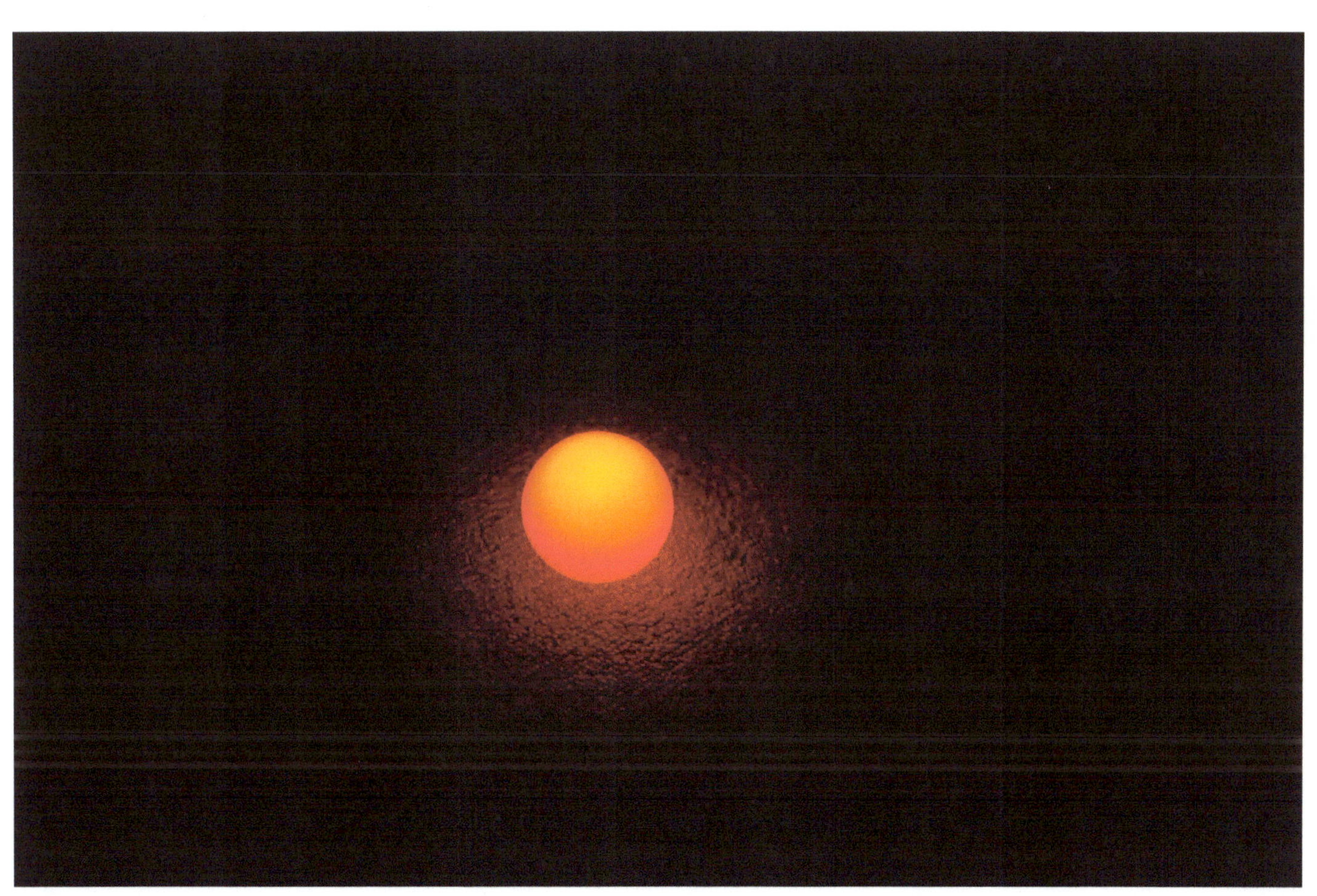

Untitled, 2012, LED light, 6 cm diameter

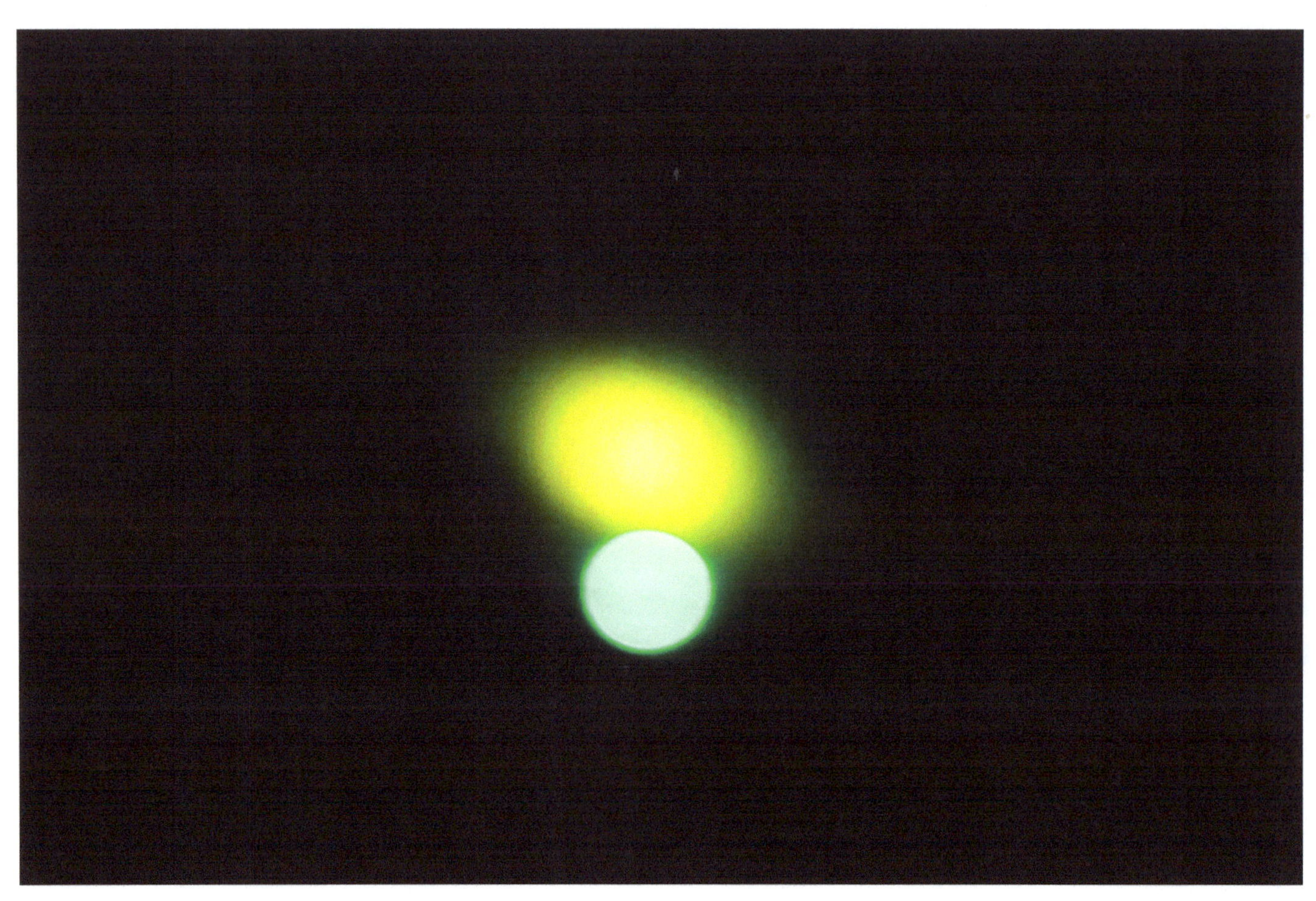

Untitled, 2012, LED lights, 6 - 7 cm

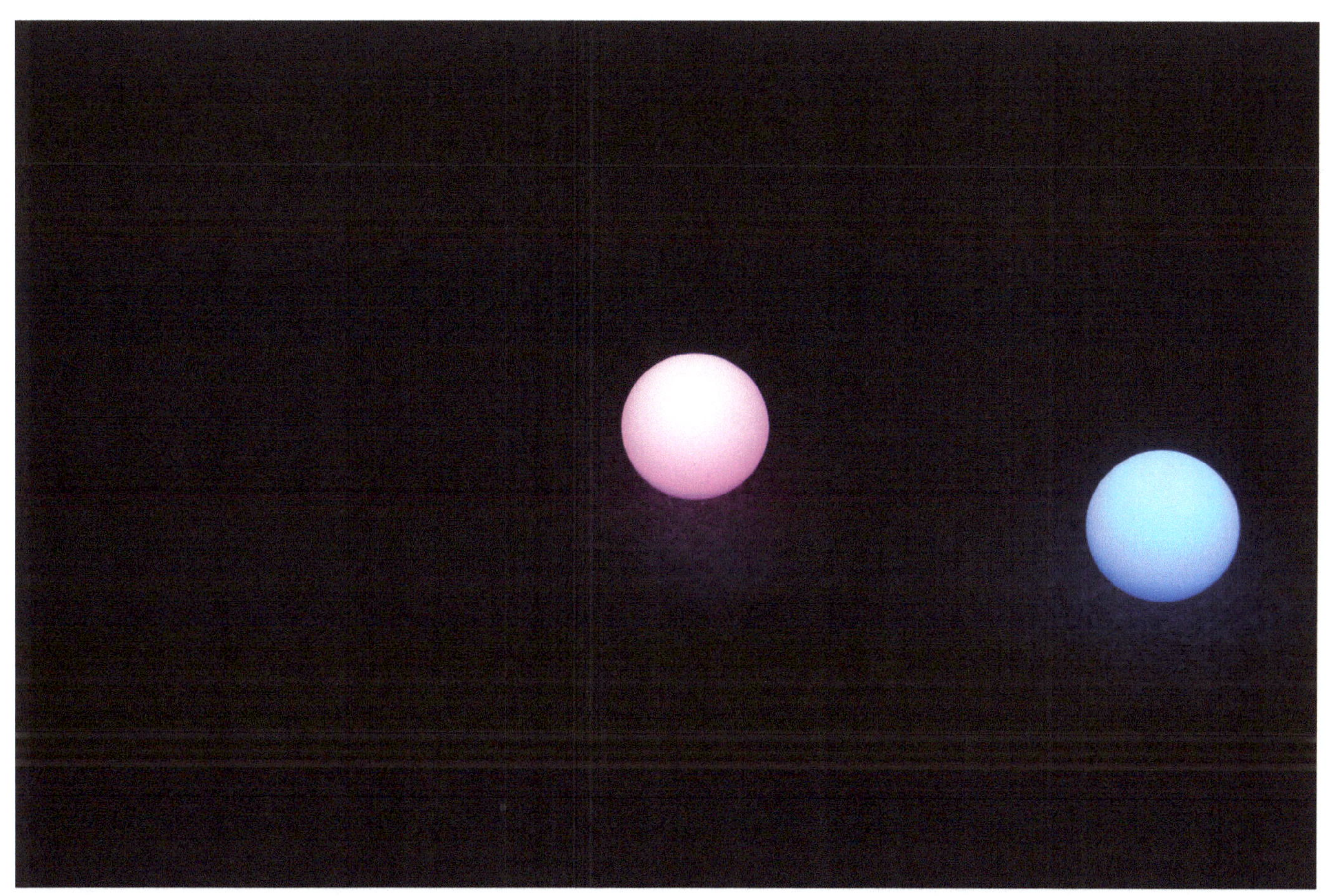

Untitled, 2012, LED lights, 2 x 6 cm diameter

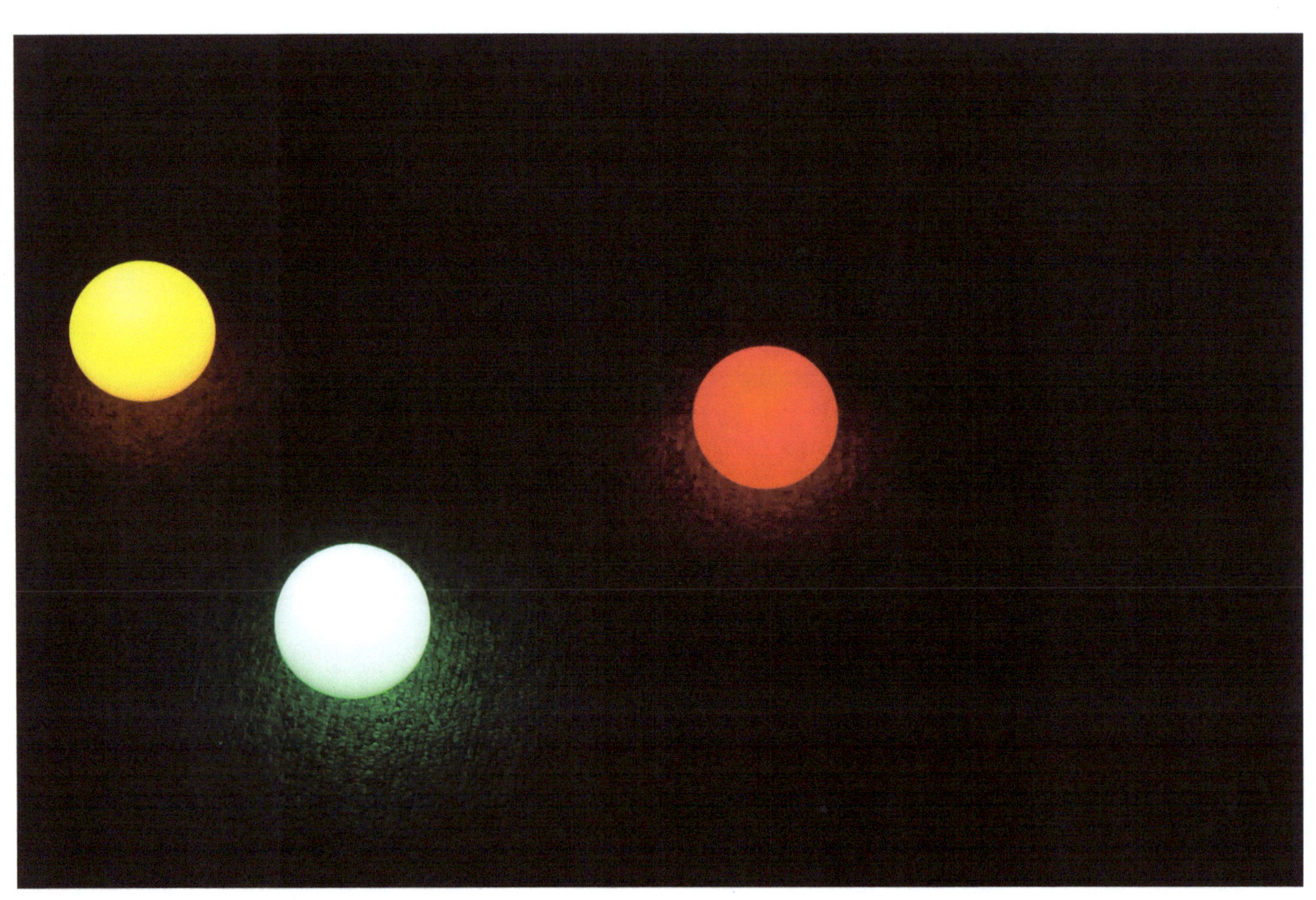

Untitled, 2012, LED lights, 3 x 6 cm diameter

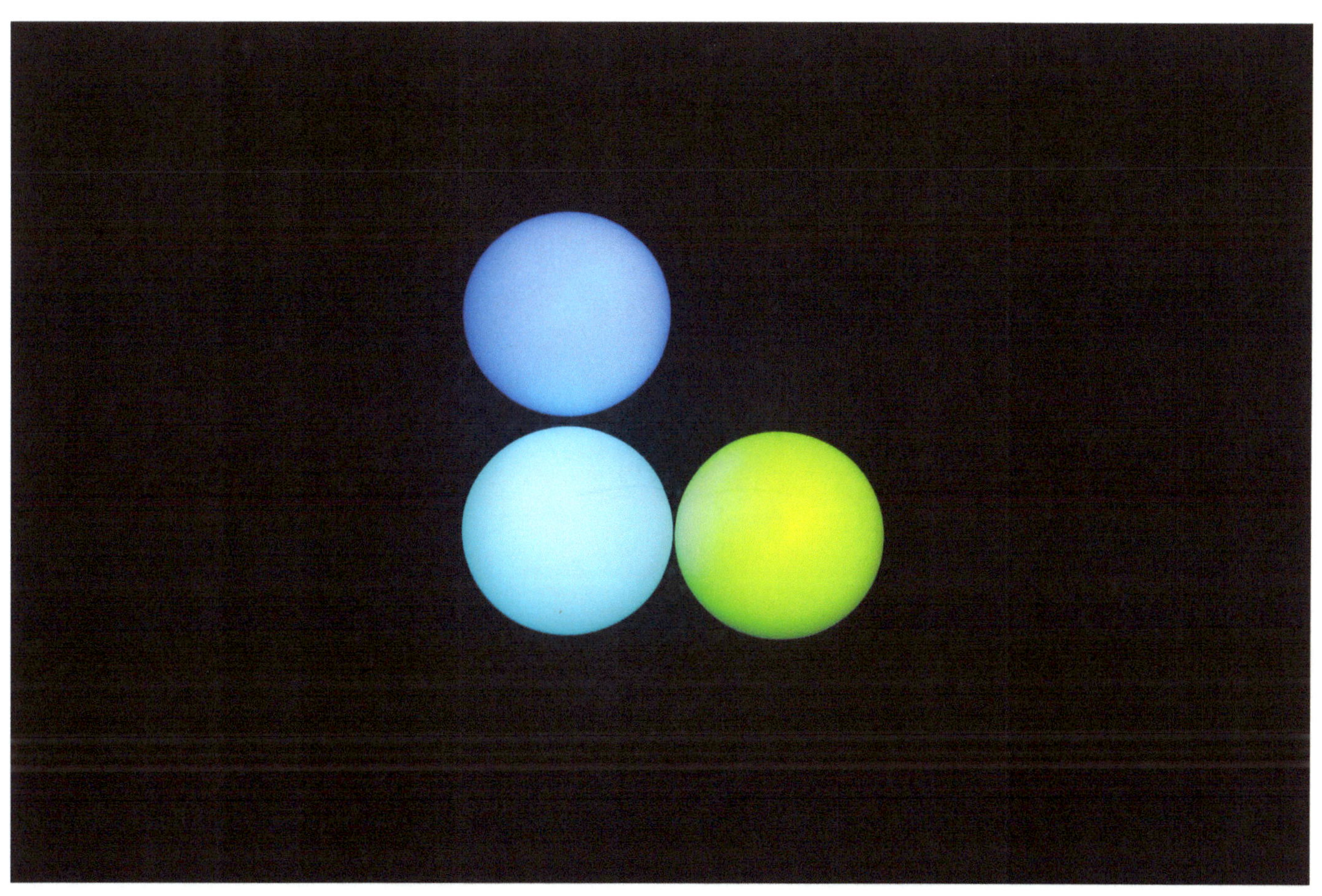

Untitled, 2012, LED lights, 3 x 6 cm diameter

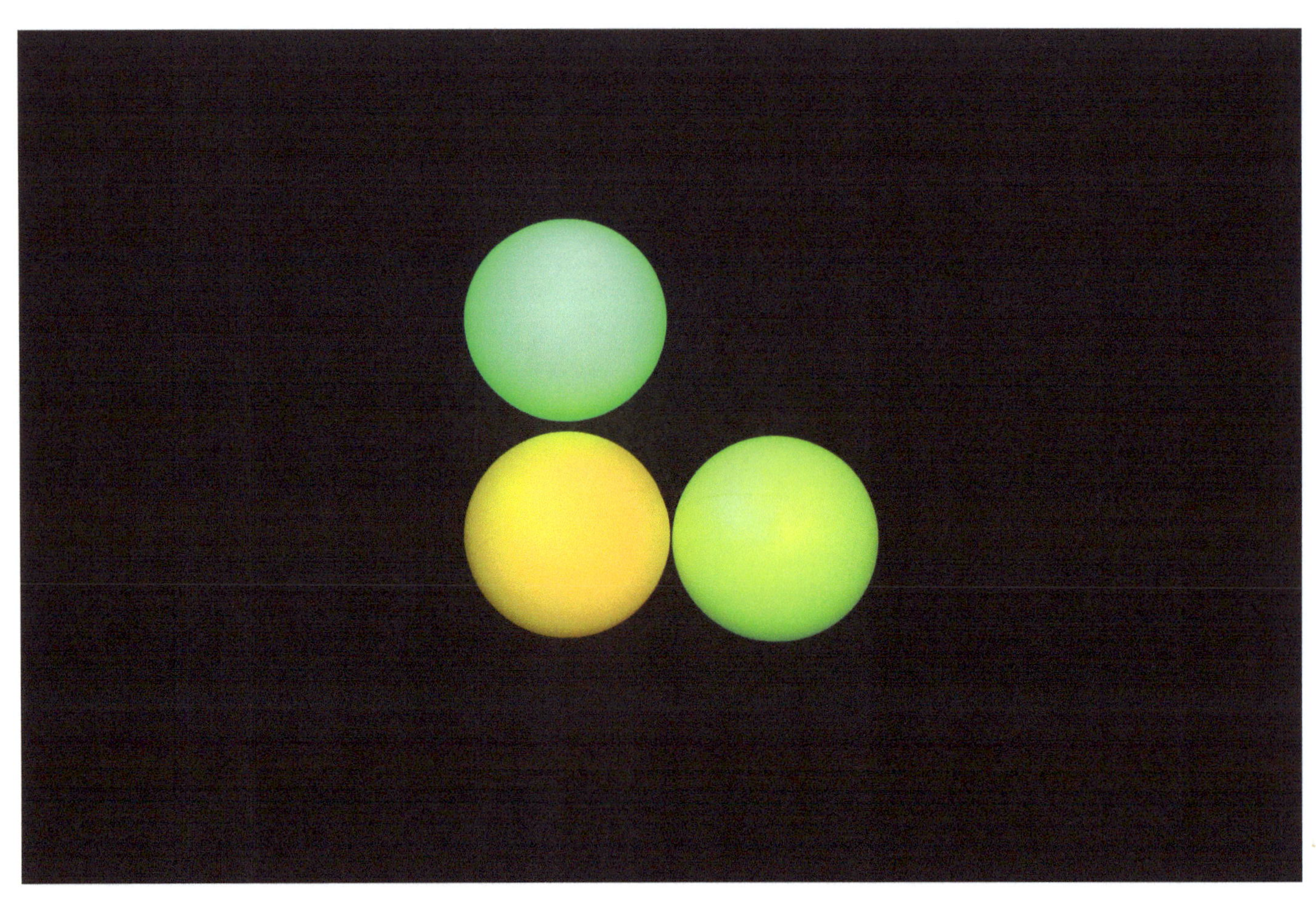

Untitled, 2012, LED lights, 3 x 6 cm diameter

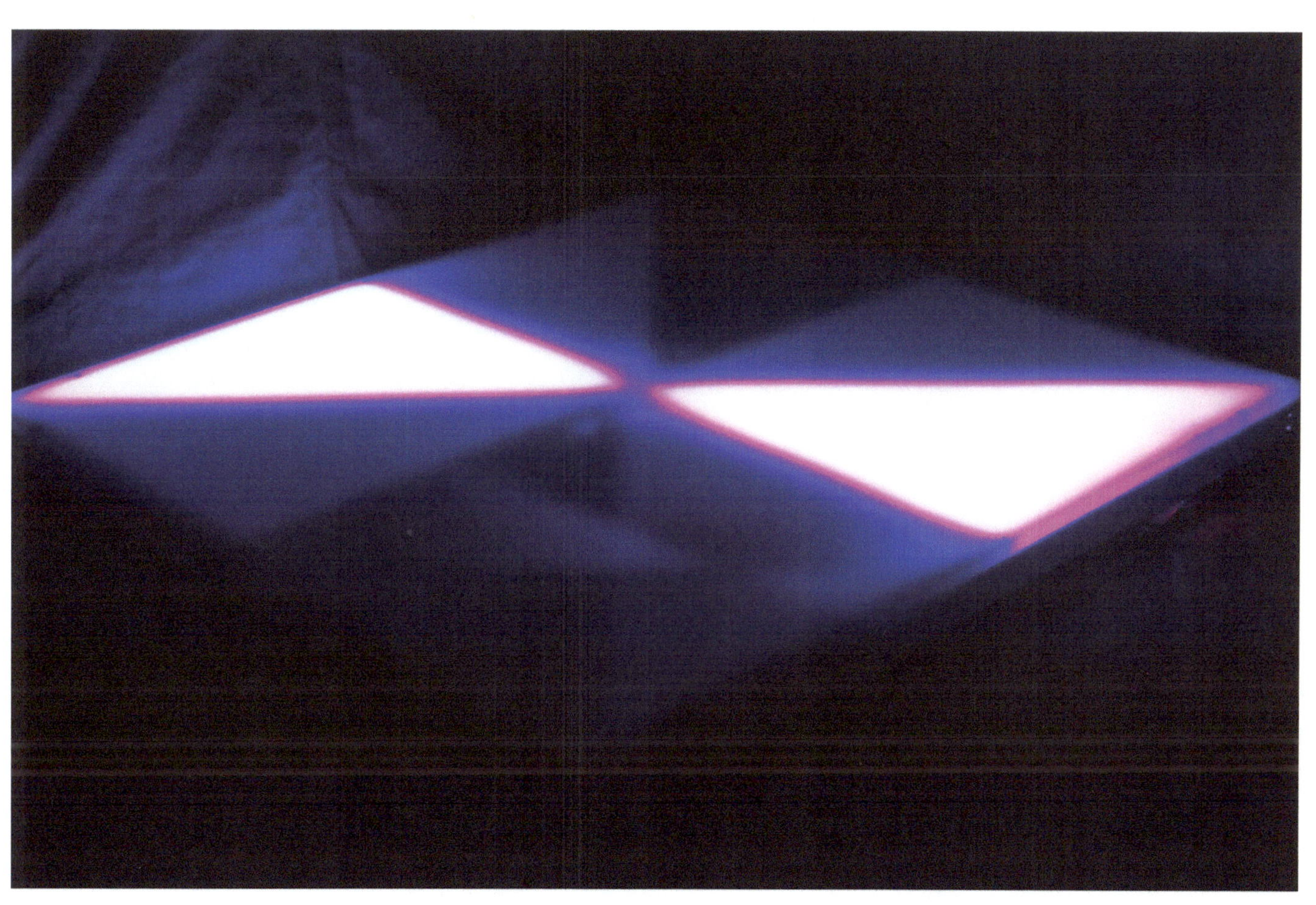

Untitled, 2012, LED programmed panel, 120 x 120 cm

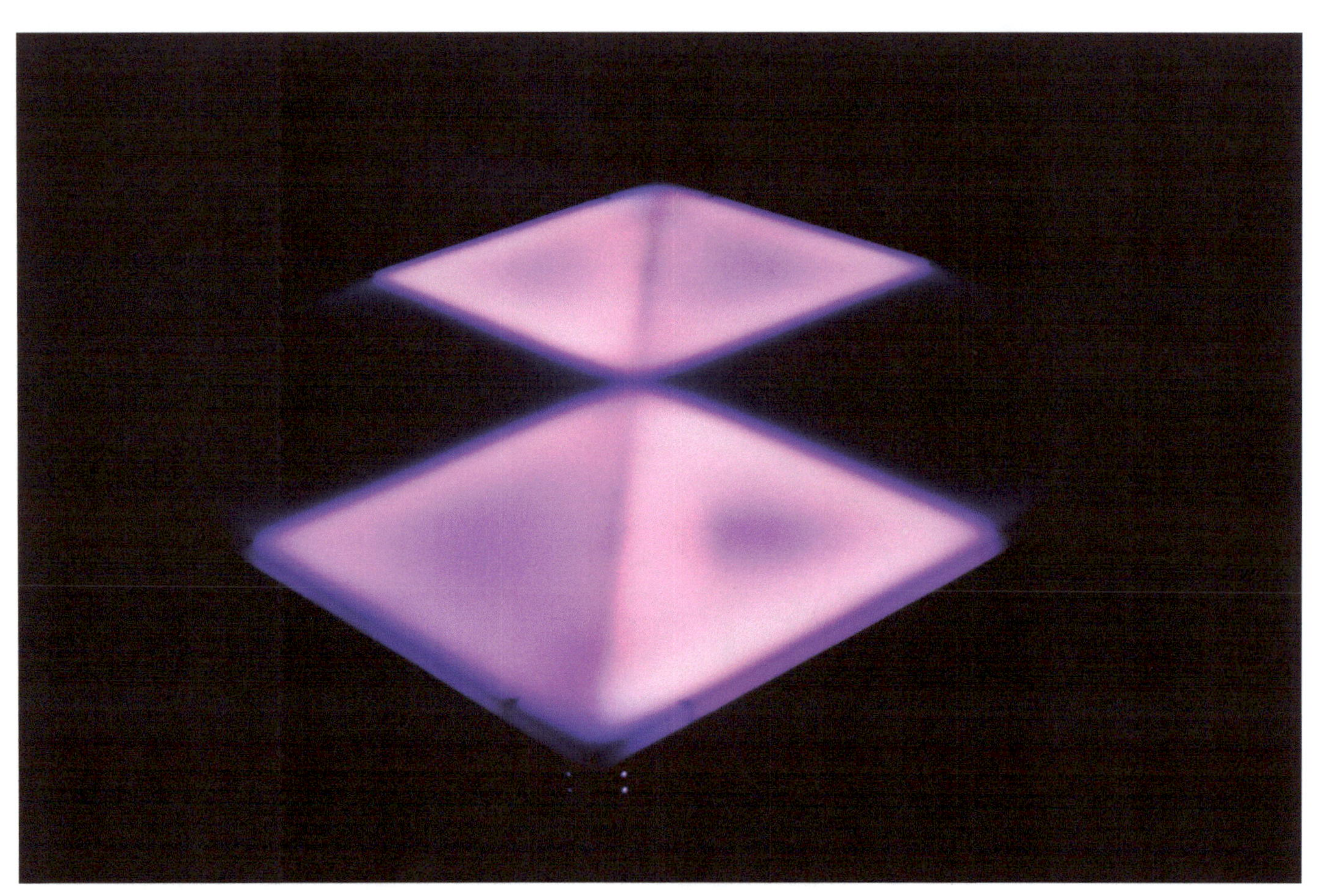

Untitled, 2012, LED programmed panel, 120 x 120 cm

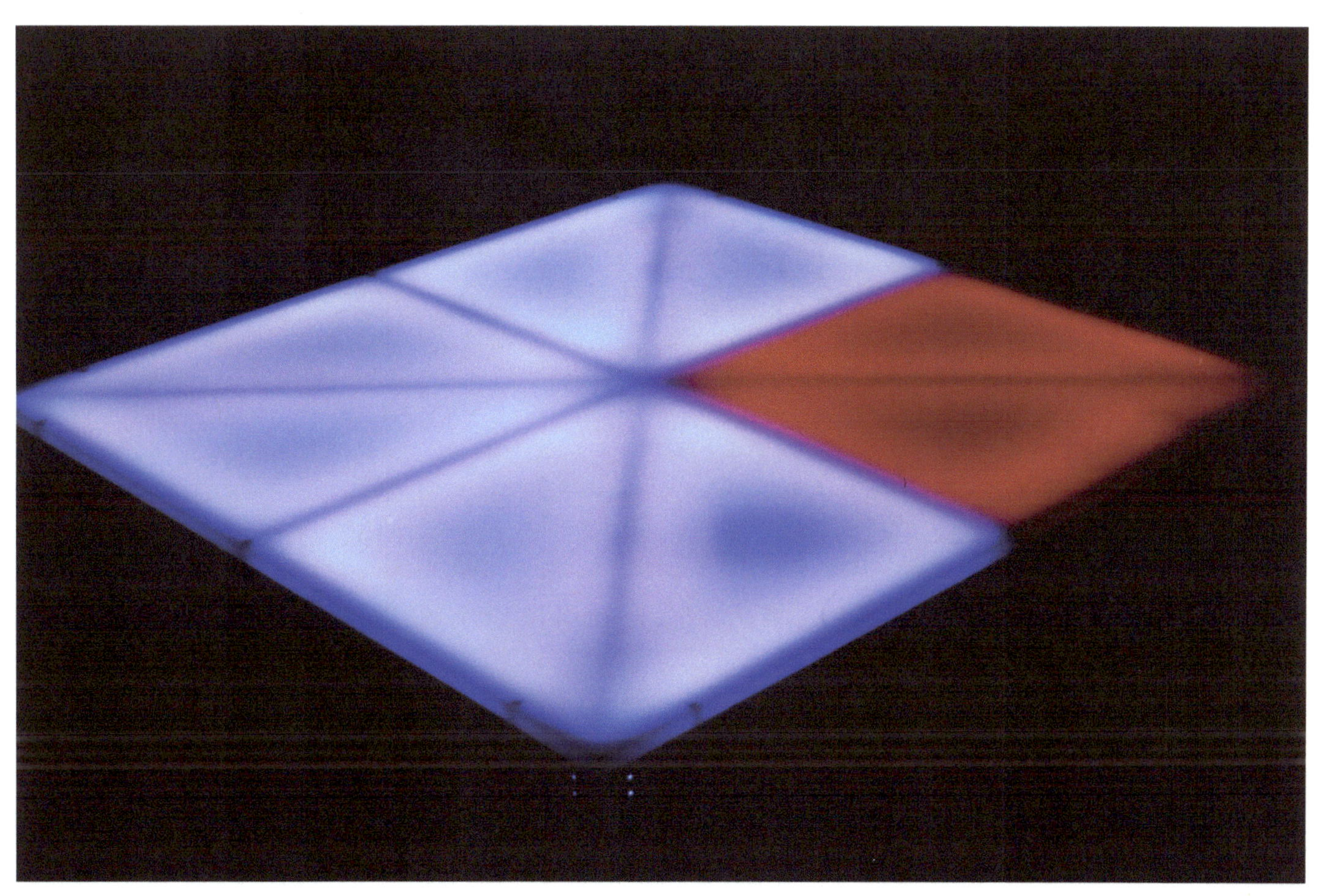

Untitled, 2012, LED programmed panel, 120 x 120 cm

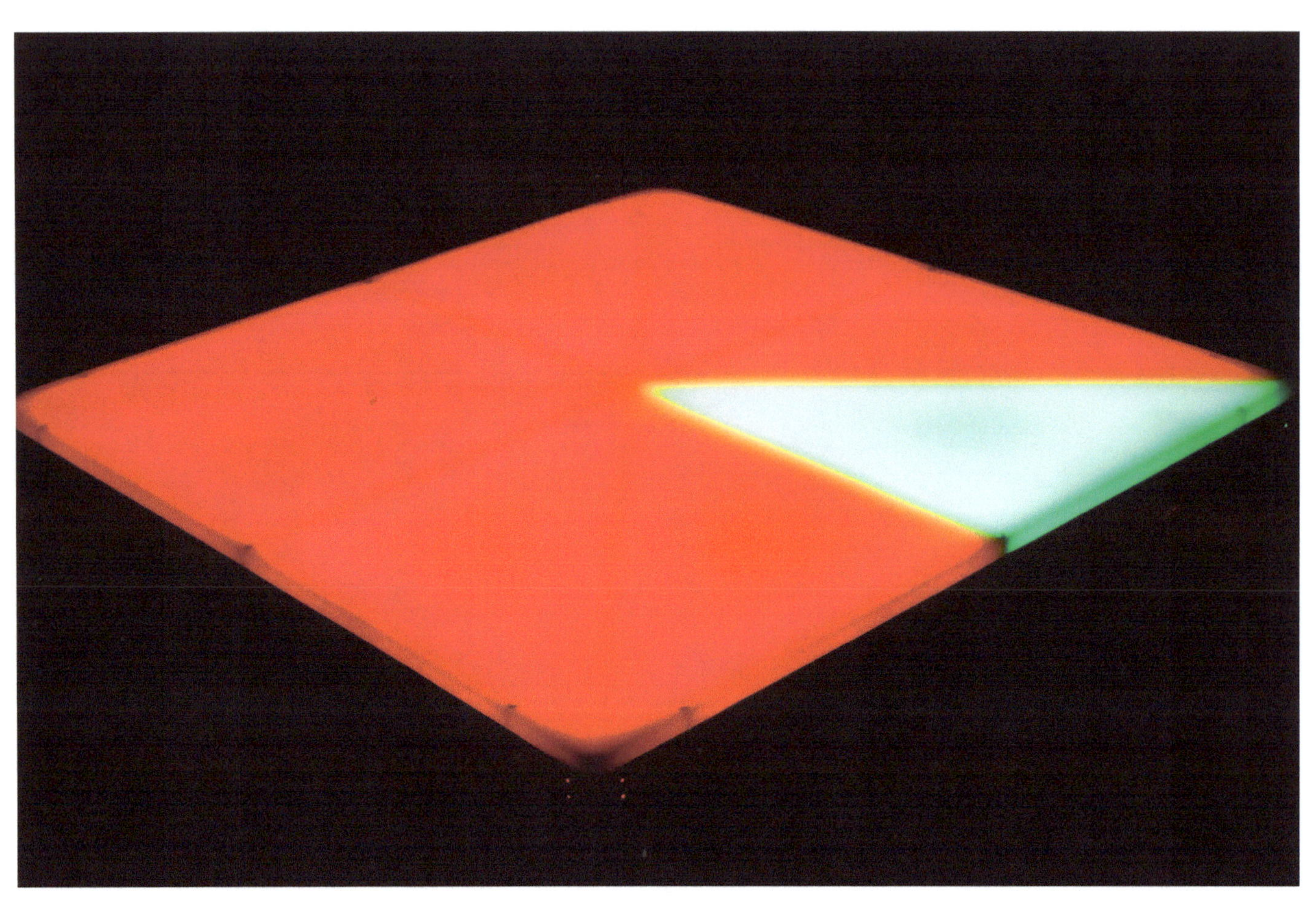

Untitled, 2012, LED programmed panel, 120 x 120 cm

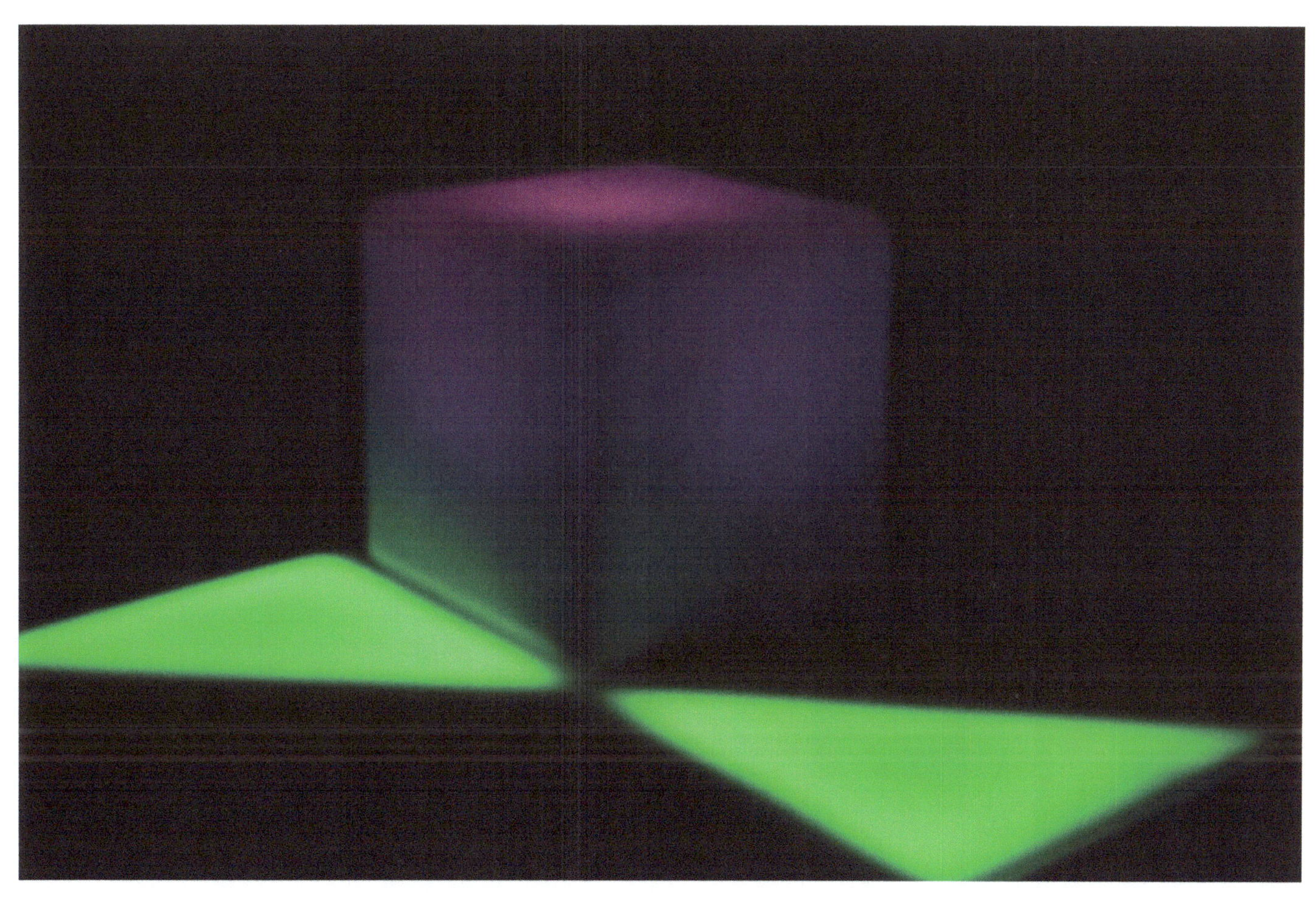

Untitled, 2012, LED programmed box and panel, 60 cm cube and 120 x 120 cm panel

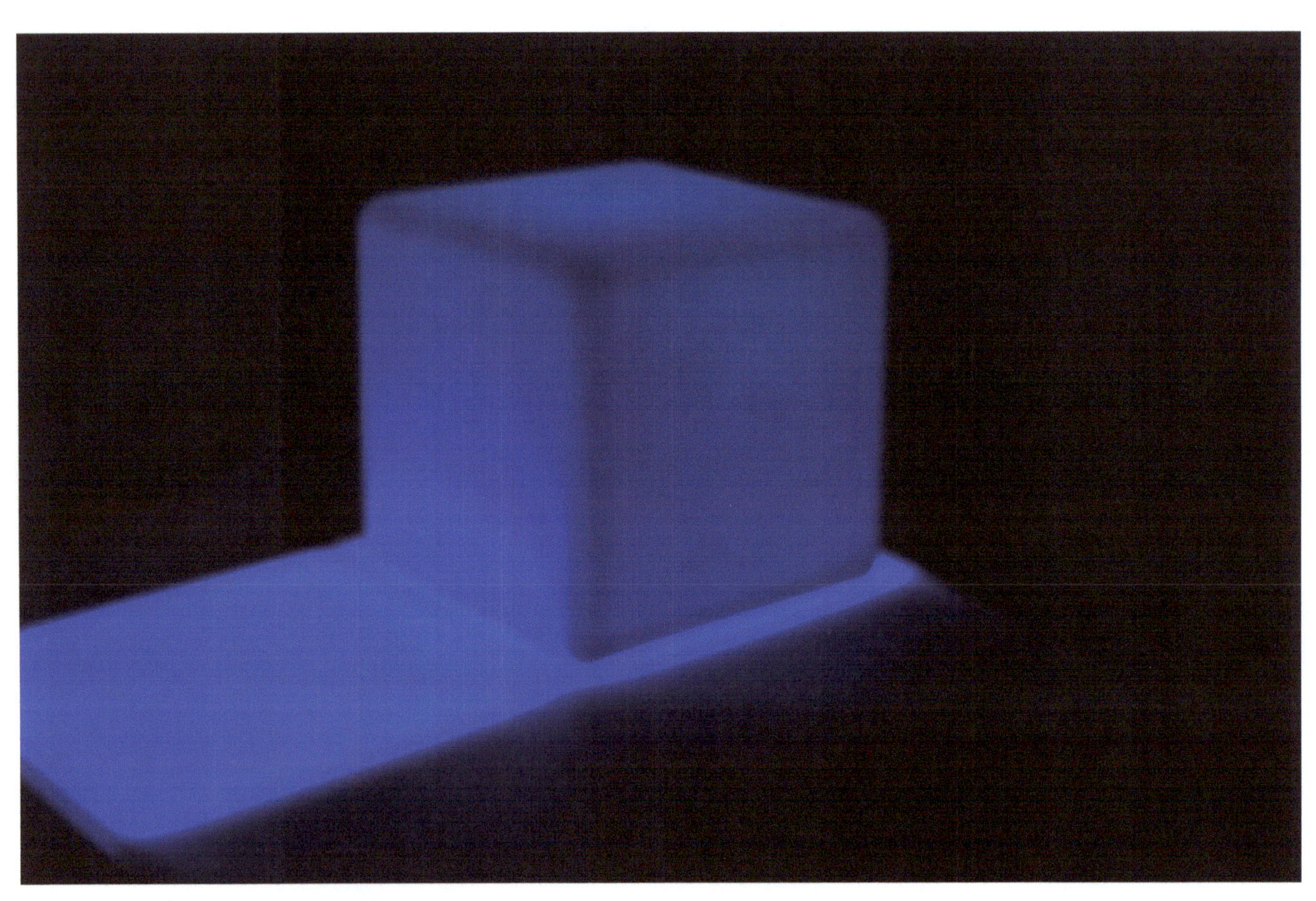

Untitled, 2012, LED programmed box and panel, 60 cm cube and 120 x 120 cm panel

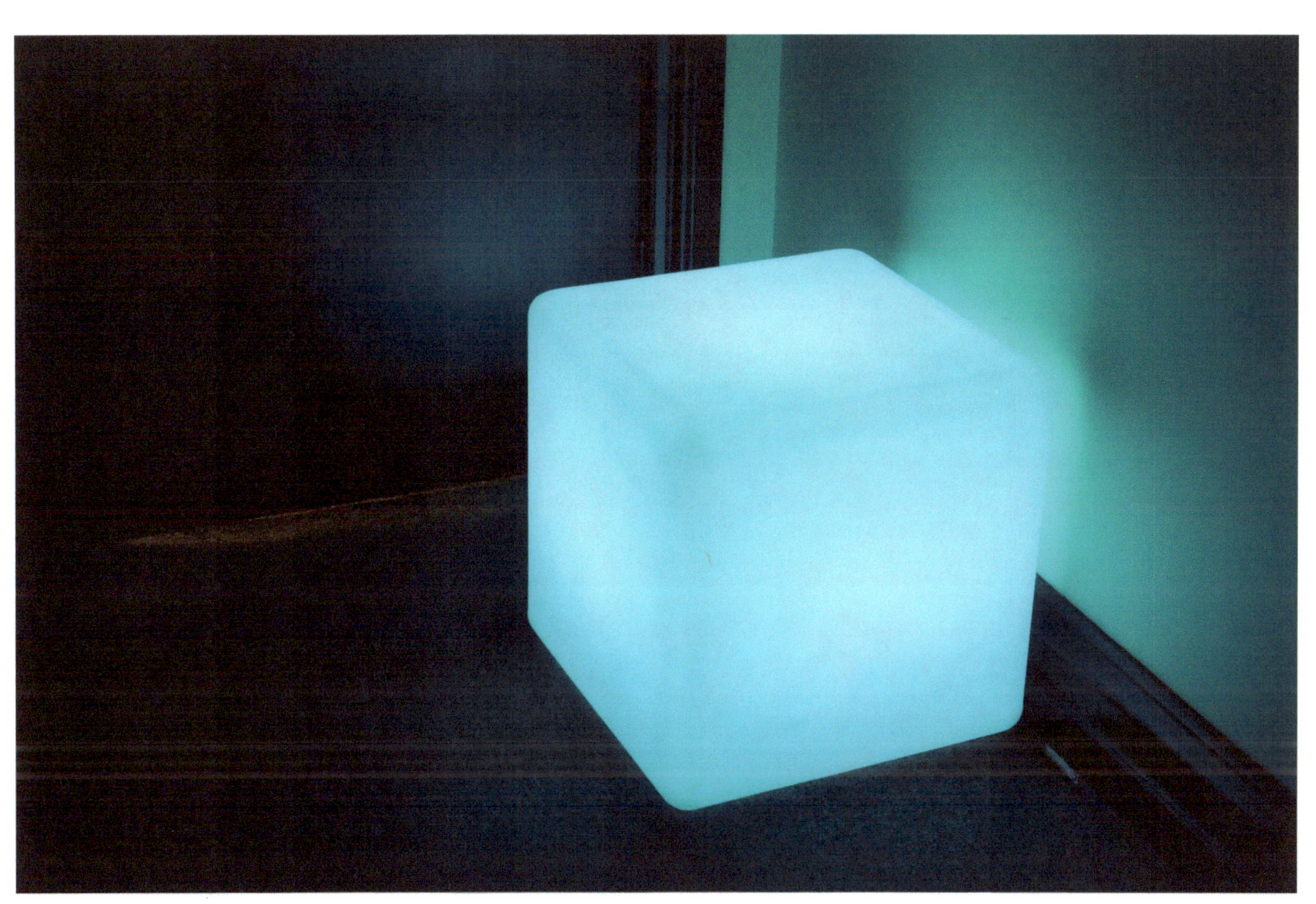

Untitled, 2012, LED programmed cube, 60 x 60 x 60 cm

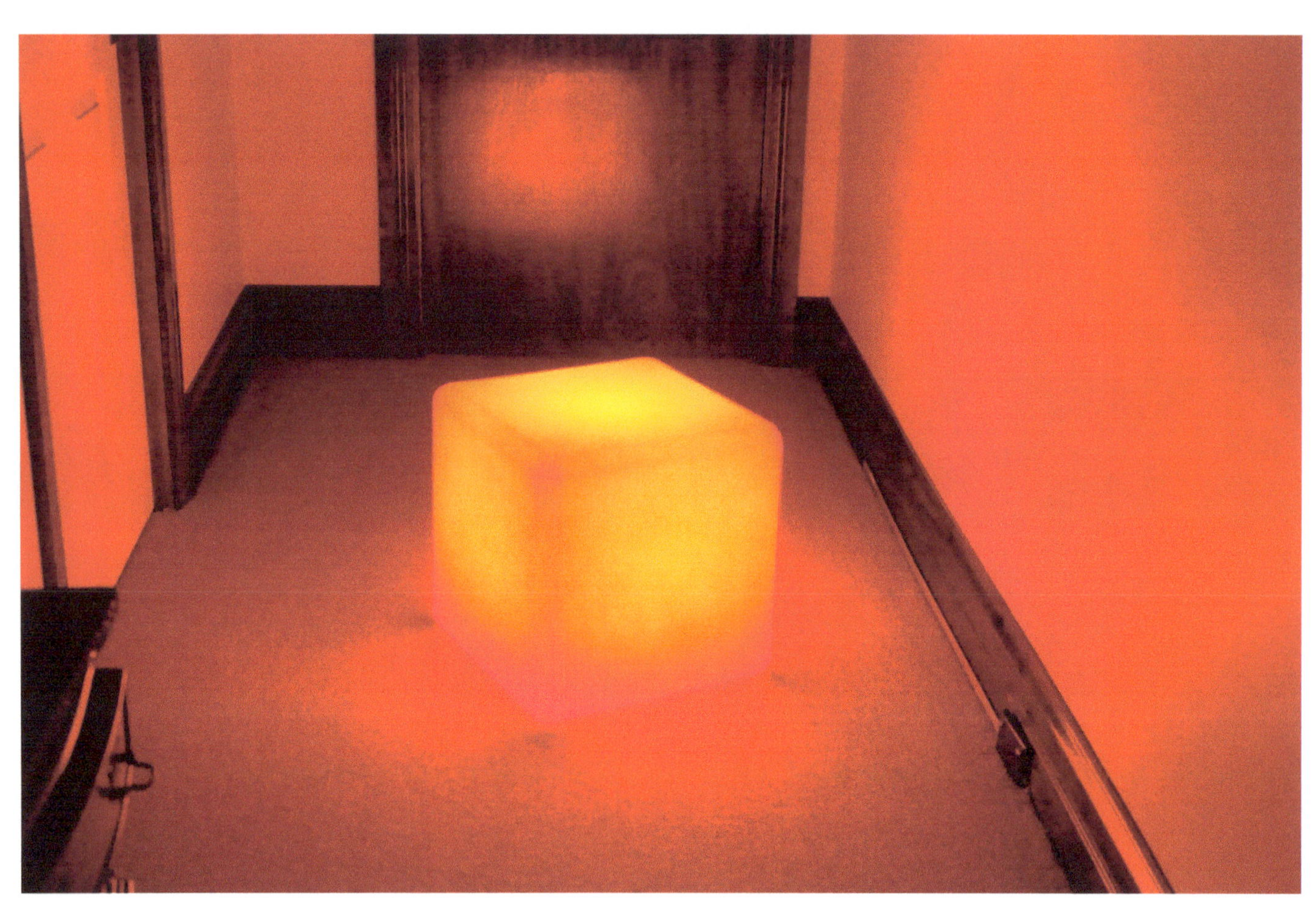

Untitled, 2012, LED programmed cube, 60 x 60 x 60 cm

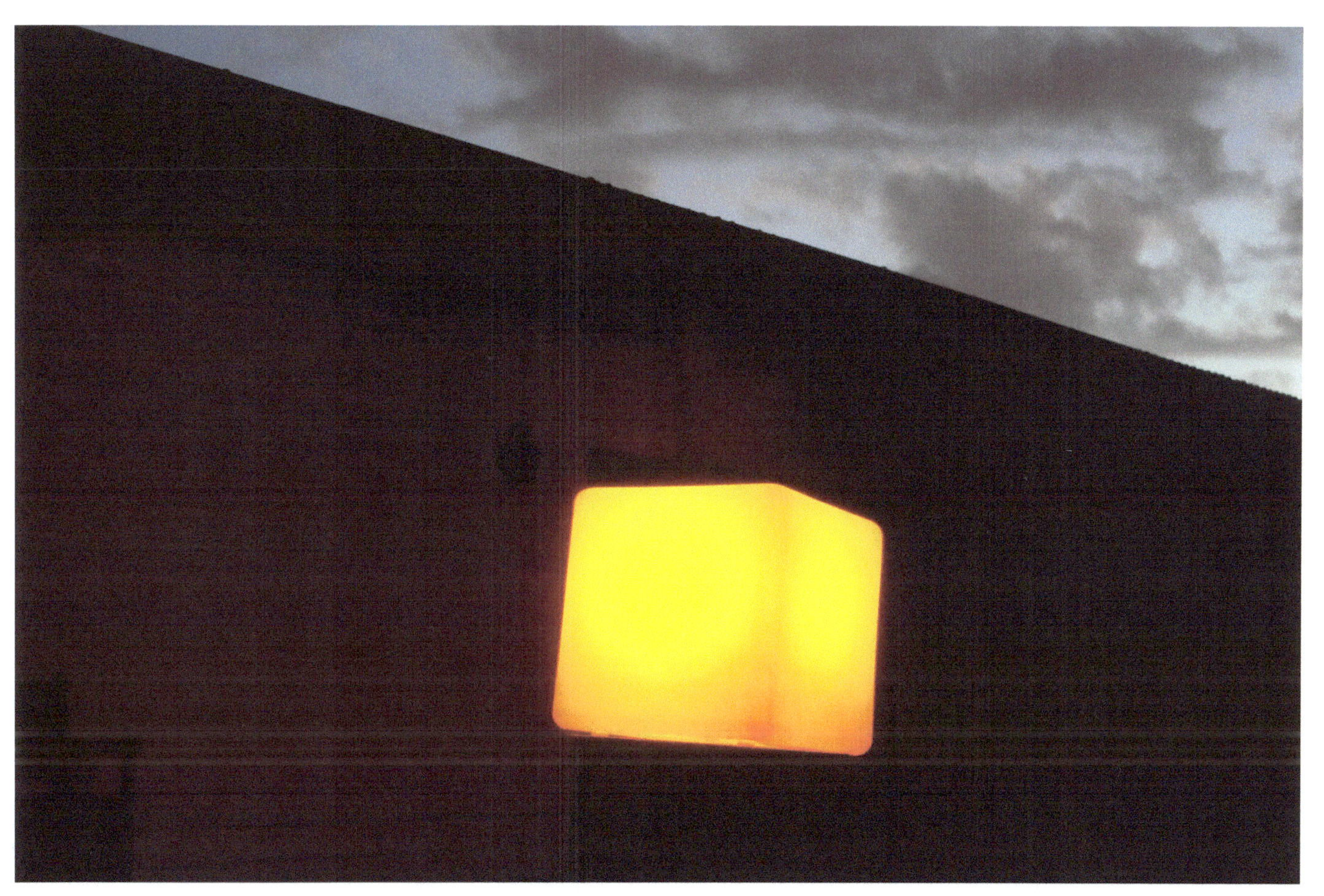

Untitled, 2012, LED programmed cube, 60 x 60 x 60 cm

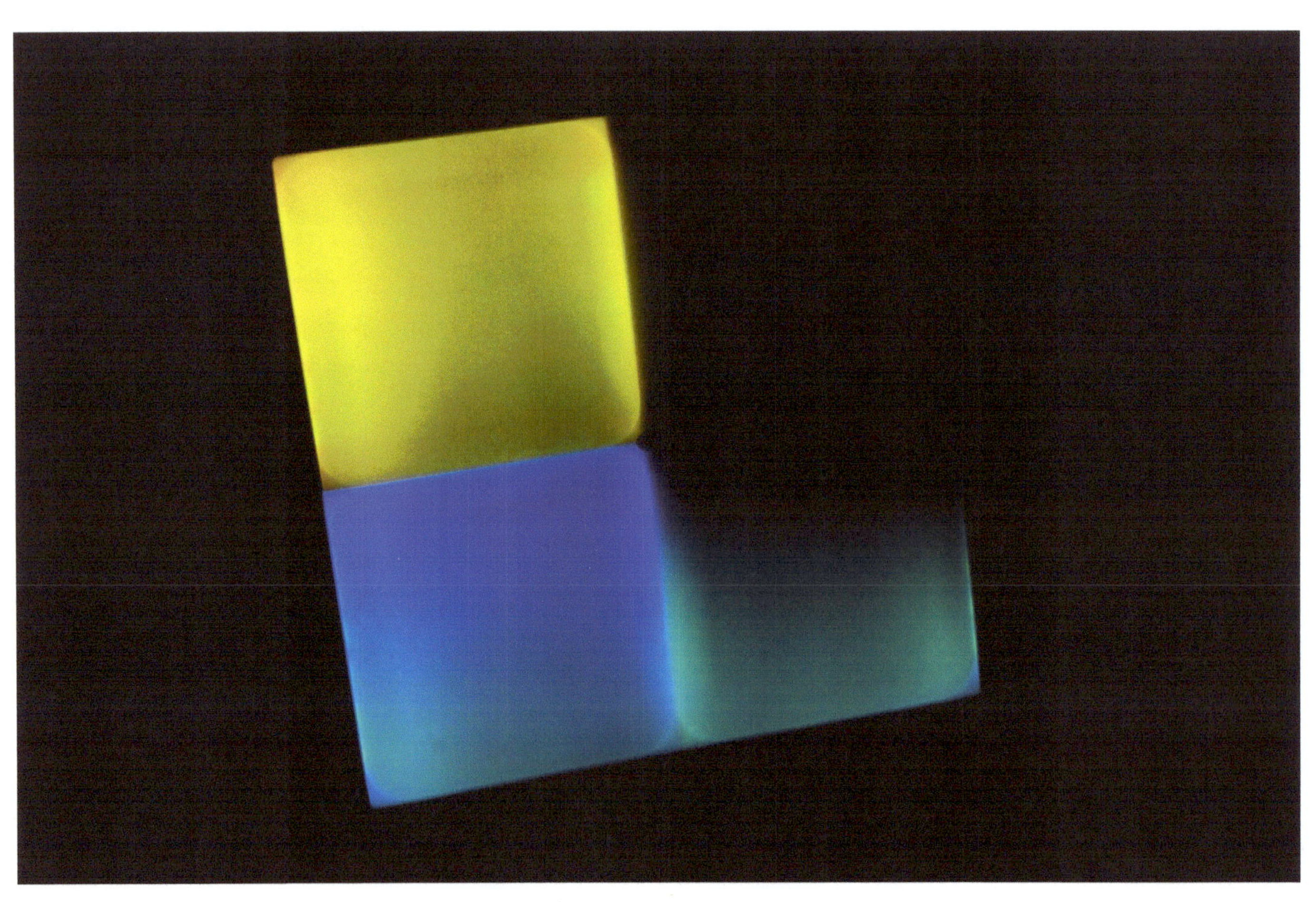

Untitled, 2012, LED programmed panel, 50 x 50 cm

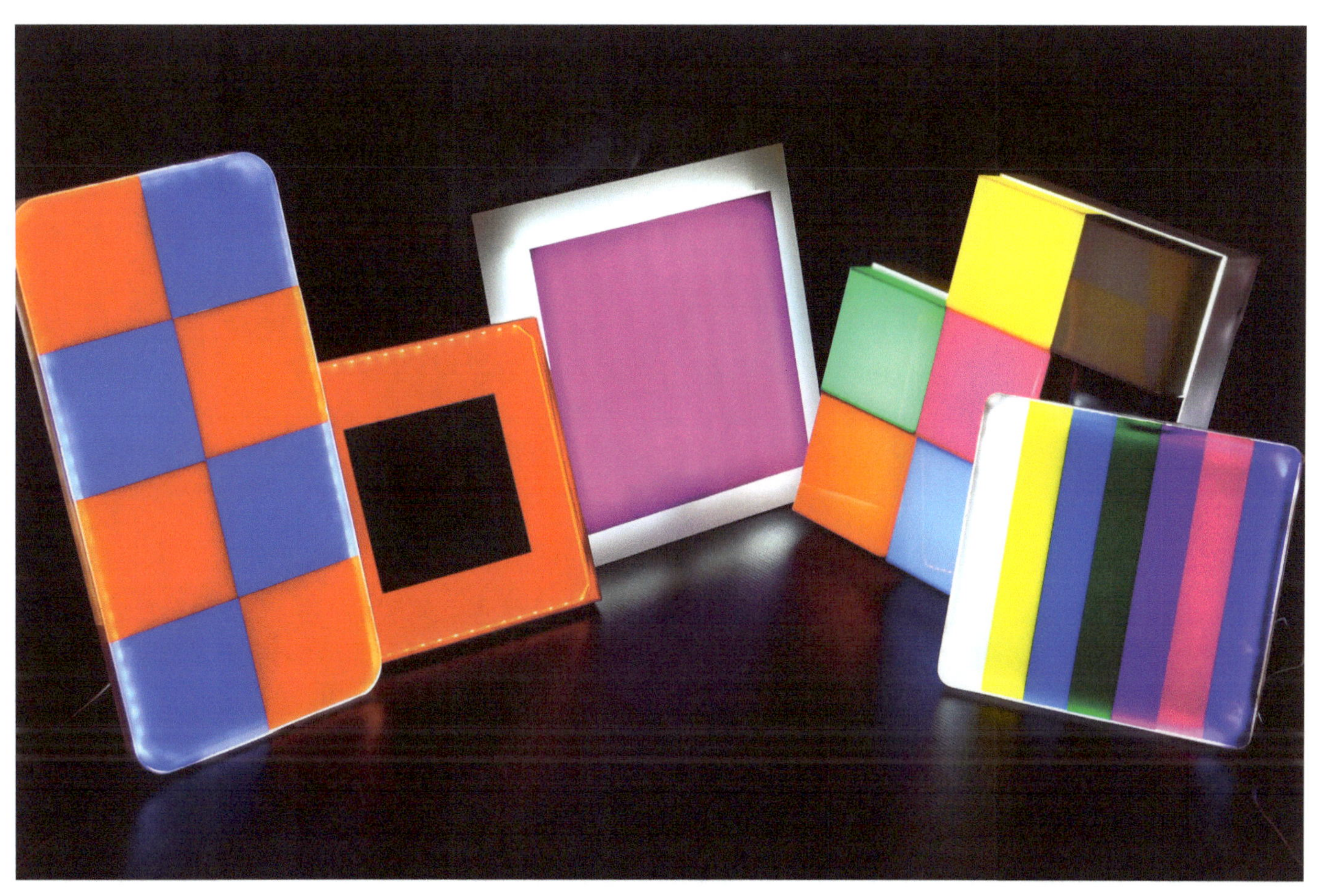

Untitled, 2012, LED light boxes, acrylic sheet and vinyl, various dimensions 35 to 75 cm

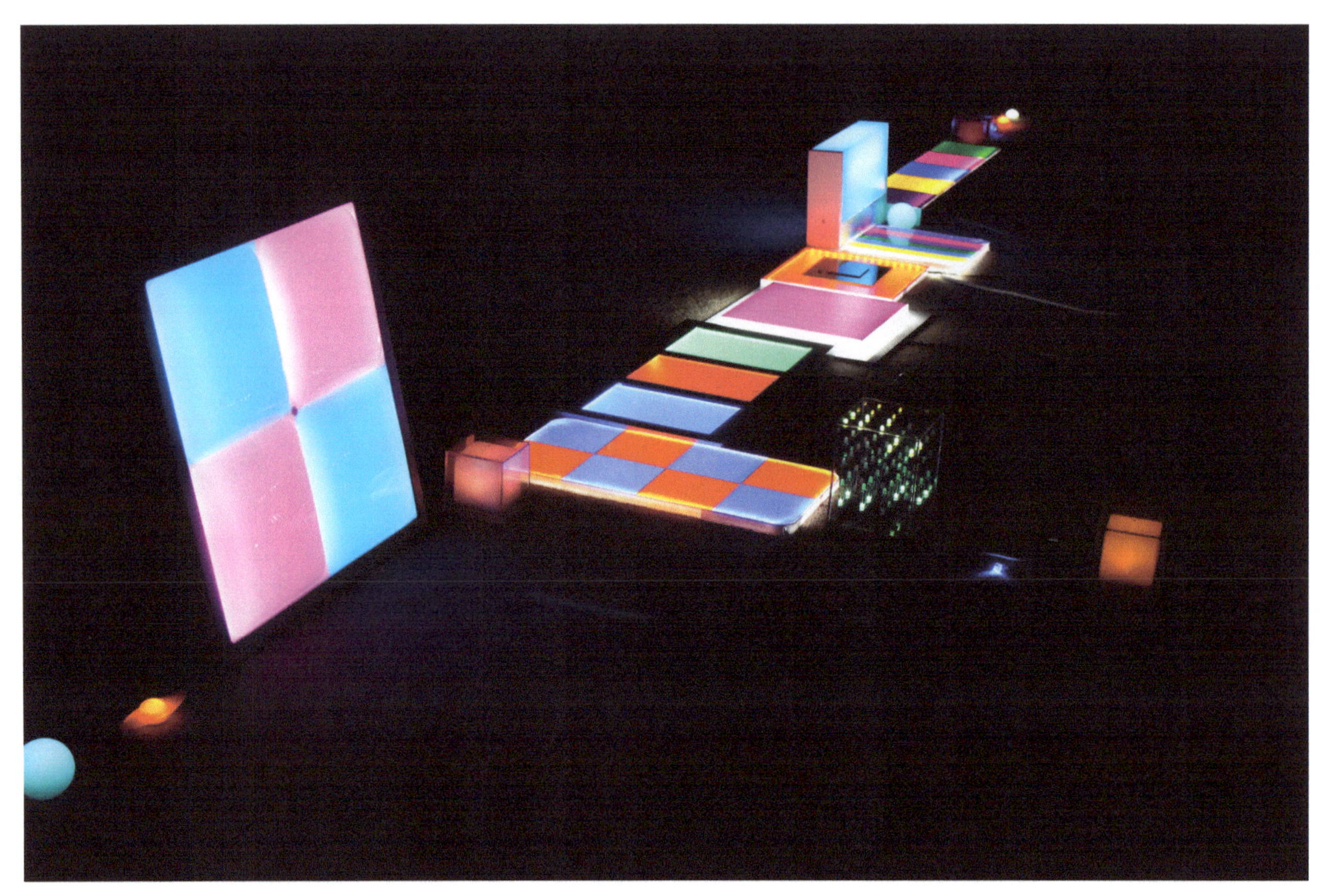

Facing east, 2012, LED lights and programmed lightboxes

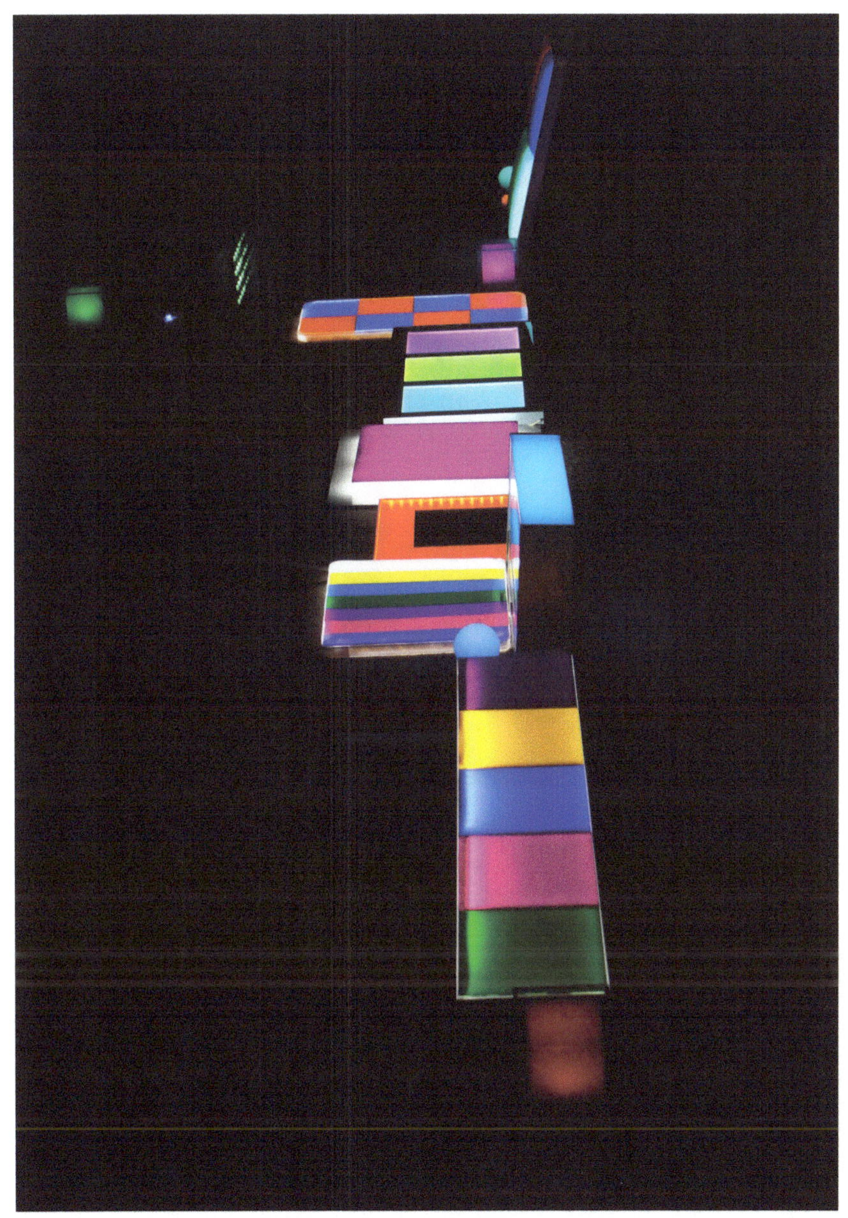

Facing east, 2012, LED lights and programmed lightboxes

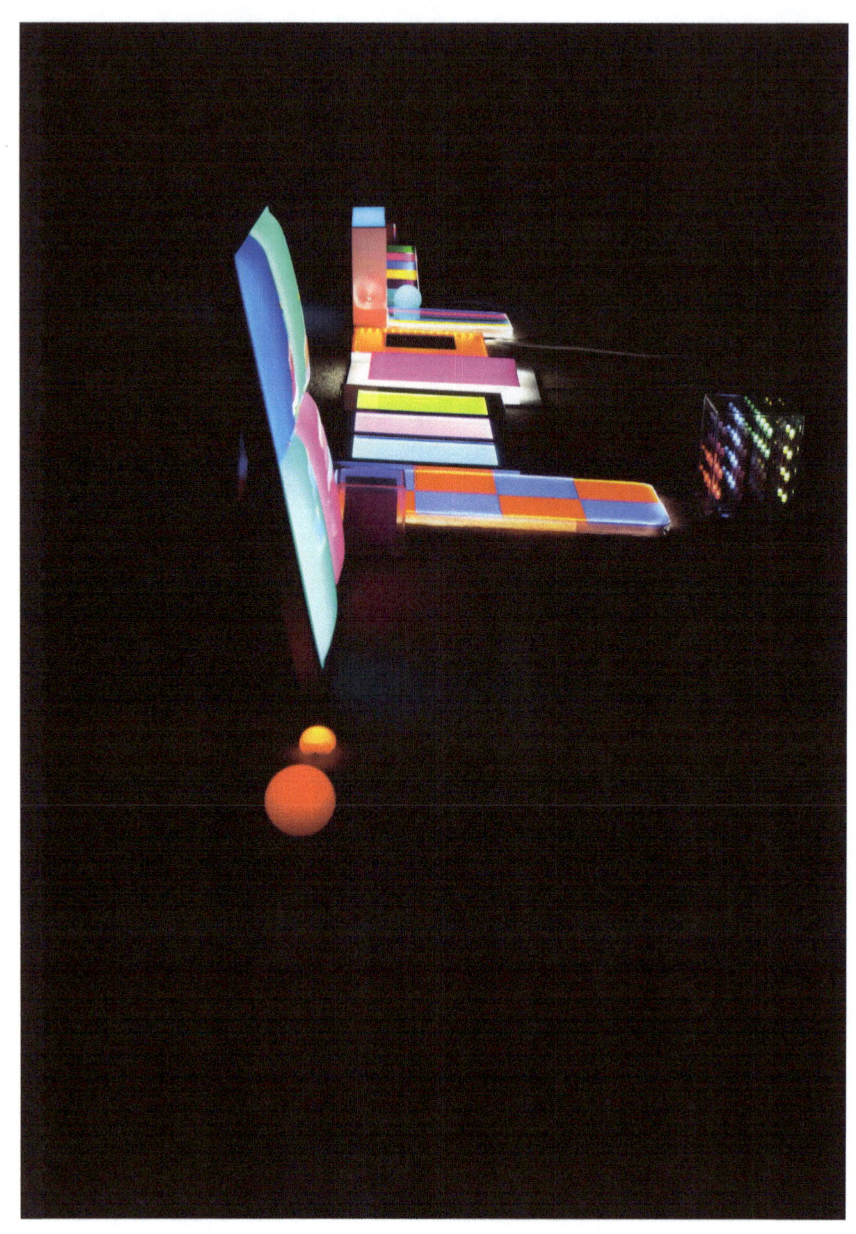

Facing east, 2012, LED lights and programmed lightboxes

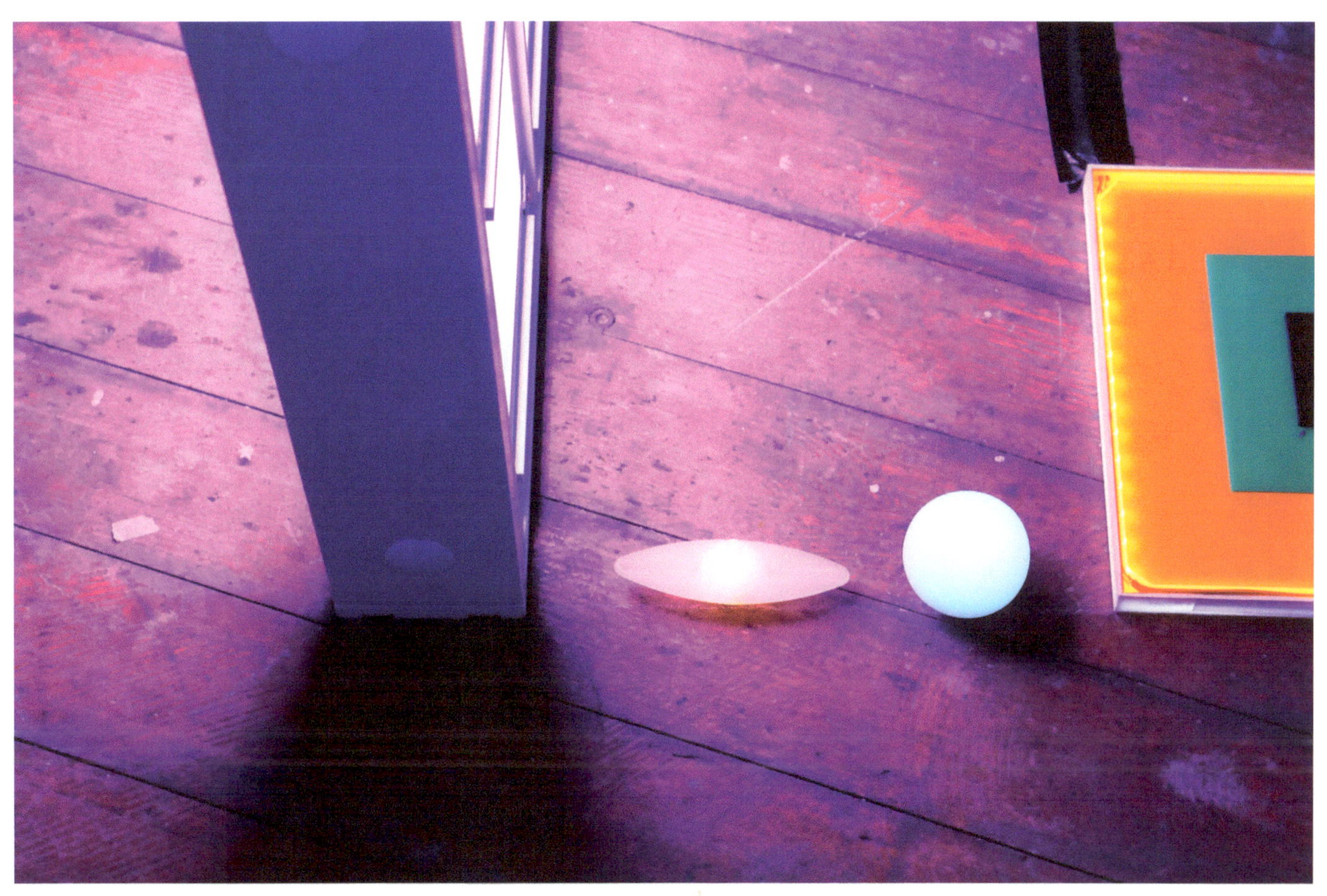

Facing east (detail), 2012, LED lights and programmed lightboxes

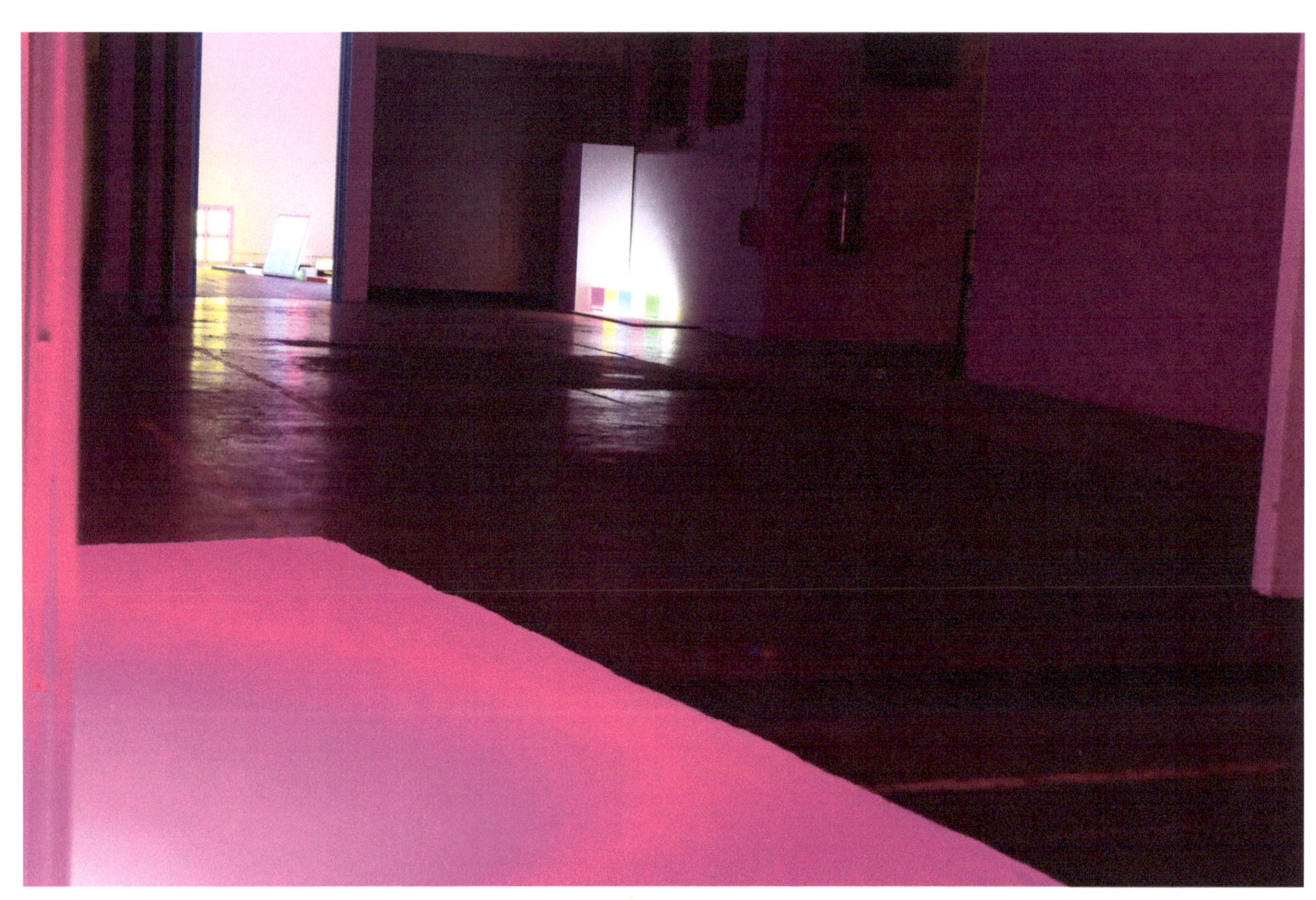

North-west, 2012, LED lights and programmed lightboxes, 74 x 74 cm, MADA

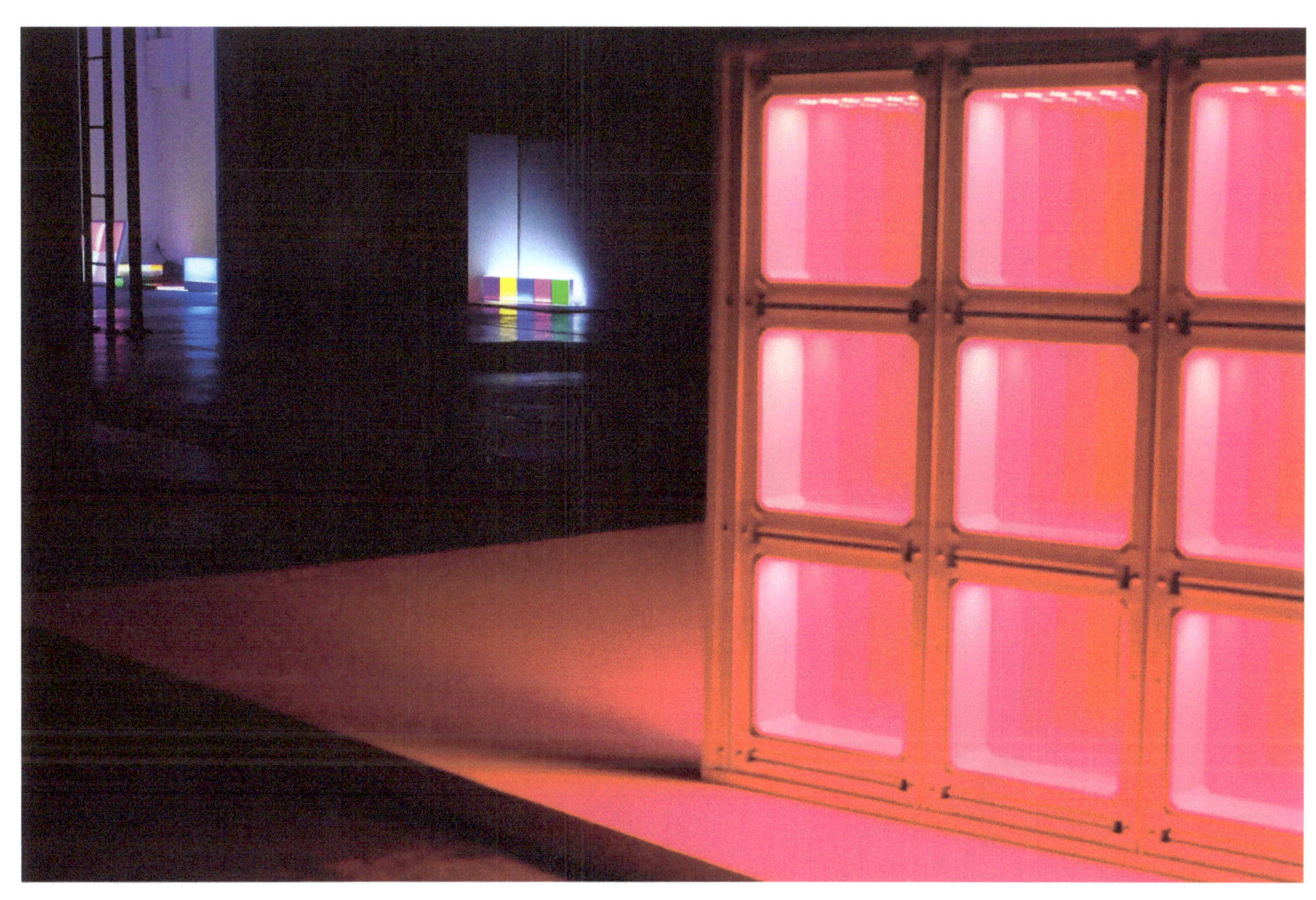

North-west, 2012, LED lights and programmed lightboxes, 74 x 74 cm, MADA

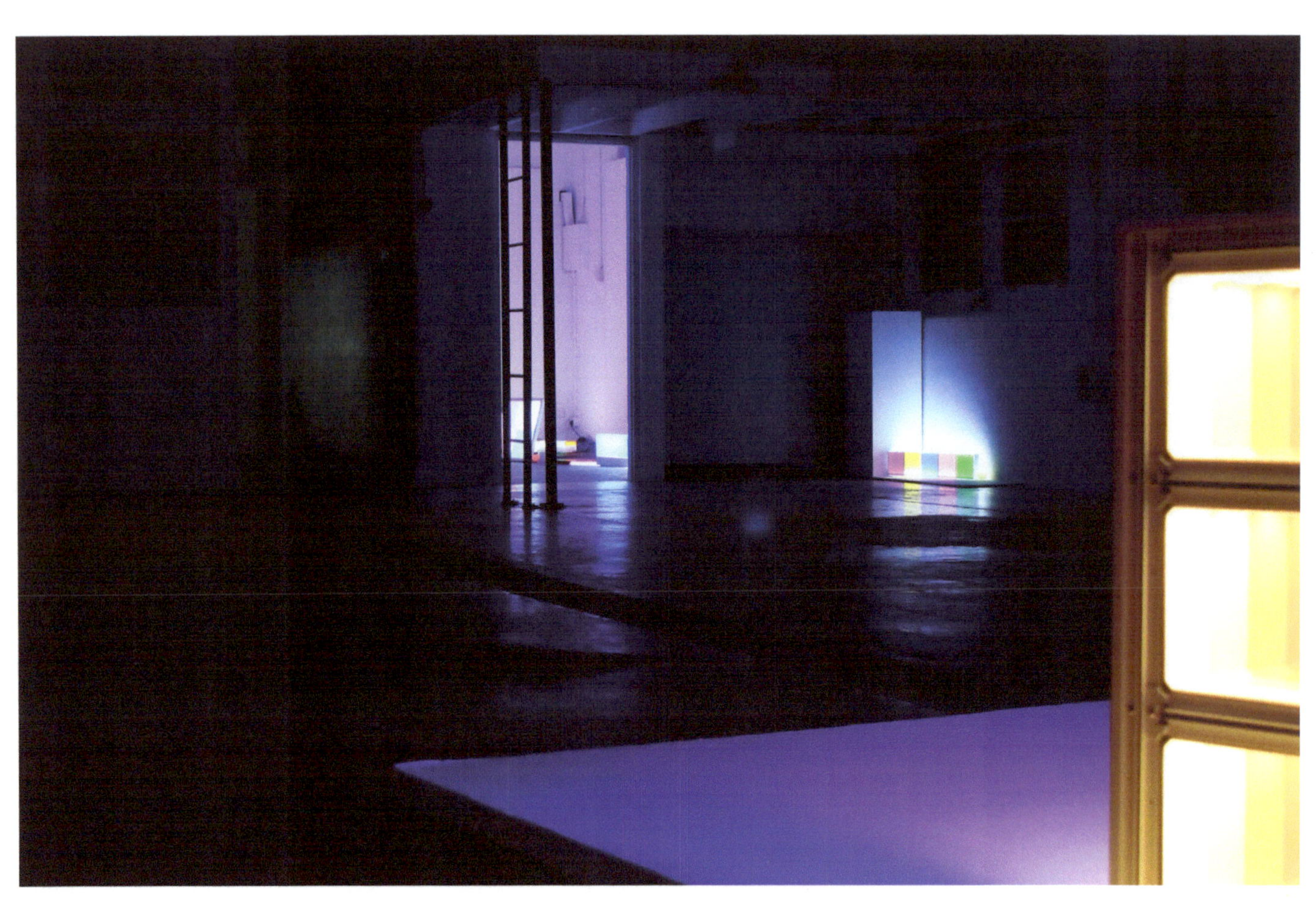

North-west, 2012, LED lights and programmed lightboxes, 74 x 74 cm, MADA

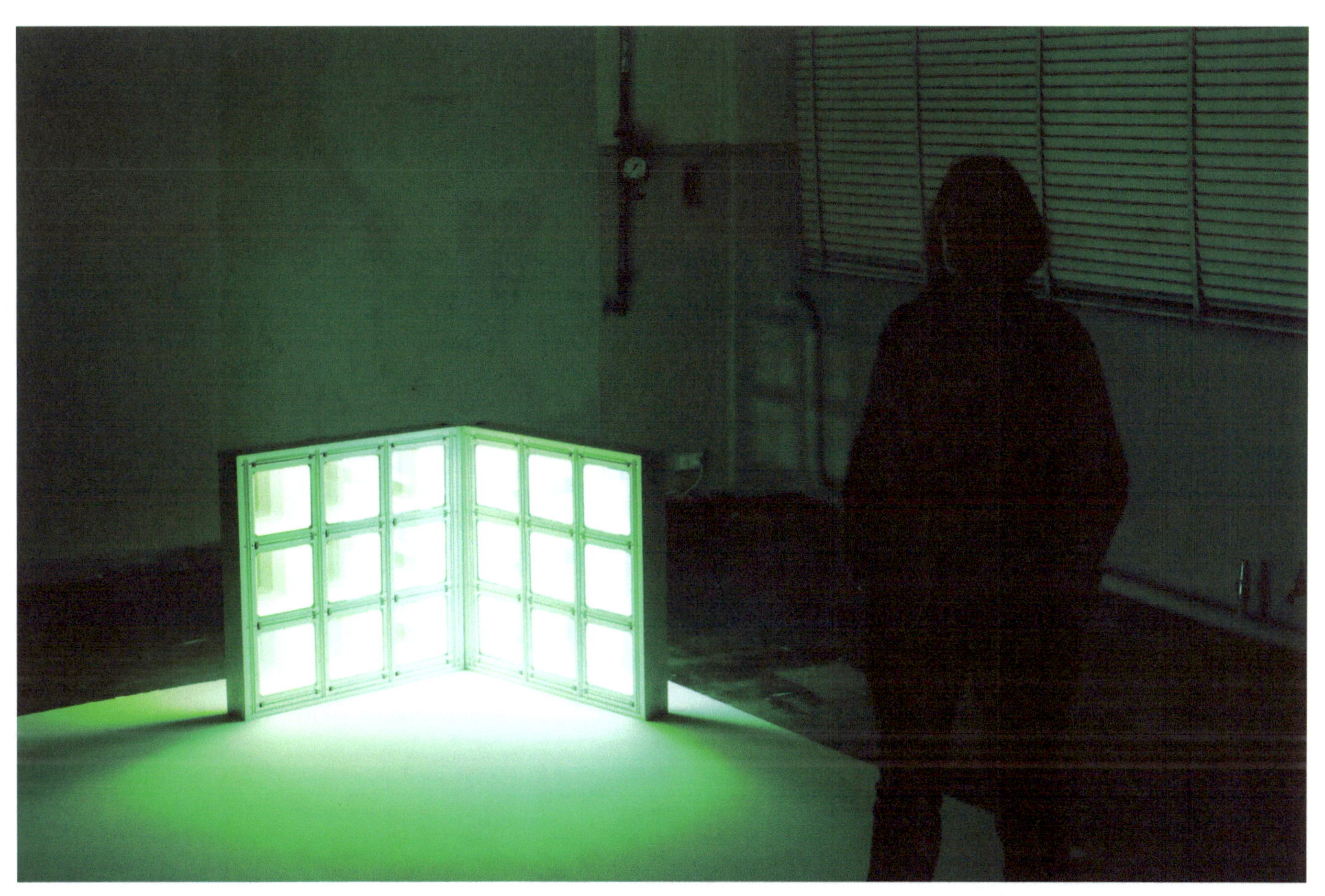

North-west, 2012, LED programmed lightboxes, 74 x 74 cm, MADA

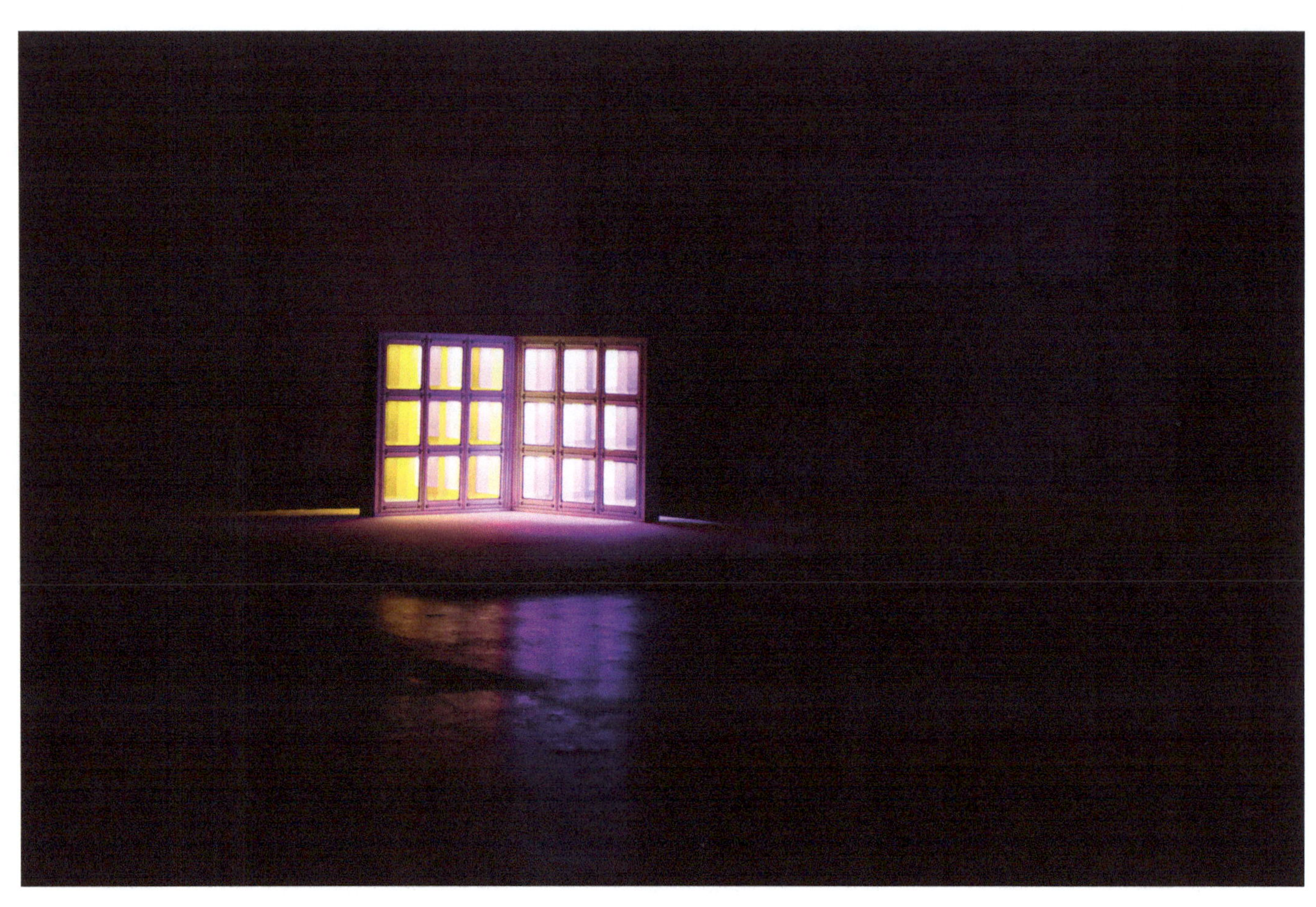

North-west, 2012, LED programmed lightboxes, 74 x 74 cm, MADA

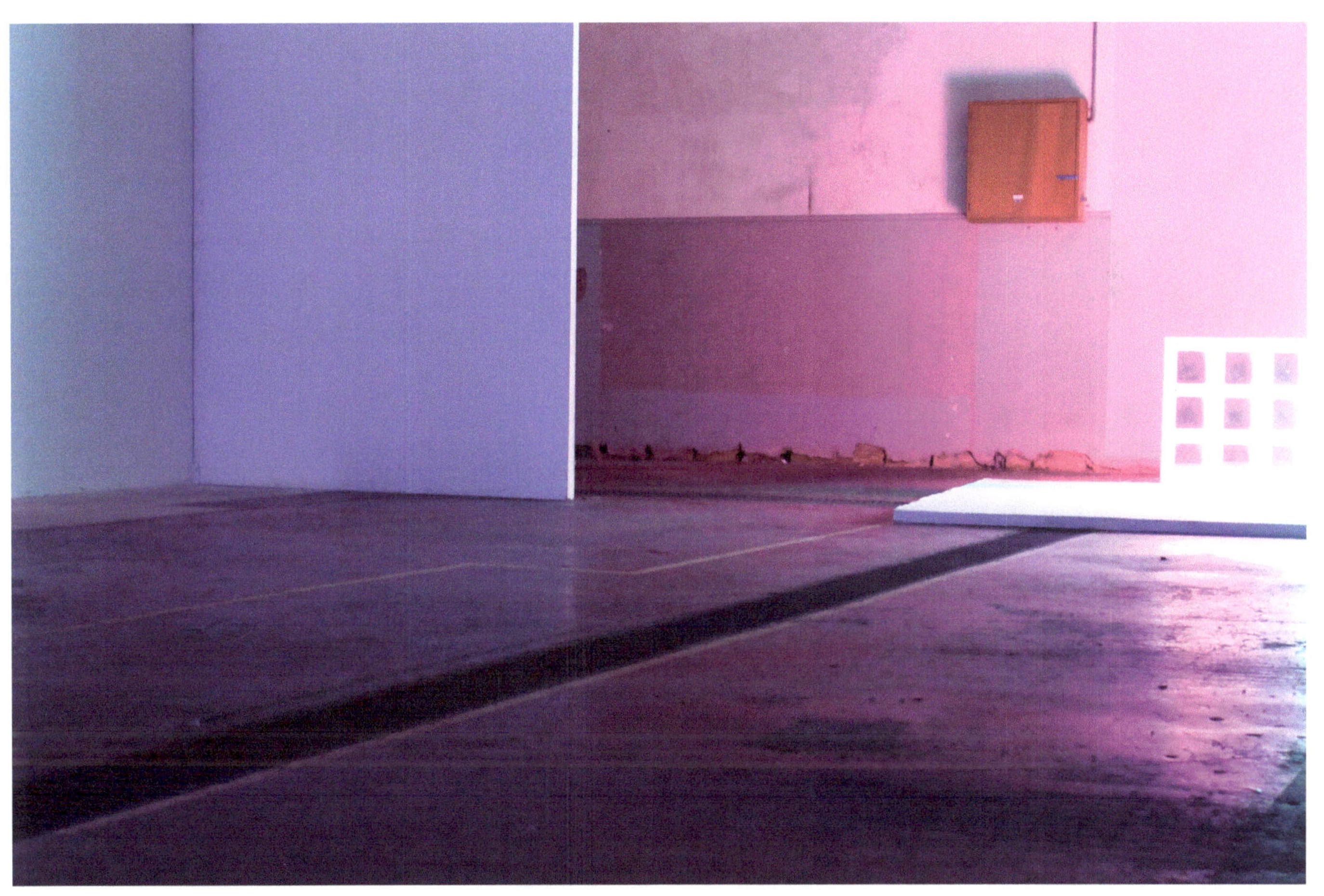

North-west, 2012, LED programmed lightboxes, 74 x 74 cm, MADA

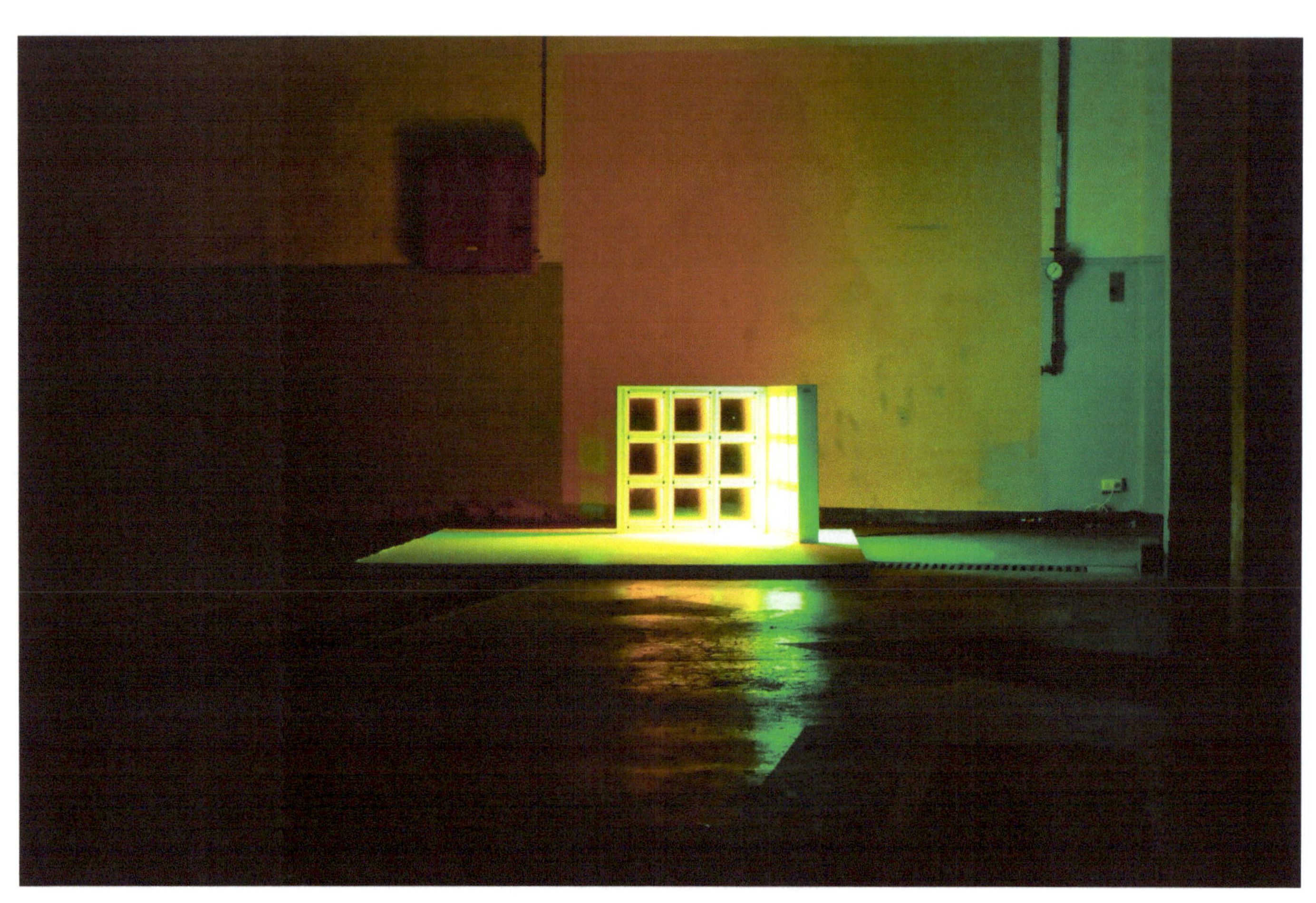

North-west, 2012, LED programmed lightboxes, 74 x 74 cm, MADA

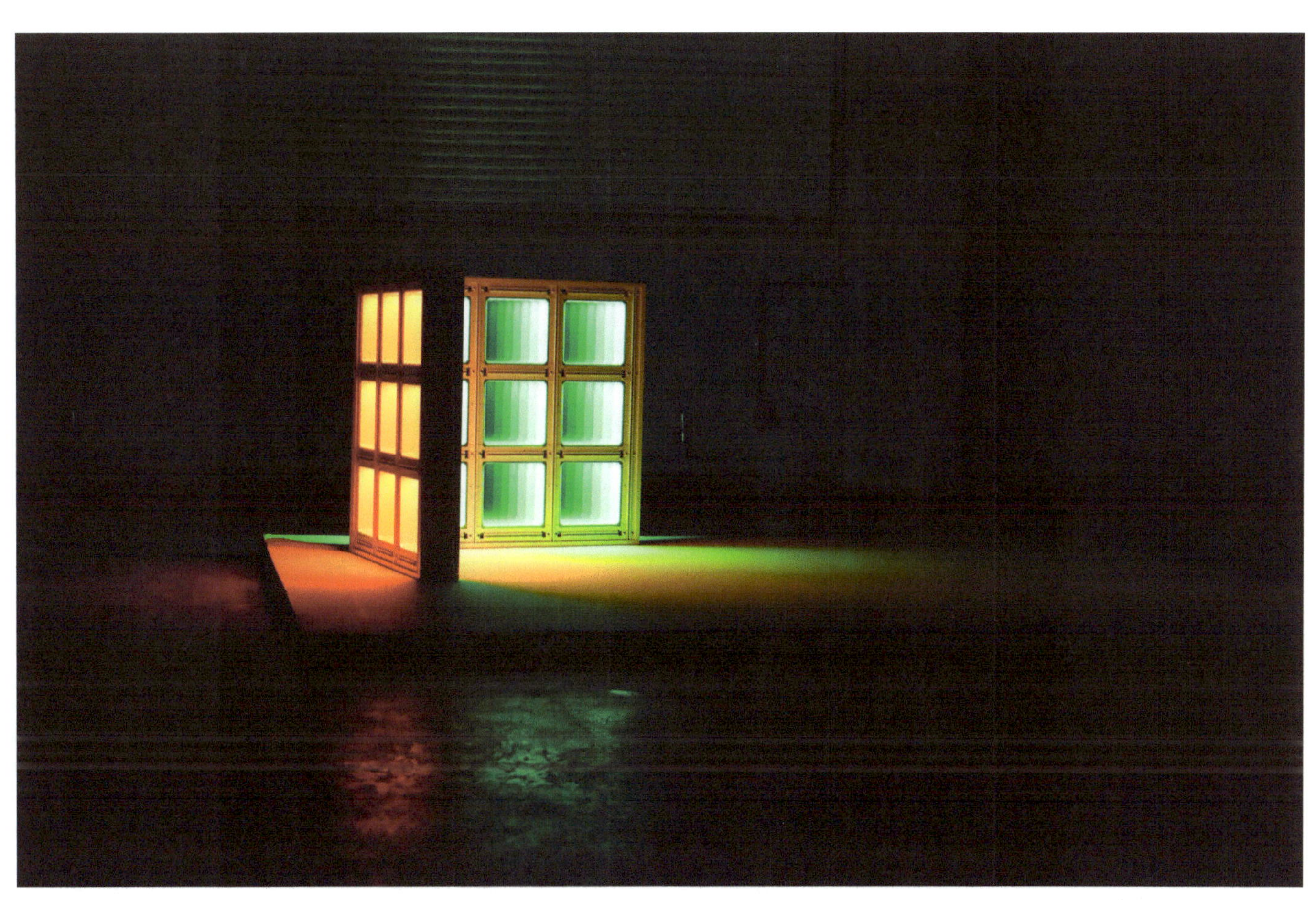

North-west, 2012, LED programmed lightboxes, 74 x 74 cm, MADA

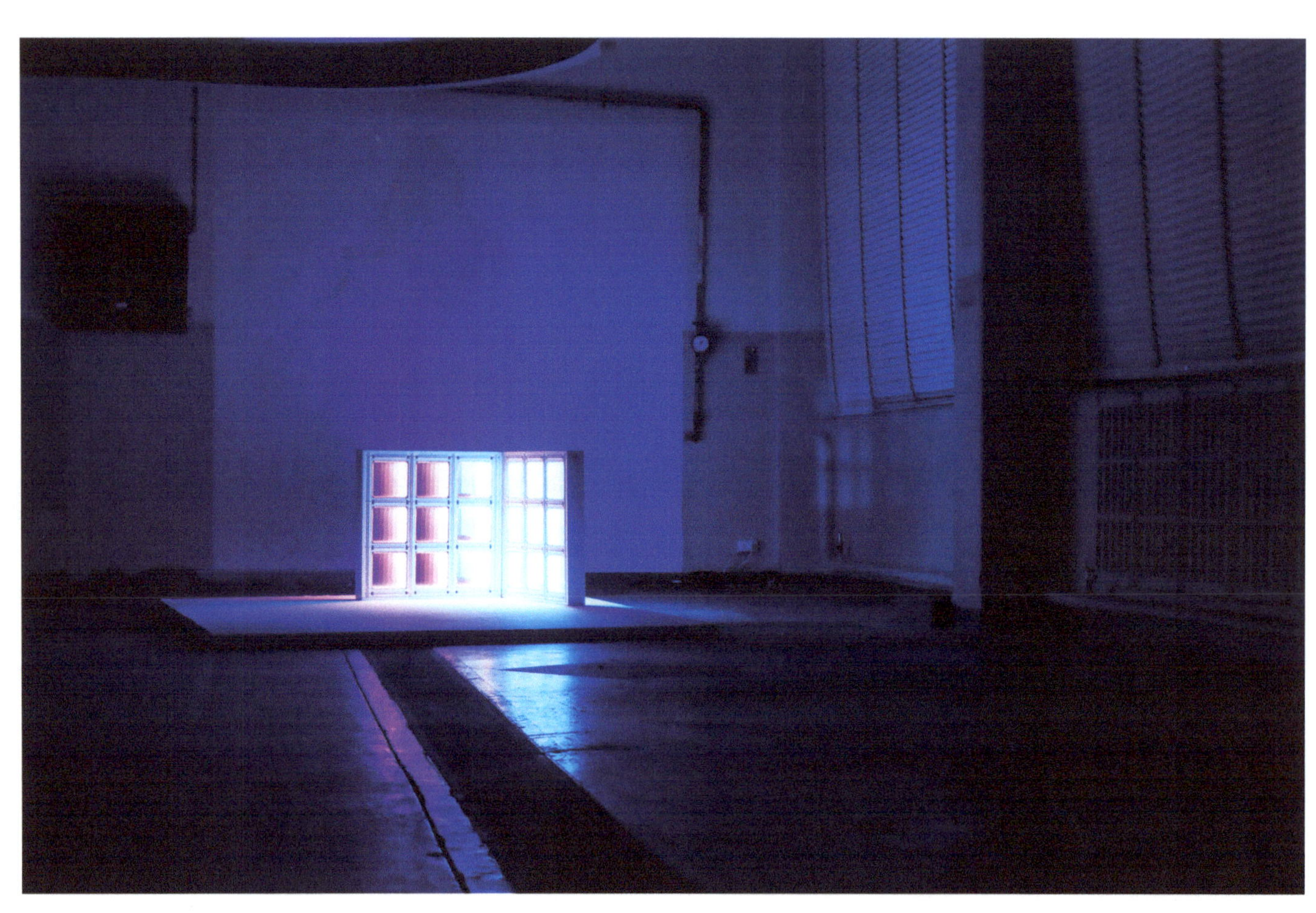

North-west, 2012, LED programmed lightboxes, 74 x 74 cm, MADA

2013

Square, 2013, programmed LEDs in aluminum frame, 60 x 60 cm

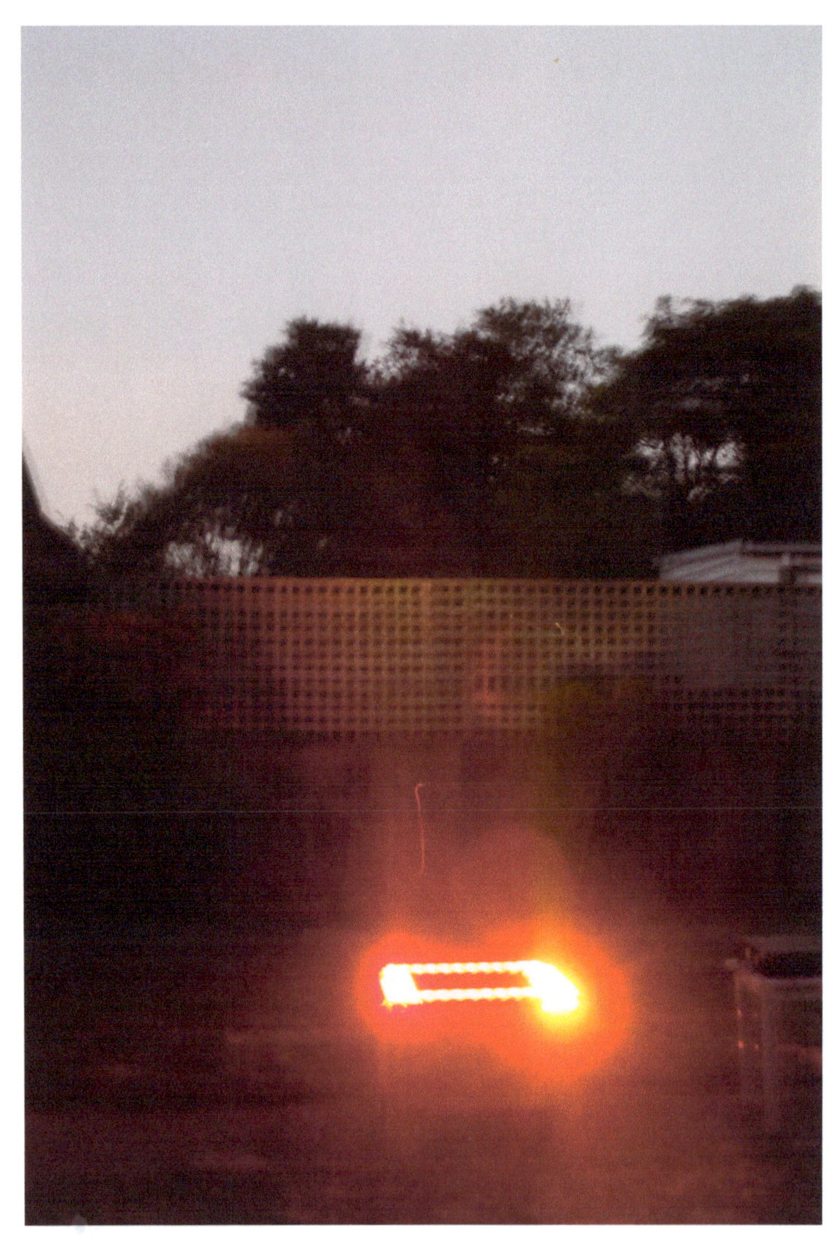

Square, 2013, programmed LEDs in aluminum frame, 60 x 60 cm

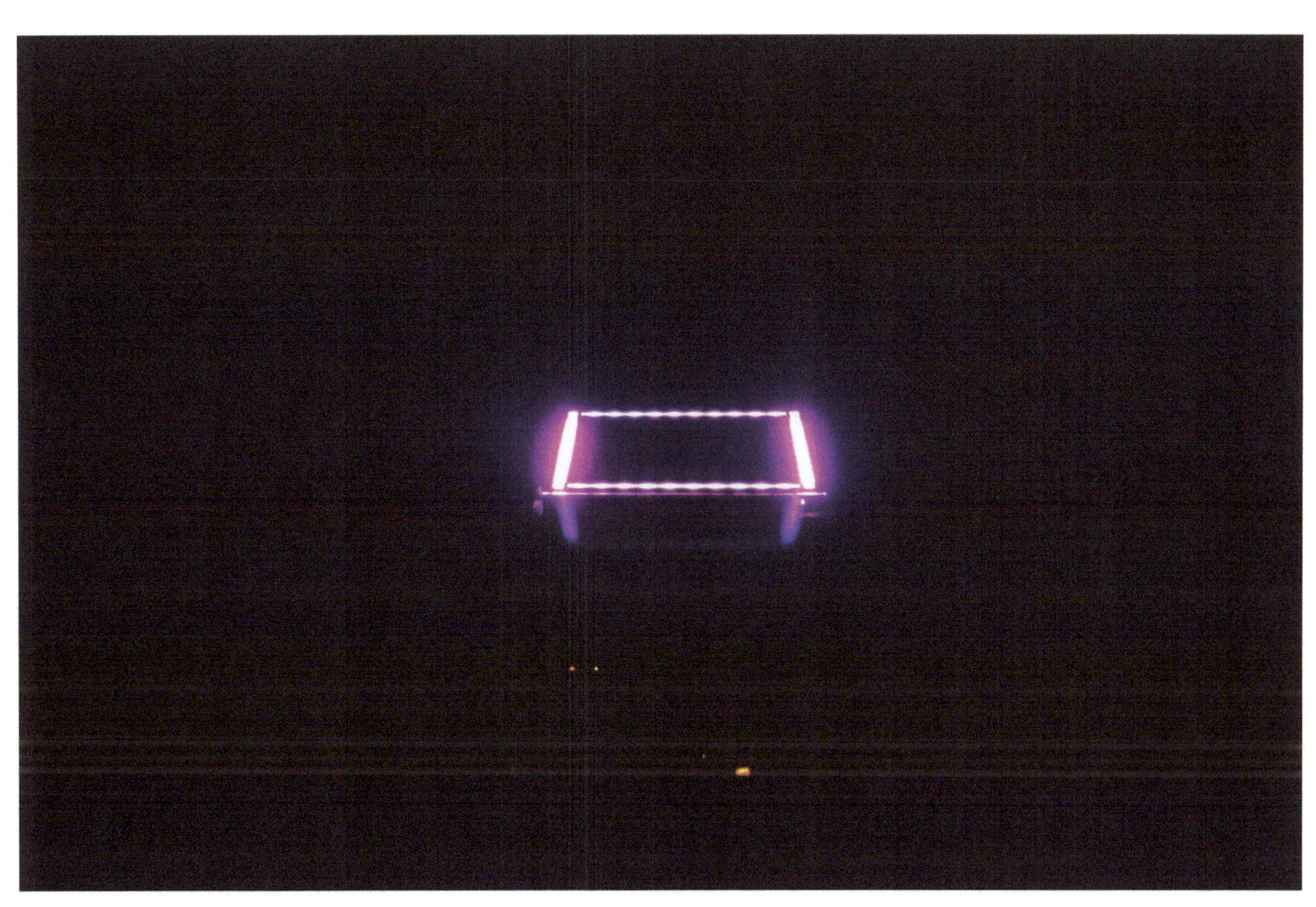

Square, 2013, programmed LEDs in aluminum frame, 60 x 60 cm

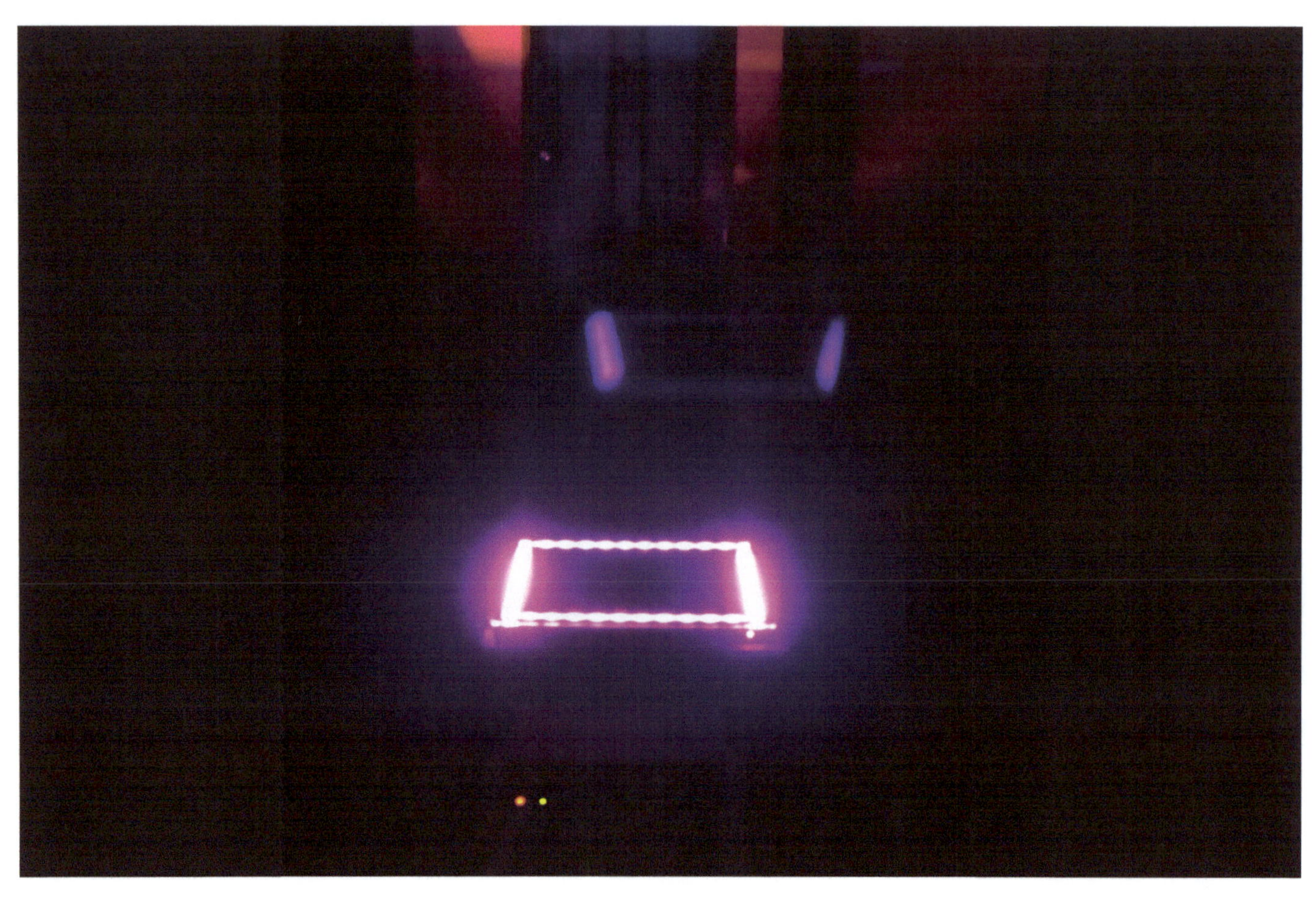

Square, 2013, programmed LEDs in aluminum frame, 60 x 60 cm

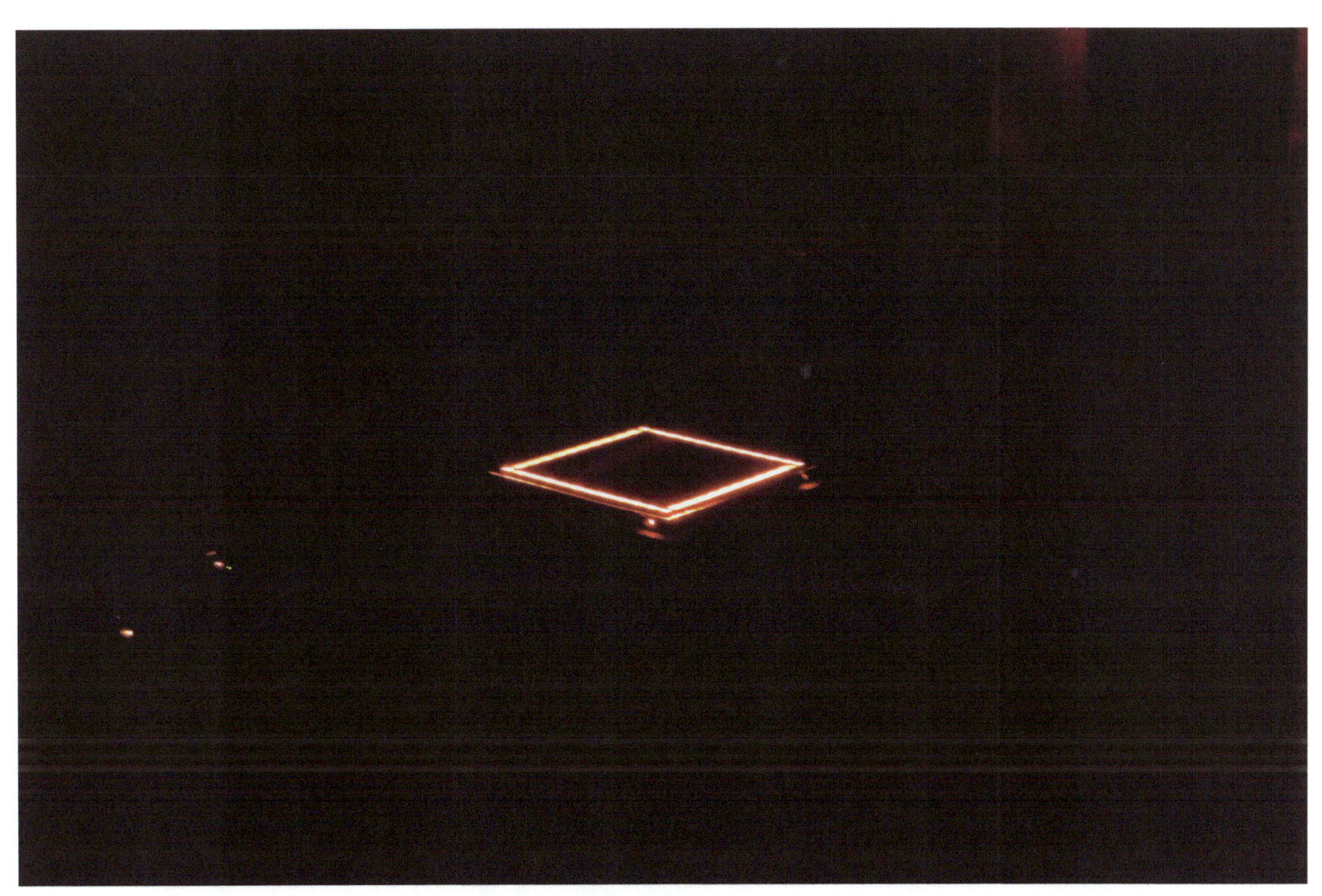

Square, 2013, programmed LEDs in aluminum frame, 60 x 60 cm

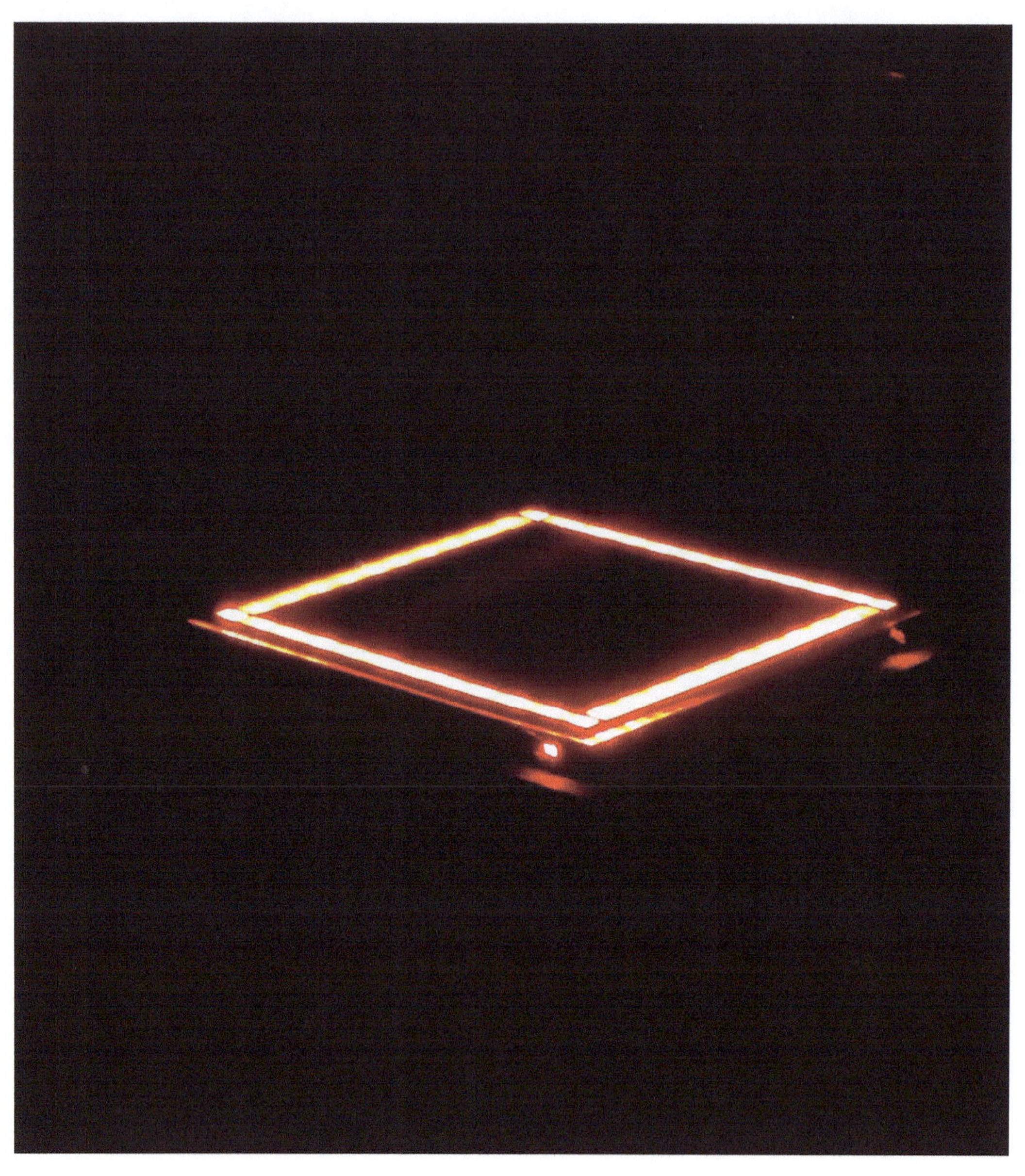

Square, 2013, programmed LEDs in aluminum frame, 60 x 60 cm

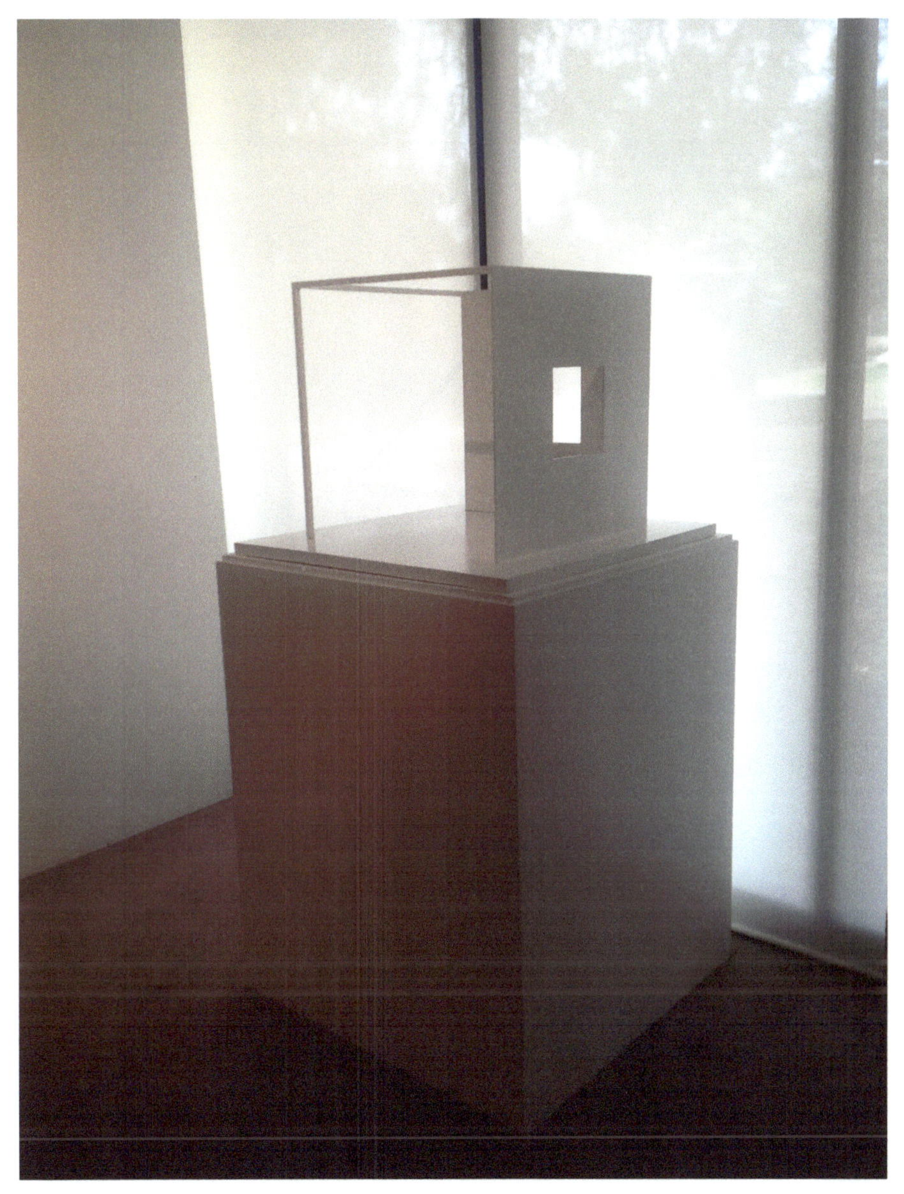

Sun always wins 2, 2013, powder coated aluminium, 52 x 74 cm,
Mary & Lou Senini Award, McClelland Sculpture Park and Gallery, Langwarrin

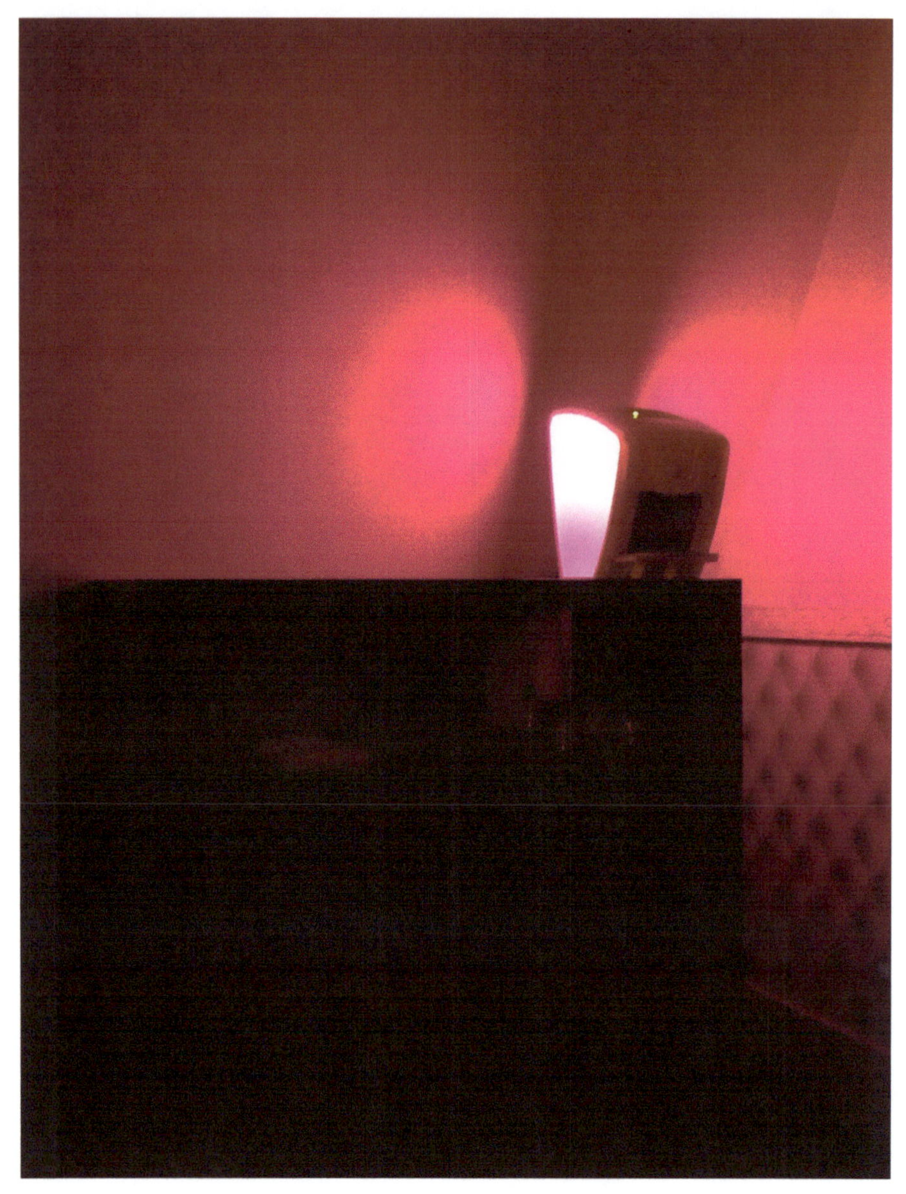

Paris hotel room, 2013, video still

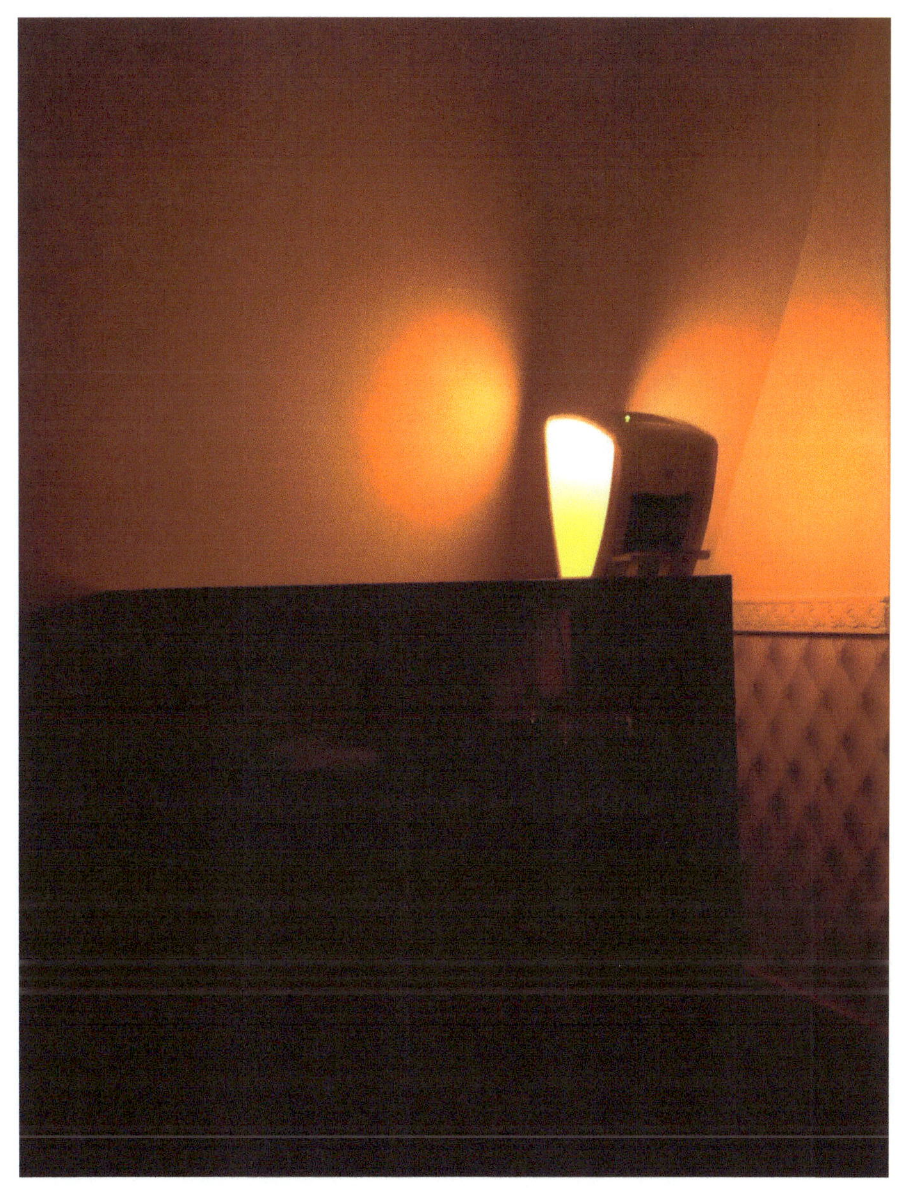

Paris hotel room, 2013, video still

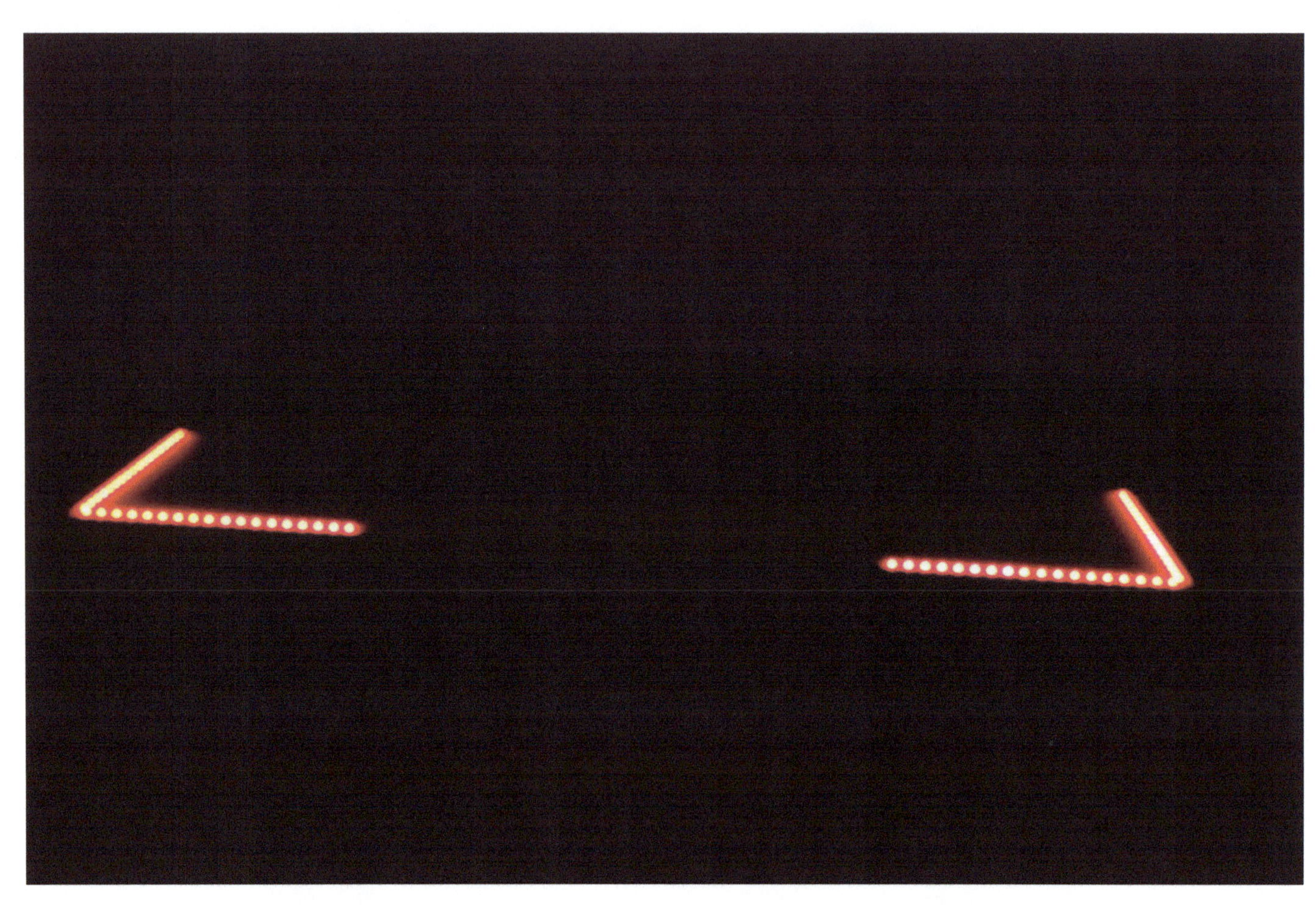

Space signifiers, 2013, LED ropes, acrylic sheet and wood, 2 x 48 x 48 cm

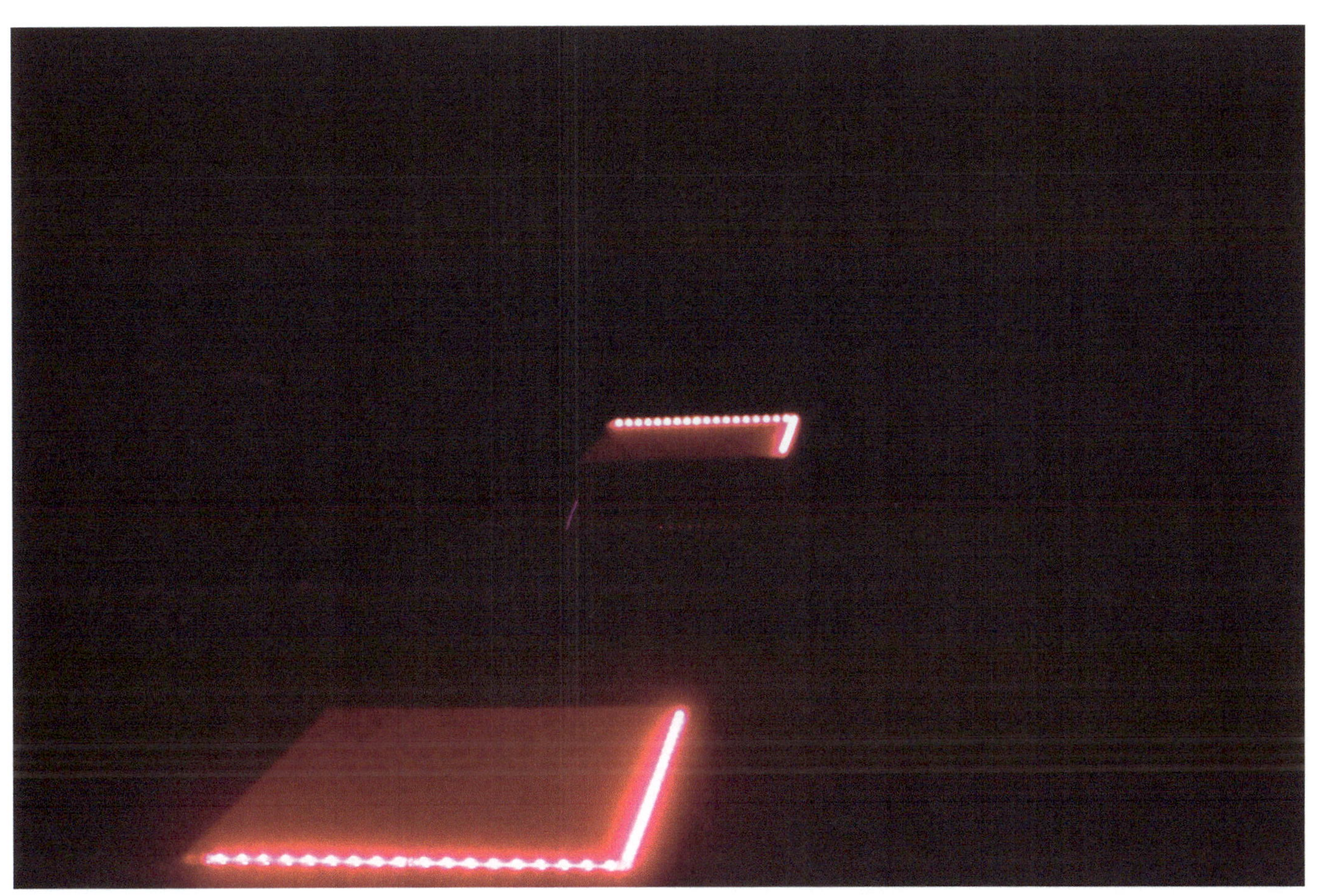

Space signifiers, 2013, LED ropes, acrylic sheet and wood, 2 x 48 x 48 cm

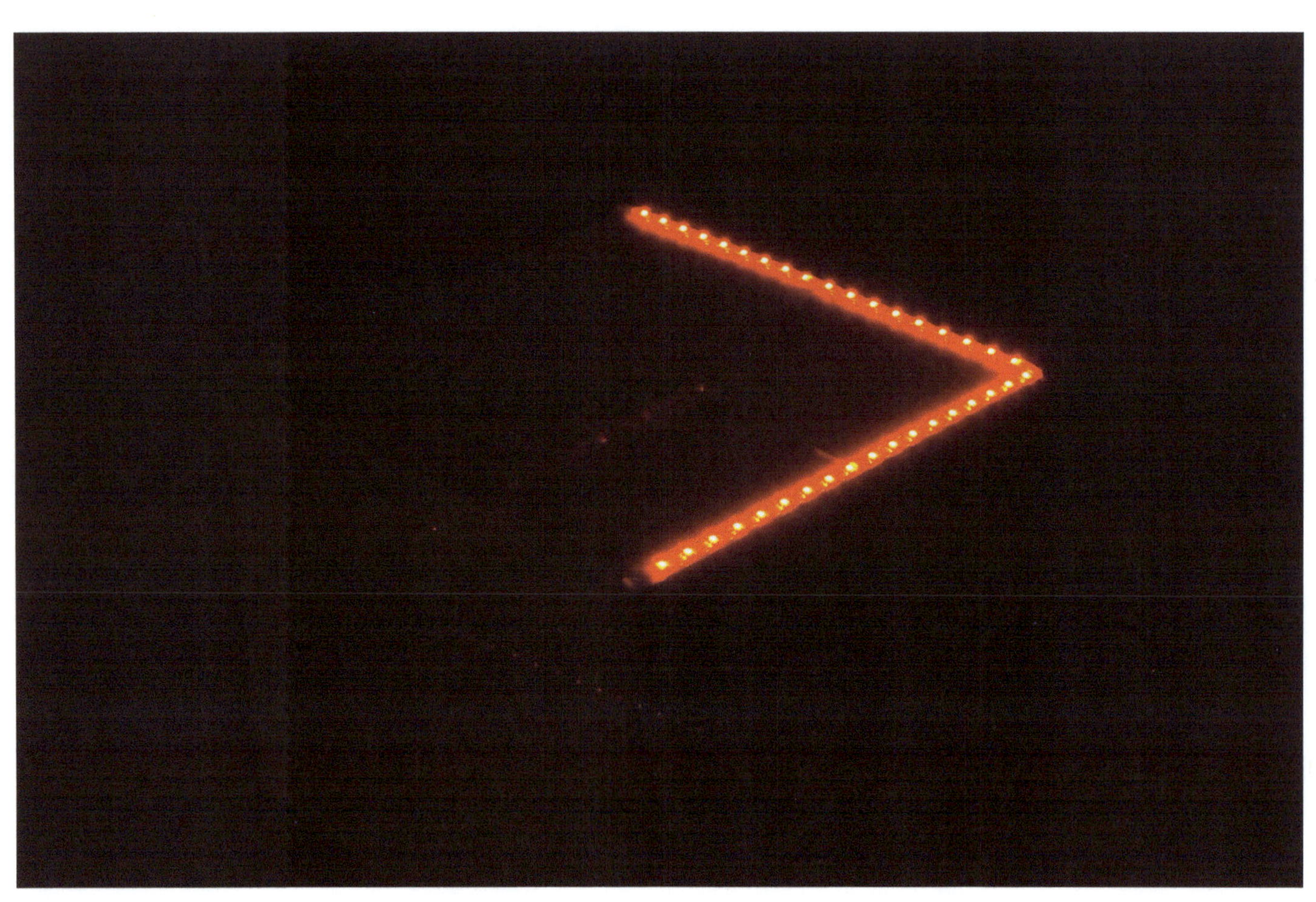

Space signifier, 2013, LED ropes, acrylic sheet and wood, 48 x 48 cm

Centre point, 2013, wood and LED spotlight.

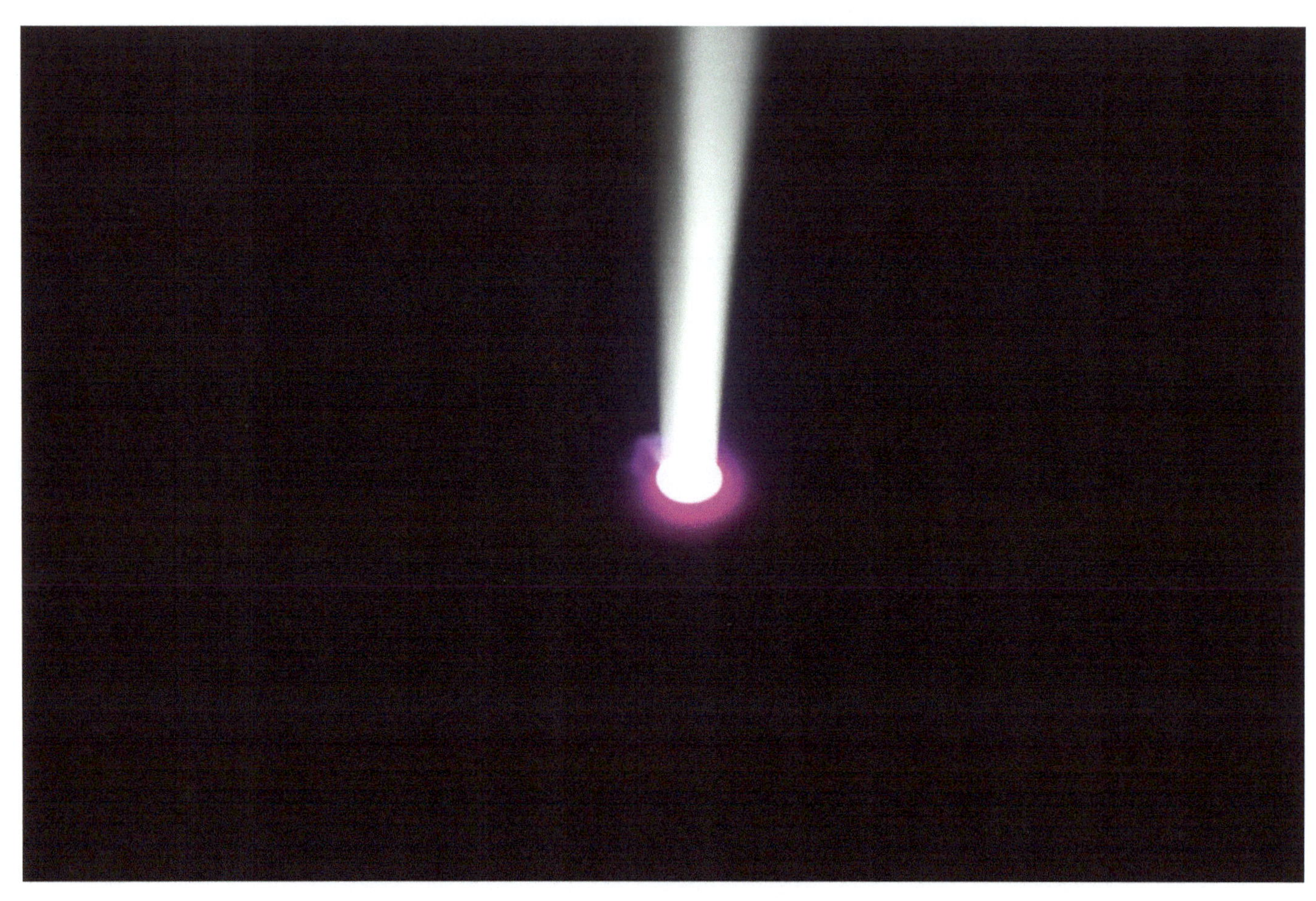

Centre point, 2013, wood and LED spotlight.

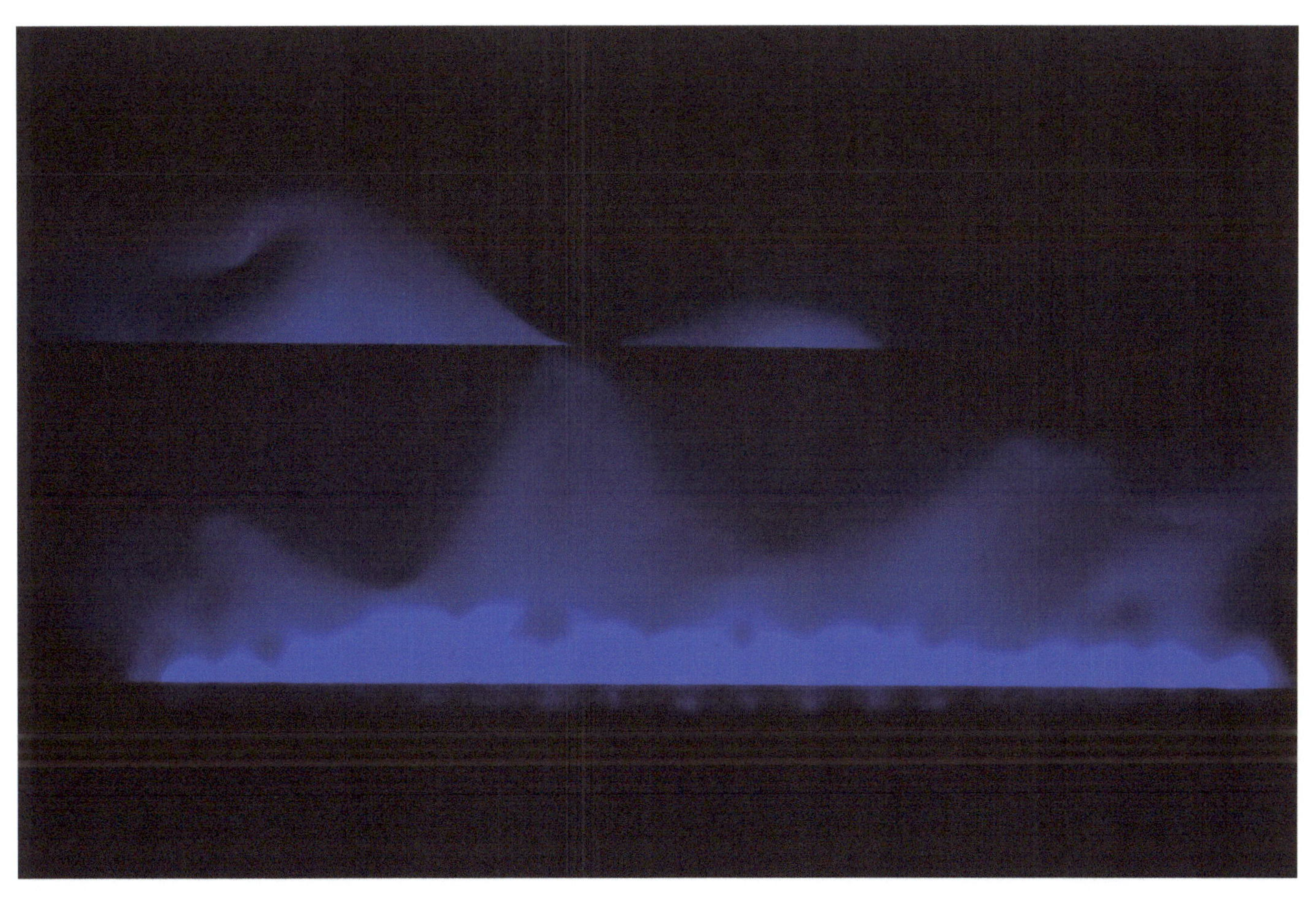

Untitled, 2013, acrylic sheets, wood and LEDs.

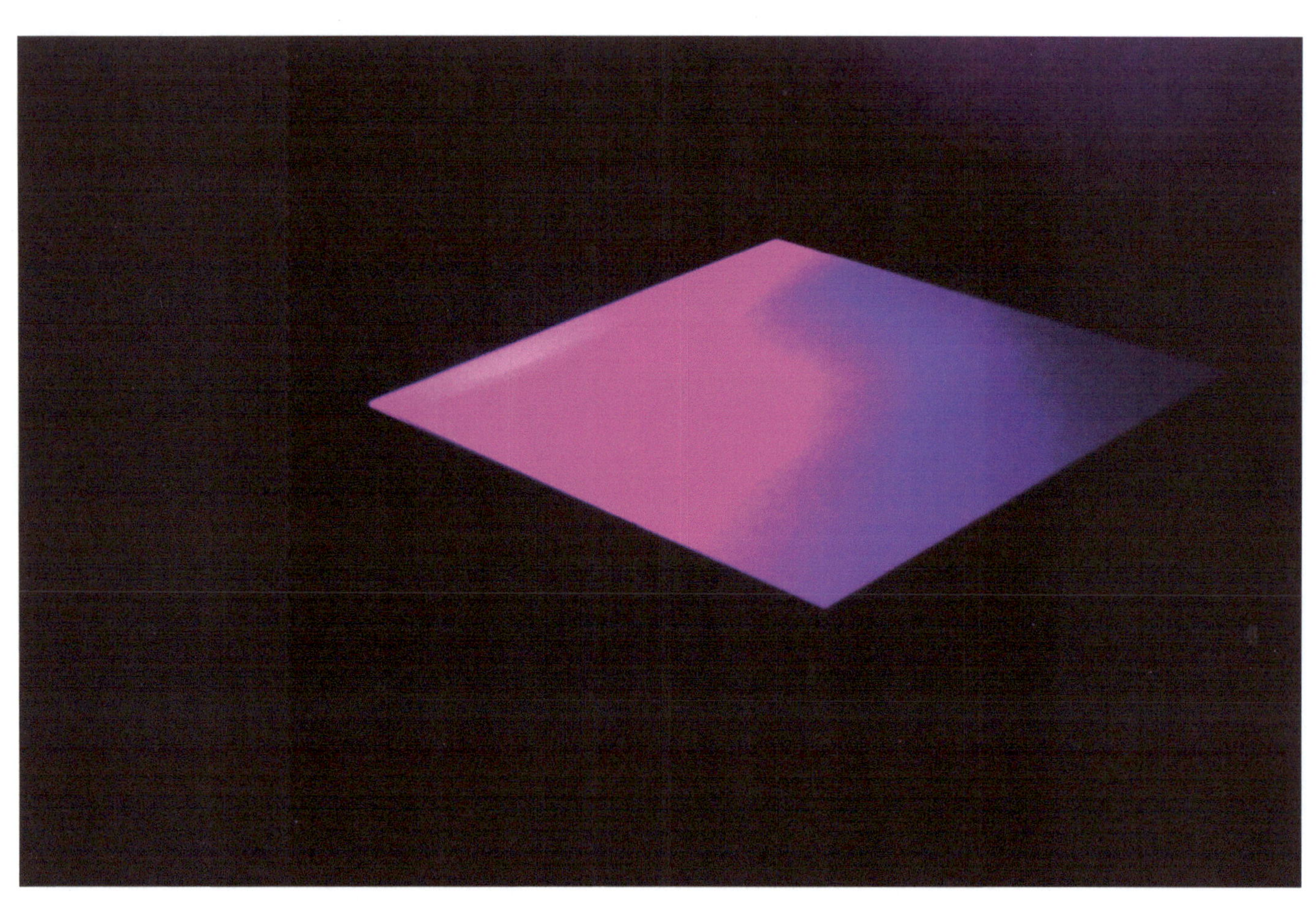

Light in plinth, 2013, acrylic sheet and LEDs, 48 x 48 x 48 cm

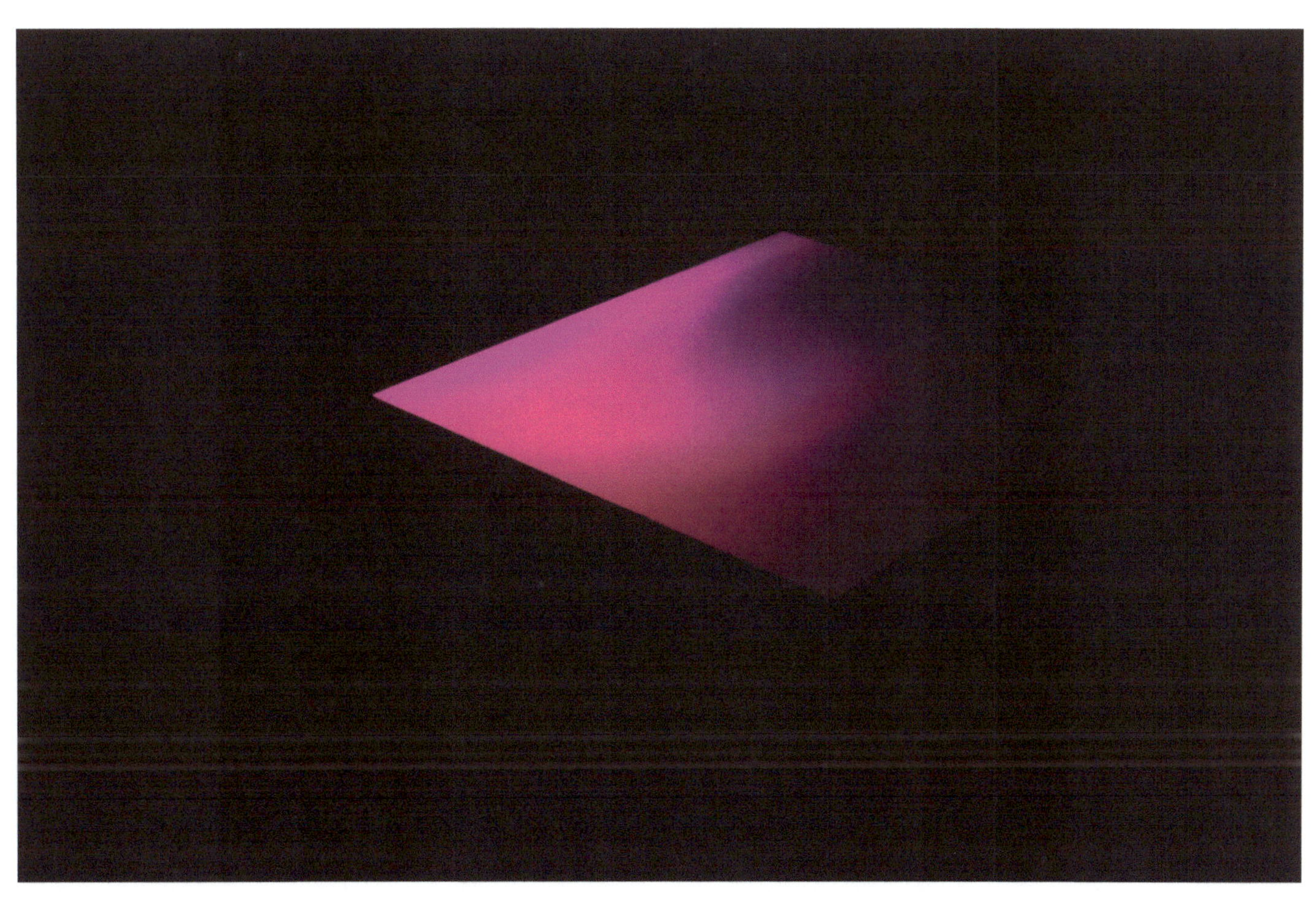

Light in plinth, 2013, acrylic sheet and LEDs, 48 x 48 x 48 cm

Light in plinth, 2013, acrylic sheet and LEDs, 48 x 48 x 48 cm

Light in plinth, 2013, acrylic sheet and LEDs, 48 x 48 x 48 cm

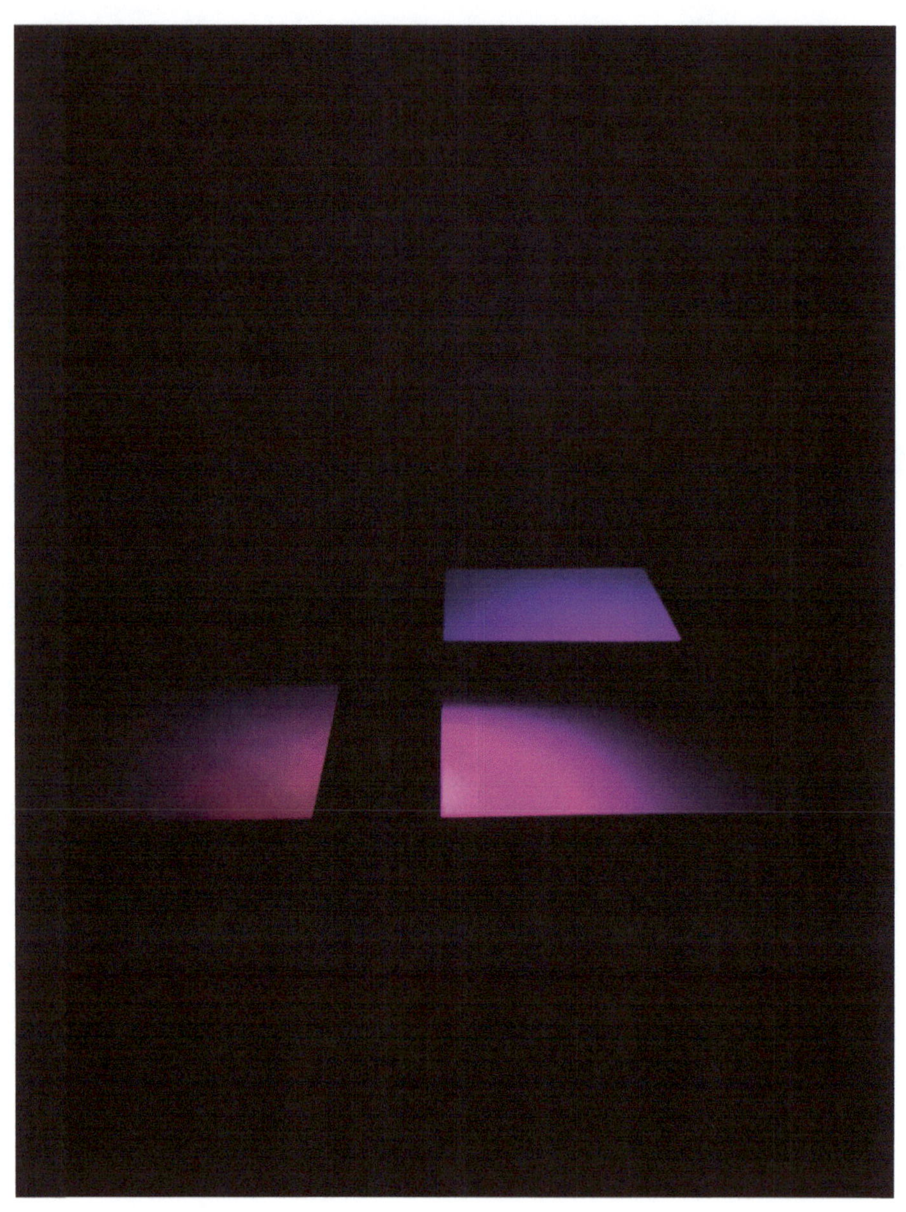

Light in plinths, 2013, acrylic sheet and LEDs, 3 x 48 x 48 x 48 cm

Untitled, 2013, programmed LED light boxes, 2 x 24 x 24 cm

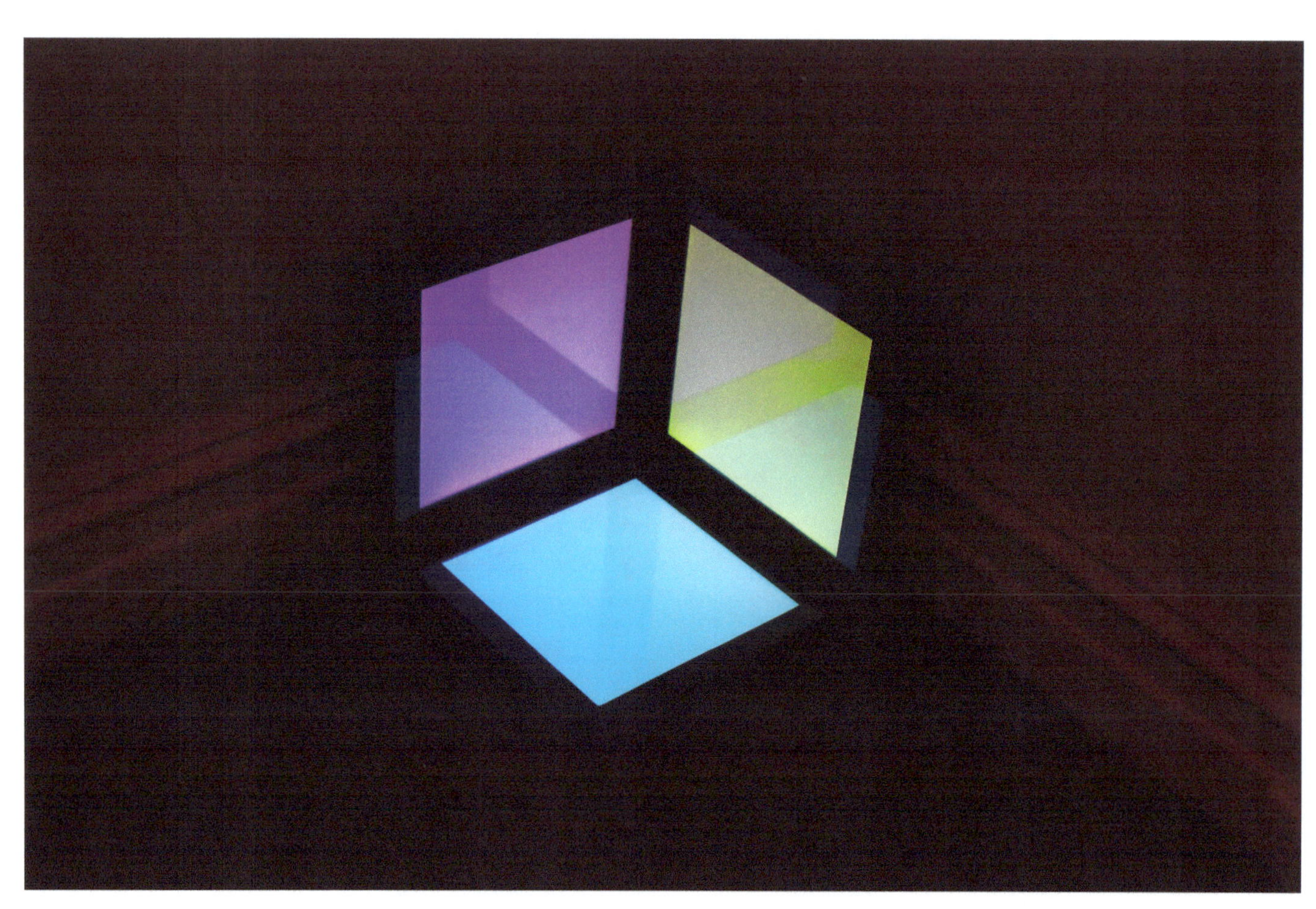

My fireplace, 2016, programmed LED triple screen light box, 32 x 32 x 32 cm

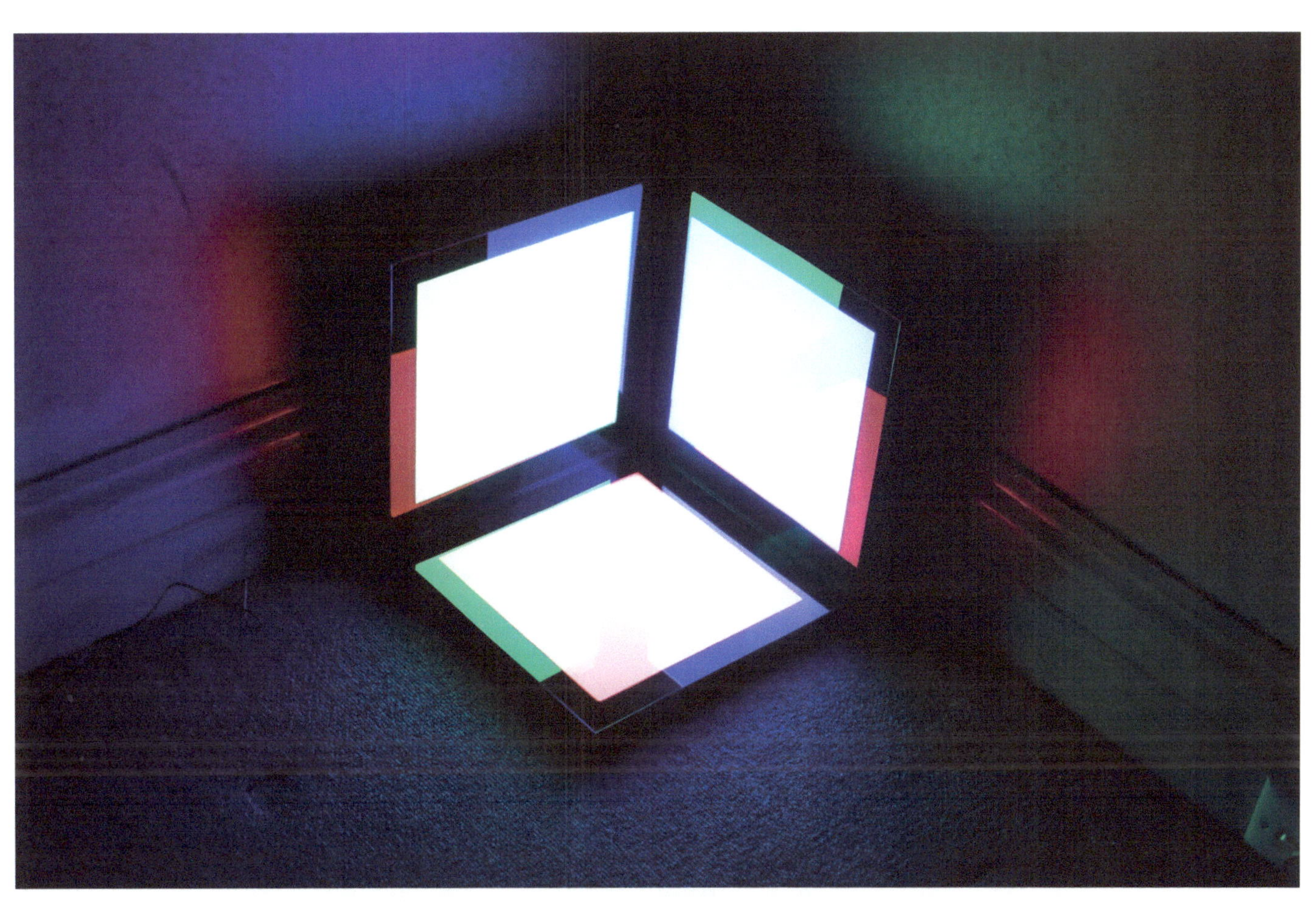

My fireplace, 2016, programmed LED triple screen light box, 32 x 32 x 32 cm

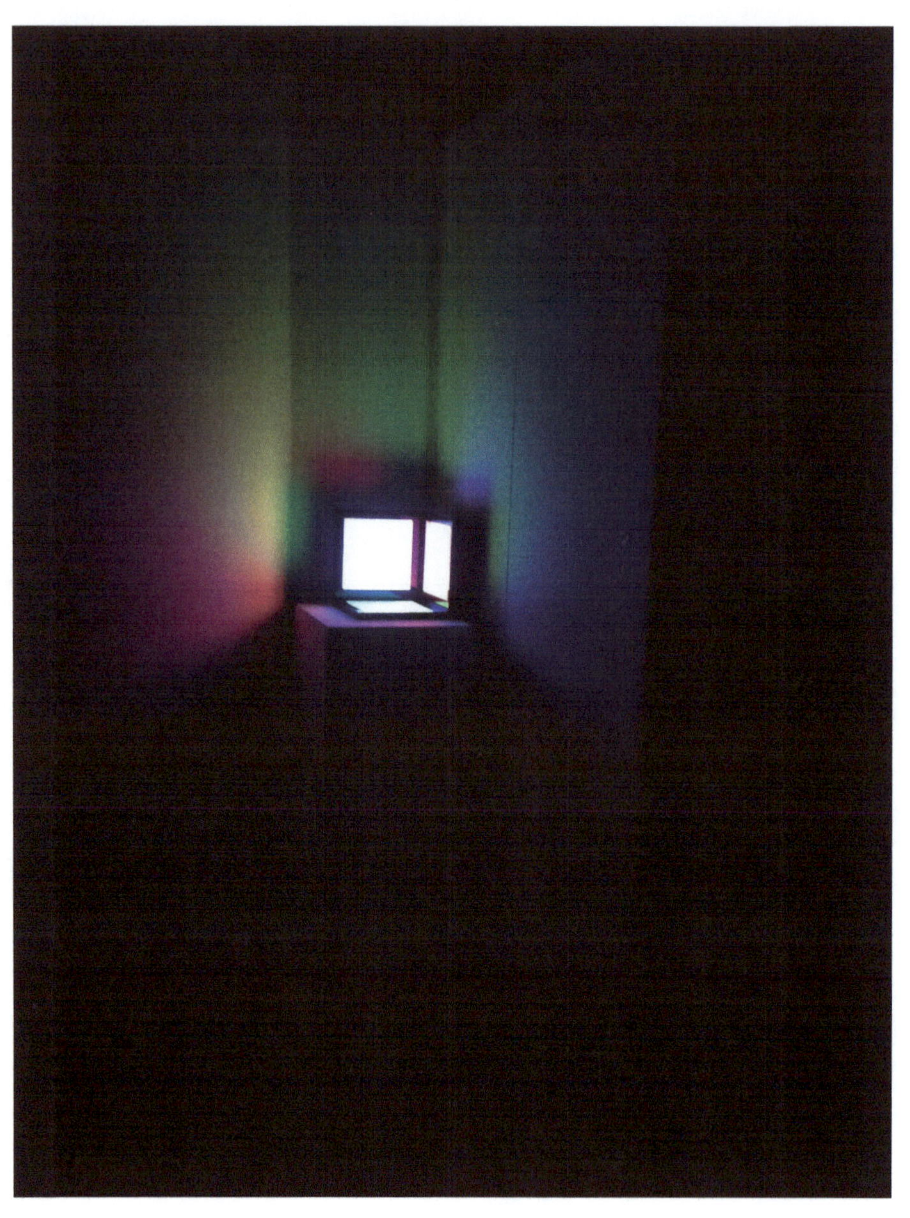

My fireplace, 2016, programmed LED triple screen light box, 32 x 32 x 32 cm

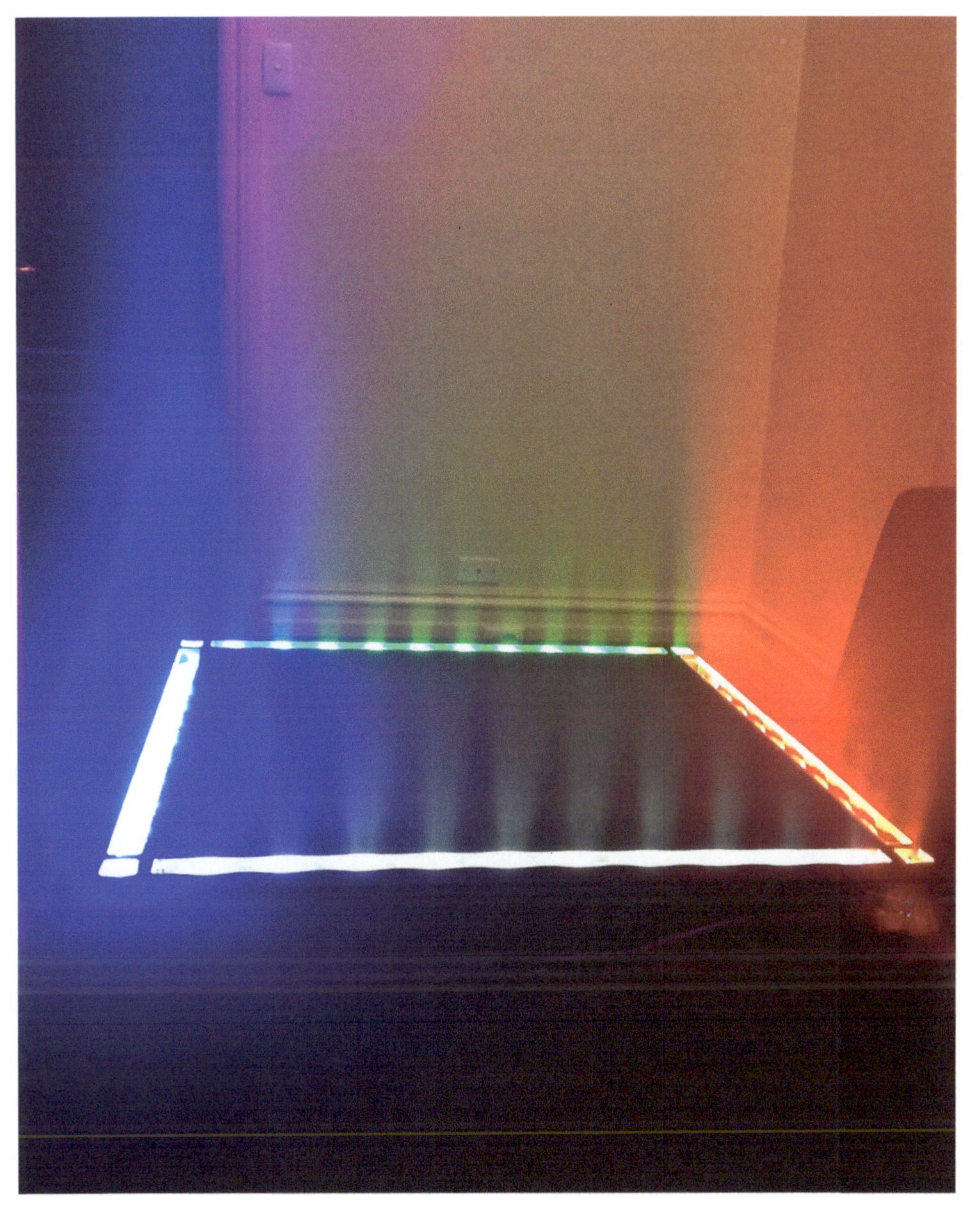

Square, 2013, programmed LEDs in aluminum frame plus haze, 60 x 60 cm

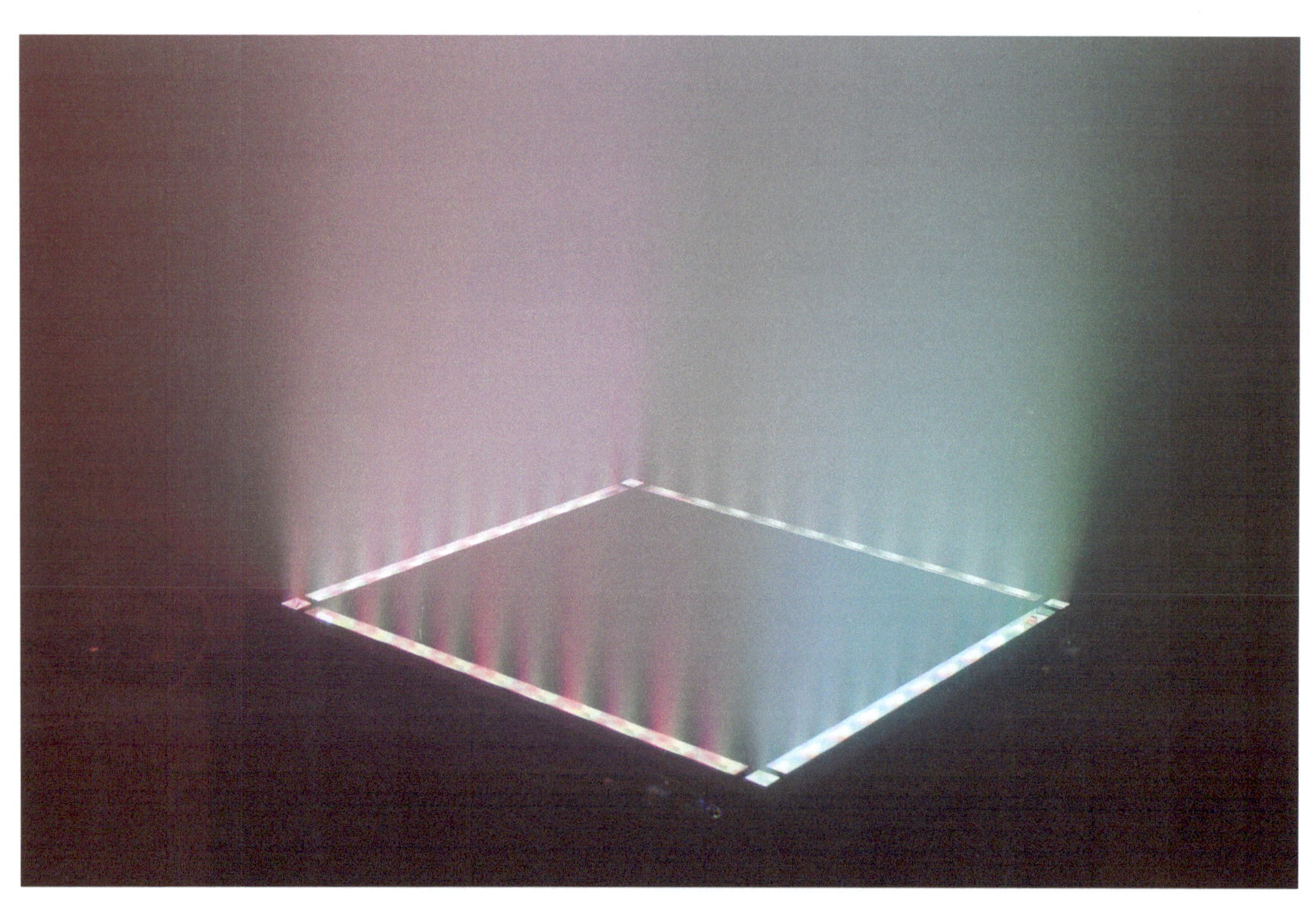

Square, 2013, programmed LEDs in aluminum frame plus haze, 60 x 60 cm

Square, 2013, programmed LEDs in aluminum frame plus haze, 60 x 60 cm

Square, 2013, programmed LEDs in aluminum frame plus haze, 60 x 60 cm

Square, 2013, programmed LEDs in aluminum frame plus haze, 60 x 60 cm

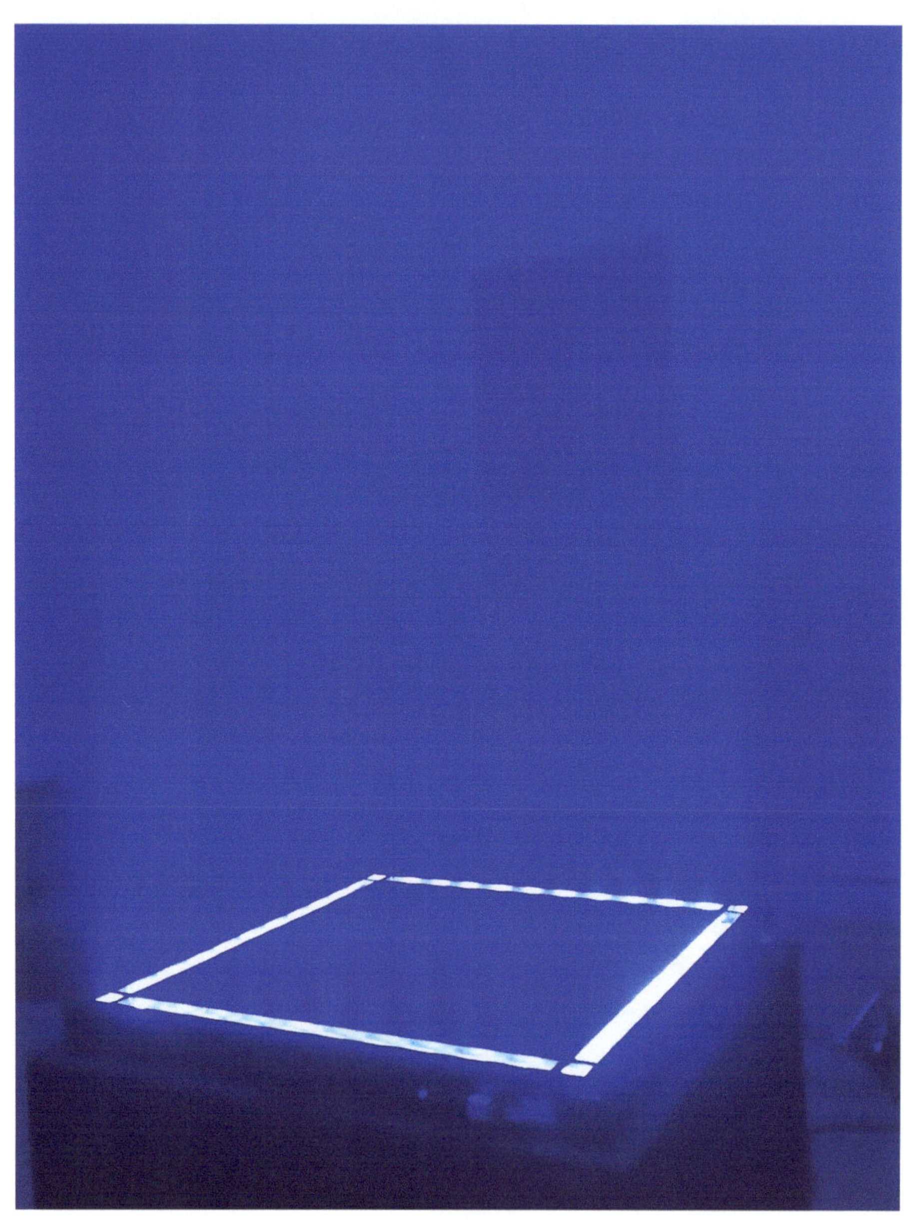

Square, 2013, programmed LEDs in aluminum frame plus haze, 60 x 60 cm

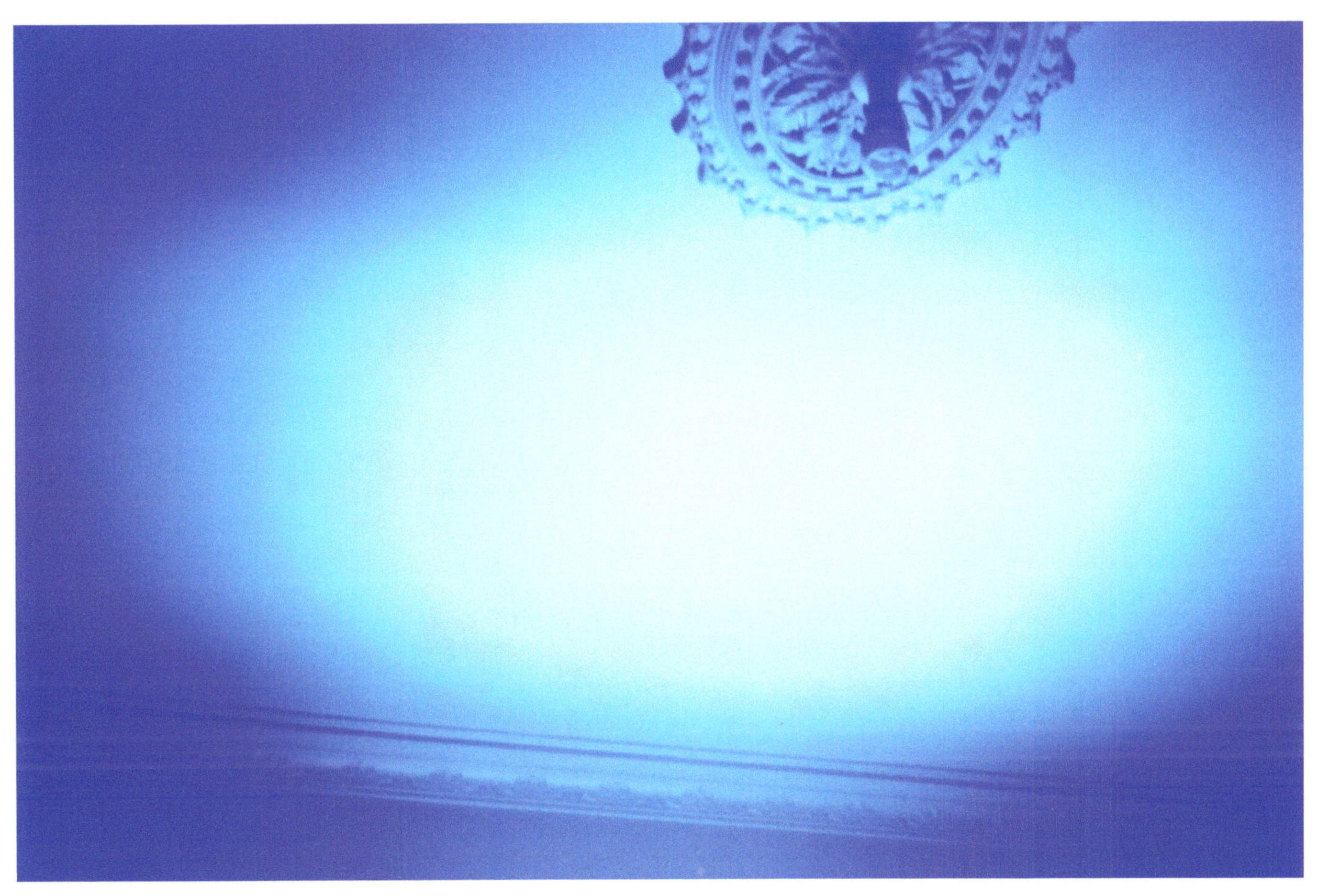

Shaft of light, 2013, programmed LEDs in aluminum frame on plinth plus haze, 60 x 60 cm

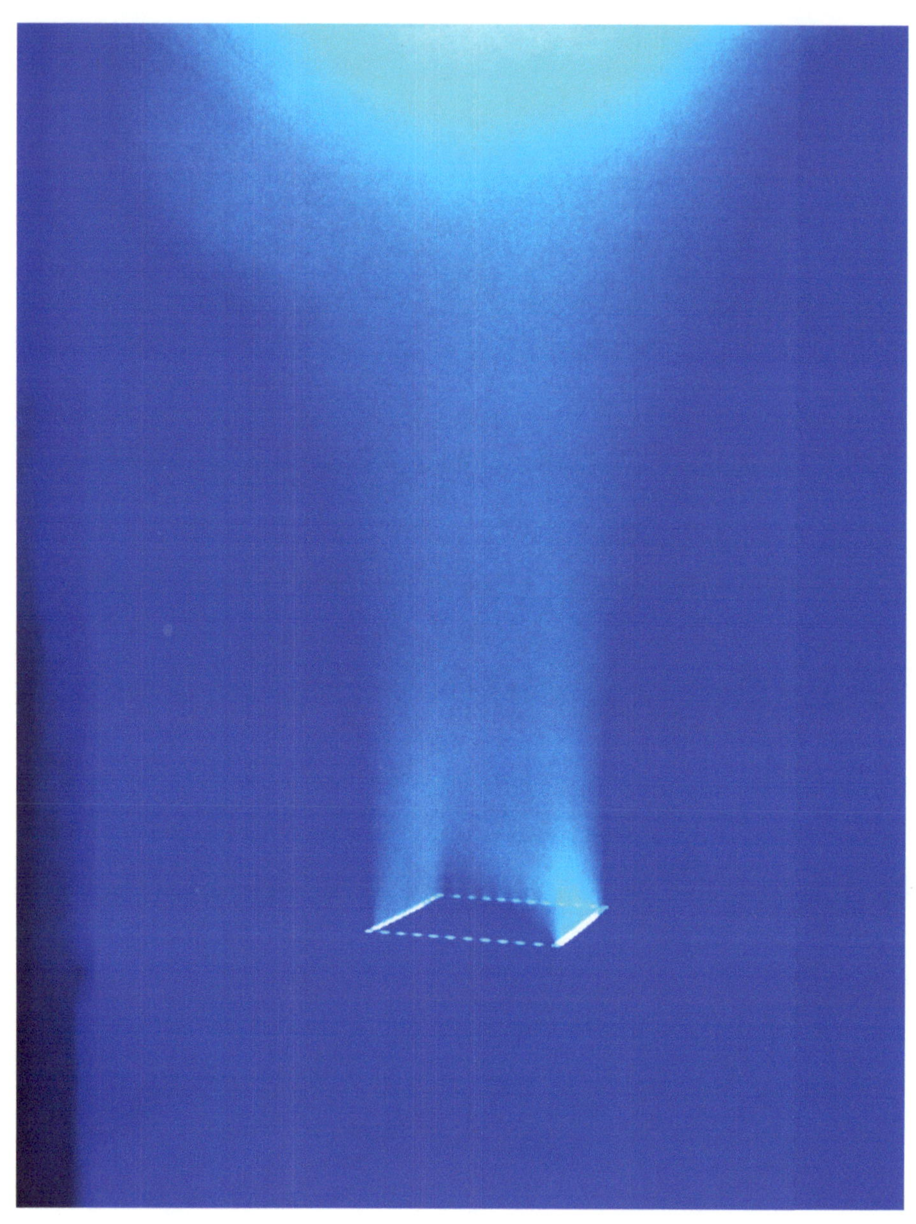

Shaft of light, 2013, programmed LEDs in aluminum frame on plinth plus haze, 60 x 60 cm